MANDY

Also by the same author

Gordon Brown: The Biography
Scargill: The Unauthorised Biography
Madame Speaker: A Life of Betty Boothroyd
John Hume: A Biography

MANDY

The Unauthorised Biography of Peter Mandelson

Paul Routledge

SIMON & SCHUSTER
A VIACOM COMPANY

First published in Great Britain by Simon & Schuster UK Ltd, 1999
A Viacom company

1 3 5 7 9 10 8 6 4 2

Simon & Schuster UK Ltd
Africa House
64-78 Kingsway
London WC2B 6AH

Simon & Schuster Australia
Sydney

A CIP catalogue record for this book is available from the British Library

ISBN 0-68485175-X

Typeset by SX Composing DTP, Rayleigh, Essex
Printed and bound in Great Britain by
Butler & Tanner, Frome, Somerset

CONTENTS

PREFACE

Peter Mandelson is a difficult man to write about. Indeed, he made the process more difficult than it need have been, by instructing his friends not to co-operate with an unauthorised biographer. Perhaps he is motivated by a natural desire to secure his privacy. Perhaps he fears the impact that revelations might have on his hitherto irresistible rise to the highest reaches of power. At any rate, he has failed.

Many people who have known Mandy down the years, since his political ambitions surfaced when he was a precocious 12-year-old boy, have been only too happy to talk to me. An unusually large proportion have, however, requested that I do not name them or that I should give them at least a fig-leaf of discretion. I have done my best to respect their wishes, and I thank all of them for their co-operation.

Why they should so fear Mandelson – and it *is* fear – is sometimes difficult to comprehend. I can understand the anxiety of politicians who have an unhealthy respect for Mandy's proximity to Tony Blair, and of journalists who are afraid of the trade secretary's long reach into newspapers, radio and television. But academics? And friends from his 'socialist' years? And trade-union officials?

It is extraordinary that a middle-ranking minister, who may never go any further than his shiny office in Victoria Street, should provoke such apprehension. I suspect his baleful influence may owe more to the perception of what he might be able to do than to what he can actually do. What else would send Jeremy Paxman round to his house in west London with a handwritten note of apology after Mandy's outing as a gay man by columnist Matthew Parris on *Newsnight*? It is inconceivable that Mandelson could actually persuade his friend Sir John Birt, director-general of the BBC, to sack a star performer like Paxman.

I have never shared the Mandy neurosis, so I hope I am the right man writing the right book. A word on origins might be appropriate. This biography is the result of a chance conversation at the newsdesk late one December night with my then editor at the *Independent on Sunday*, Rosie Boycott. Over wine (mine) and cigarettes (hers) after the first edition had been put to bed, we discussed the prospects for another book on Mandelson being written by my *Independent* colleague Donald MacIntyre. Rightly or wrongly, this was said to be the Authorised Version. Certainly, he had been promised access. 'Trouble is,' I volunteered, 'who wants to read that? Don't we want to read the unauthorised version.' Ms Boycott did not hesitate – she rarely does – and shot back, 'Yes. And you should write it.'

So I did. I could not have done so without the constant encouragement of my agent, Jane Bradish-Ellames, and of Martin Fletcher, Anna Kiernan and Robert Rimmer at Simon & Schuster, so my thanks go to them. I am afraid I tried sorely the patience of my wife, Lynne. She did not mind the debris of my previous book, a biography of Gordon Brown, all over the flat. She did object to 'having Mandelson in the place'. Heartfelt apologies, and thanks for the Hartlepool journeys.

My chief object has been to tell the rattling good story that Peter Mandelson's life so far has made. He is a bit like his Millennium Dome: big and impressive on the outside, a bit of a mystery inside. And the whole show has an uncertain future.

This book was written a few hundred yards from Labour's old headquarters, which sit opposite a Southwark health centre bearing the 1930s legend 'The People's Health is the Highest Law'. Just down the road is Herbert Morrison House. It is historic Labour territory, and *Mandy* is dedicated to the memory of the socialists who built the party that Mandelson inherited. → ouch !

Walworth, South London
December 1998

DOWNFALL

His fall from grace and power was as spectacular as his meteoric rise to success. Peter Mandelson resigned from his Cabinet post as Secretary of State for Trade and Industry at 10 a.m. on 23 December 1998, barely 36 hours after the scandal of his secret loan became known.

Mandelson's departure from high office took place amid turmoil in the government, an inquiry into his financial affairs by the Parliamentary Commissioner for Standards, and an opposition campaign to undermine Labour as the party of sleaze and 'cronyism.' It was Tony Blair's worst day since New Labour gained power 18 months earlier. Mandygate soured his administration's image, and damaged his own credibility as Prime Minister.

It had all started so differently. The slick, disciplined general election campaign of April 1997. The heady expectation that 'Things can only get better'. The phenomenal popularity of New Labour, month after month leading the Tories in the opinion polls by a huge margin. The sense that a radical new Third Way was being driven forward by the brightest and the best. Peter Mandelson, the golden boy of his political generation, had everything going for him.

And it ended in two brief letters – 'Dear Tony', and 'Dear Peter'. After less than 6 months in the Cabinet, where he was on track to realise his childhood ambition to become a Labour Prime Minister (as his grandfather, Herbert Morrison, never had) he was cast into the outer darkness of the Commons' back benches. His career in public life was checked, perhaps terminally, by his own hubris.

The manner of his going was classic Mandelson. First, he claimed he had done nothing wrong by borrowing £373,000 from his friend, the wealthy Labour MP Geoffrey Robinson, and not declaring it, either to the Prime Minister or to the parliamentary Register of Interests. Then he conceded, with an ill grace, that he might have made 'an error of judgment' in arranging the secret loan in the autumn of 1996, to buy a luxury Georgian town house in a fashionable area of west London.

He toured the radio and television studios on 22 December, desperately trying to 'spin' himself out of trouble. He accepted every interview request, confident that his legendary powers of persuasion would get him out of trouble. But when they were put to the final test the mystical properties of spinning were found wanting.

There were simply too many unanswered questions. Not merely, why did a bachelor minister need a four-bedroom house in one of the most expensive parts of Notting Hill? But also: had Mandelson broken the law by deceiving the Britannia Building Society when he applied for a £150,000 mortgage on 9 Northumberland Place?

When first asked if he had completed the application form properly, Mandelson said he was sure he would have 'sought to answer the question properly'. Within hours, he was backtracking, claiming that he could not recall if he had revealed the Robinson loan to the building society, as he was legally obliged. He continued to equivocate, telling the BBC: 'It was nearly two years ago and I can't remember every question or every answer. Having tried to find the copy of the form and failed to do that I cannot clarify that even now.' The *Mirror* also disclosed that Mandelson had an account at the Queen's bank, Coutts, holding nearly £50,000. The Conservatives pressed hard for more details, ensuring that the scandal would not die a natural death.

It was against this background of deepening sleaze that Mandelson telephoned Blair at Chequers at 10 p.m. on 22 December. In an emotional exchange the Trade Secretary said he was angry with himself for getting the government into trouble. He wished he had never borrowed the money from Robinson, and he wished he had come clean about the loan to his officials and the Prime Minister. But he had done nothing wrong. He had only been unwise.

Mandelson offered to resign on the spot. Blair asked him to sleep on it and talk again the next day. Mandelson repeated his resignation offer 12 hours later, and this time the Prime Minister did not seek to dissuade him. A senior government official was quoted as saying: 'You could see he knew he was doing the wrong thing in trying to hang on. He now feels ghastly, but relieved he's done the right thing. He's made a colossal error, and paid a colossal price.'

Mandy did not see it quite that way. He still felt robbed. In his resignation letter, he wrote:

Dear Tony,

I can scarcely believe I am writing this letter to you. As well as being one of my closest friends you are a close colleague whose leadership and political qualities I value beyond all others.

As you have, I have reflected overnight on the situation concerning the loan I took from Geoffrey Robinson and I have decided to resign from the Government.

As I said publicly yesterday, I do not believe that I have done anything wrong or improper. But I should not, with all candour, have entered into the arrangement. I should, having done so, told you and other colleagues whose advice I value. And I should have told my permanent secretary on learning of the inquiry into Geoffrey Robinson, although I had entirely stood aside from this.

I am sorry about this situation. But we came to power promising to uphold the highest possible standards in public life. We have not just to do so, but we must be seen to do so.

Therefore with huge regret I wish to resign. I am very proud of the role I played in helping you and previous leaders of the Labour Party to make our party electable and to win our historic victory last May. I am proud of the trust you placed in me both at the Cabinet office and at the DTI. In just 18 months you have helped to transform this country and the Government has made huge progress delivering on our manifesto and its programme of modernisation.

I will always be a loyal Labour man and I am not prepared to see the party and the Government suffer the kind of attack this issue has provoked.

You can be assured, of course, of my continuing friendship and total loyalty.

Yours ever, Peter.

In reply, the Prime Minister wrote:

Dear Peter,

You will know better than anyone the feelings with which I write to you. You and I have been personal friends and the closest of political colleagues.

It is no exaggeration to say that without your support and advice we would never have built New Labour.

It was typical of you, when we spoke last night, that your thought was for the reputation of the Labour Party and the Government and that you believed that since there had been a misjudgment on your part, then, as you said to me 'we can't be like the last lot' and that what we are trying to achieve for the country is more important than any individual.

But I also want you to know that you have my profound thanks for all you have done and my belief that, in the future, you will achieve much, much more with us.

Yours ever, Tony.

This theme, namely that Mandelson was only out of favour temporarily, was taken up by the *Guardian*. Supposedly his tormentor, but in reality the most supportive conduit for his spin. The paper's splash headline on 24 December was 'Goodbye for now', signaling its belief that the Svengali of politics would stage a political recovery at some future date.

Mandelson will bounce back. He has limitless reserves of self-esteem. He is still in his early 40s. He is disgraced, but he still has the support of New Labour's ruling clique of modernisers, as well as the backing of the Prime Minster. Margaret McDonagh, General Secretary of the Labour Party, said: 'I am sure Peter will, in due time, resume a central role in Labour's continued modernisation, as the party that represents the hopes and aspirations of hard working people.' Denis MacShane, another modernising Labour MP predicted simply: 'He will be back.'

Why Tony Blair should want him back, beyond the call of friendship, is one of the mysteries of politics. His supposedly unique powers of media manipulation have been shown to be worthless in a real crisis. His judgment has been exposed as poor. He admitted himself: 'I should have been open about the loan. I should have informed my colleagues and my permanent secretary, and in so doing I should have protected myself against the appearance of a conflict of interest. It was my fault and I paid a very big price' His fault, surely, was to believe that the dark arts of spin-doctoring could save him.

The role of this biography in Mandelson's downfall should not be underestimated. For months prior to publication , his aides had been expressing a mixture of apprehension and contempt. Contempt towards an 'Old Labour' author, but apprehension about what might be revealed – not just about Mandy's private life, but his financial affairs. This had proved the most elusive area for previous investigators.

On 23 December, the *Daily Telegraph* reported a friend of Mandelson as saying: 'The loan was known only to a very small number of people. But we knew it was in the Routledge book so there could have been a case for pre-empting the book. But the

Guardian got in before us.'

On the same day *The Times* said that at Westminster a report was circulating that 'a journalist', a sworn enemy of Mr Routledge, had managed to obtain a leak from a draft of the biography and had published it in order to ruin its launch. The Mandelson camp conceded that 'if the leak scuppered the Routledge book, it would be the "silver lining" to the cloud enveloping him (Mandelson).'

Both these theories have some validity. It is true that the secret loan was known only to a handful of people – among them this author. And it does appear in this book.

What's more a copy of the page proofs of *Mandy* was mysteriously tampered with after having been delivered to the high-security Palace of Westminster. The 300-page draft was delivered to the House of Commons in early December, addressed to the author. Due to an oversight by a member of the Commons staff it was delivered to the office of the *Independent on Sunday*, where I formerly worked. Coincidentally, this is also the office where Donald MacIntyre, *Independent* columnist and author of a rival, authorised biography, works, but whom I exonerated entirely from this underhand behaviour.

The parcel appeared the following day in the parliamentary office of the *Mirror*, ripped open, with the contents exposed. The text had clearly been rifled through by persons unknown. It could easily have been photocopied overnight. Friends of Mandelson were in a position to pass details on to him, or even a copy of the text. He was then able to launch a pre-emptive strike of the kind discussed by his 'friend' in the *Daily Telegraph*.

This is not a fanciful scenario. Indeed it was confirmed in the *Guardian* on 24 December, by Seumus Milne, a media acolyte of Mandelson. He wrote that on 15 December, Ben Wegg-Prosser, Mandelson's 24 year-old political adviser, took an urgent call from a 'media friend' who had managed to look through Mr Routledge's book proofs for 20 minutes. The Geoffrey Robinson loan was in Chapter One: 'Scandal!' – and the fuse was lit for the events that culminated in yesterday's conflagration.'

The political bonfire also consumed Geoffrey Robinson, the Paymaster General, whose secrecy from two years earlier set in train the Christmas melodrama. He was compelled to resign a few hours after Mandelson. Robinson had been under fire from the media for more than a year, and had already been forced to apologise to the Commons for 'oversights' in the registration of his business interests.

In his resignation letter Robinson, whose financial affairs are under investigation by DTI officials, said: 'In the case of the loan to Peter Mandelson, I merely considered myself, in 1996, as someone in a position to help a long-standing friend, with no request for anything in return.'

And he got nothing in return, except removal from a ministerial job (for which he took no salary) that he loved doing. His political demise – he is too old to expect another post in government – demonstrates the danger of undue proximity to the Prince of Darkness.

1

SCANDAL!

Peter Mandelson lives his life on the edge. He relishes challenge, and is magnetised by danger. With his political pedigree and withering intelligence, he could have opted for the easy route through public life, but he chose the path of controversy. 'I love people who are different, exotic, or dangerous,' he once confessed. 'I don't like conformity.'

But he does not unlock his innermost feelings, not even on the television psychiatrist's couch. It is still a matter of speculation why he is ineluctably drawn to a socially and politically risqué way of life. His motive may be a burning desire to do better than his famous grandfather, Labour's post-war deputy leader Herbert Morrison, one of the most hated politicians of his generation. Or perhaps it is an exhibitionist function of his homosexuality: the sheer daring of the gay world that attracts him to newspaper headlines like a moth to the flame.

Like most politicians, he is deeply ambitious. His eyes are firmly fixed on a place much higher up the Cabinet table. Even in the school playground, and with his grinning approval, the other boys used to chant, 'PM for PM.' His appetite for power would be unexceptional were it not for the chance of history that placed him at the right hand of the prime minister, in a position of such influence that other ministers practically weep with rage and envy.

The tragic death of Labour leader John Smith in 1994 drew Mandelson out from the shadows. It delivered him unrivalled access to Tony Blair, who famously said, 'My project will be complete when the Labour Party learns to love Peter Mandelson.'[1] Blair's closeness to his trade secretary is the key to Mandy's unique role under New Labour. The prime minister relies on him, leans on him and trusts him in a way that suggests dependency. Yet Mandy's political skills are no greater than those of most middle-ranking ministers. His oratory is wooden, and his speaking manner patronising. He is a clumsy, unoriginal writer, and he attracts fear and loathing in about equal measure from most of the people who cross his path.

And, most dangerously for a prime minister who wants his government to be squeaky-clean, in contrast to John Major's sleaze-riddled administration, Mandelson's name regularly emerges when Labour is hit by scandal. He even gets a walk-on part in Matthew Parris's definitive *Great Parliamentary Scandals* for his role at the time of the break of Foreign Secretary Robin Cook's marriage break-up. He was in the thick of the trouble over Formula One motor-racing magnate Bernie Ecclestone's £1 million gift to the party, which had to be repaid. He was drawn into 'Dollygate', the cash-for-access scandal that broke in 1998, as was his long-time friend Roger Liddle, a policy adviser in 10 Downing Street. And when Welsh Secretary Ron Davies was forced to resign in October 1998 because of an indiscretion at the gay end of Clapham Common, Mandelson was inevitably dragged into the affair. His homosexuality was exposed again, this time on live television.

Fittingly, Mandelson's obsessive personal secrecy ensures that the media (and public) interest in him – what he is, where he came from and what he is up to – perpetuates an insistent search for information. He does not want us to know, ergo we must find out. The search for scandal goes right back to his childhood, when Mandelson was a keen Boy Scout. Tall, even as a boy, he cut rather a gawky figure in shorts, long woolly socks and a woggle. He went on camps, and later recalled that he was always sad when the week under canvas came to an end. Always one to be out in front, he graduated to be leader of his 'six' in leafy Hampstead Garden Suburb.

But there was something nasty going on in his cub scout troop. Many of the boys, then aged around 10, were subject to sexual abuse by a scoutmaster, who was twice their age. One fellow cub scout, who knew Mandelson from the age of 5, said the scoutmaster used to sit them on his knee while he masturbated. The boys talked about it among themselves, and one finally plucked up the courage to tell his parents. They in turn informed other parents. These were different, less abuse-conscious days. The parents decided not to call in the police, but to report the abusive group leader to the scouting authorities. They investigated, and removed the abuser; there was no prosecution.

Mandelson's fellow-scouter, who asked not to be identified, was abused over a period of months in this way. He believes that Mandelson was drawn into the web of abuse. 'We were both victims of the same perpetrator of sexual abuse,' he told me. 'It happened to me, and it happened to him.'[2] However, Mandelson himself has never made any reference to such an experience, which is not surprising, given his blanket refusal to discuss the sexual side of his life.

The first real political scandal in which Mandelson was involved, played out in the mid 1970s, still reverberates today. Mandy joined the Young Communist League – and possibly the parent Communist Party of Great Britain – in his late teens, and took part in a Soviet-dominated World Festival of Youth in Havana, Cuba, in 1978. His role has been variously interpreted down the years. Some intelligence experts believe he may have been an MI6 'agent of influence' working, perhaps innocently, for the West during a critical period of the Cold War. He certainly came to the attention of MI5, which held a file on him for more than a decade because of his communist days.

The scandal of his bit-part role in world communism returned to haunt him after New Labour came to power, when a renegade MI5 agent, David Shayler, revealed the existence of his security file. This lifted the affair into a long and embarrassing parliamentary conflict with the Conservatives over his precise involvement in revolutionary politics. He demanded that his file be pulped, and claimed (almost certainly wrongly) that his telephone had not been tapped. The scandal died down, and then flared up again in the autumn of 1998 when Shayler was held in a French jail pending extradition moves by the British authorities. Rumours surfaced at Westminster that, if he was compelled to stand trial in Britain for breach of official secrets legislation, then facts would emerge relating to Mandelson that would sink the government.

The readiness with which political correspondents wanted to believe these stories testifies to more than exasperation with Mandelson's long campaign to control the media. Experience over recent years indicates that where there is Labour scandal, papers like to mention Mandy's name. For instance, in the months after the general election, he was sucked into a scandal surrounding his former constituency agent and friend, Bernard Carr. Mandy had befriended Carr soon after becoming the Labour parliamentary candidate in Hartlepool in late 1989. Carr was a local councillor, representing a ward in the old part of the town, the Headland. He was also president of the local Labour Party, and was known among constituency stalwarts as an ambitious man with a good opinion of himself. In time, he became Mandelson's constituency agent, never far from his side in the 1992 general election campaign.

But there was a flamboyant side to Carr. He enjoyed being in the public eye, and in 1996 his ostentation got him into trouble. In August that year, he travelled to London to take part in a *Sunday Telegraph* weekend competition to find Britain's worst cook. Carr took second prize with an appalling turnip-and-fish soup. After the contest, held at Brown's Hotel in the West End, Carr spent two nights in the Dolphin Hotel in Pimlico. On the following Monday, he attended a two-hour meeting on housing organised by the Tudor Trust Housing Group. And on his return to Hartlepool he put in an expenses claim for £150. The money had been advanced to him before he left for the capital.

A fellow councillor 'shopped' Carr, arguing that the claim was bogus. He demanded an inquiry. John Walton, the council's chief financial officer, investigated, and concluded that Carr's claim was false. The links between the housing trust and Hartlepool Council business were too tenuous to support reimbursement. Carr repaid the money, plus a further amount previously paid for another visit to the same housing trust. Moreover, it emerged, Carr had misled the inquiry. Initially, he told council officers he had travelled to and from London on the day of the Tudor Trust meeting. The truth was established by a simple check with the hotel.

The amount of money involved was small, but the affair was big news in Hartlepool. Carr was obliged to stand down from his key positions on the council, chairman of the ruling Labour Group, and of the Housing Services Committee. Then, on 6 September, Cleveland police were called in to probe further allegations of financial irregularities involving Carr and his council expenses. Ten days later, he was ordered out of his house by a county court judge for non-payment of his weekly rent. Finally, on 15 November, he was charged with six offences of deception and one of attempted deception over an eighteen-month period, and stood down from the presidency of Hartlepool Labour Party.

The case aroused considerable interest because of Carr's closeness to Mandelson. It was expected that Mandelson would appear, bizarrely, as a witness both for the prosecution and for the defence. But the case dragged on, and in the meantime Carr came to the notice of the police a second time. In the early hours of 16 August 1997, he was arrested in a public toilet with a 17-year-old youth and charged with gross indecency. Five months later, the charges were dropped by Hartlepool magistrates after the Crown Prosecution Service offered no evidence. Then, in February 1998 at Teesside Crown Court, Carr was cleared of the expenses fraud because the CPS once again dropped the charges. New evidence about the council's 'lax' accounting procedures emerged minutes after the trial began, compelling the Prosecution service to abandon the case.

Mandelson was enraged. He accused police and prosecutors of incompetence, saying that the evidence against his friend was flimsy and that the entire investigation, which lasted eighteen months and cost £100,000, was a waste of taxpayers' money. 'If a case gets into court and does not stand up to scrutiny for more than a matter of minutes you are bound to ask yourself why it had been brought in the first place, how it had been handled and at what wasted cost to the taxpayer.'[3] He suggested that the figure of £100,000 might be a 'very conservative' figure, and warned that someone, somewhere down the line, was going to have to ask some questions.

But not him. And certainly not in public. Mandelson first pleaded ministerial responsibility as a reason for not tabling Commons questions about the affair, and then invoked parliamentary protocol to prevent Frank Cook, Labour MP for the neighbouring constituency of Stockton North, from proceeding with questions about the case. 'This is a constituency matter and I have raised the matter directly with the Home Secretary,' said Mandelson. 'It is my job and I am doing it.'[4]

Nothing more was heard of the affair of Mandy's pal, who resumed public life. Then *Punch* magazine began investigating the background to the Carr cases. The magazine concluded that Mandy's shock and outrage at the failure of the case were curious, since he apparently knew it was going to collapse at least two days before. According to *Punch*, Mandelson's new agent, Steve Wallace, attending Labour's local government conference in Scarborough the Saturday before the trial, had 'assured at least one Hartlepool councillor present that Mandy would not be travelling north for the hearing because it was being called off'.[5] An unnamed council source helpfully added that the latest trial collapse, following so soon after the failure of the gross indecency charges, had shocked local people. 'Carr and Mandelson are still very good friends; he always attends Mandy's parties when he has them at his constituency home in Hartlepool.'[6]

The issue of Mandelson's money has often attracted the attention of muckrakers, but the truth has eluded them. The problem is that the sums do not add up. Mandelson has two homes, a four-storey Victorian semi in Hartlepool and a very desirable residence in fashionable west London. The latter was valued at £500,000 in early 1998, and the former at £70,000. Yet until he became minister without portfolio on £87,851 a year, in mid-1997, Mandy had always been a modest earner. As a researcher at the TUC in the late seventies, he earned civil service pay of a few thousand a year, and he possibly earned even less when he went on to work for the Labour Party as a researcher to shadow transport secretary Albert Booth in the early eighties. He then worked as a researcher and junior producer at LWT, before moving on to Walworth Road as Labour's director of communications on £28,000 a year.

None of these jobs made him any serious money, and his first foray into the property market was a small farmworker's cottage in the Wye Valley, costing him around a year's salary. His work for SRU, the consultancy started by style guru Peter York, in the early nineties brought him about the same salary – on his own admission. And when he entered Parliament in 1992, he almost certainly took a salary drop to the MP's £25,000 a year, even taking into account the various allowances. The purchase of his Hartlepool home – where there are pictures of himself in every room – was probably financed from the sale of his Wye Valley cottage, which had grown appreciably in value.

But how did he afford a £500,000 pad in one of the most sought-after streets of Notting Hill, where he became a neighbour of Princess Charlotte of Luxembourg, Kate Moss and Ralph Fiennes? His mortgage is reported to be £150,000, a figure that has never been denied. So where did the other £350,000 come from? Some have suggested that he inherited it from his famous grandfather, Herbert Morrison, who had been deputy leader of the Labour Party, home secretary and foreign secretary. Unfortunately for this theory, when he died in 1965, Morrison was virtually estranged from his only daughter, Mary, Mandelson's mother. He rarely visited the Mandelsons at home in north London, and on his death left only £28,000, about £300,000 at 1998 prices. In any case, Lord Morrison of Lambeth, the father of metropolitan socialism, left everything to his second wife, Edith, the golf-playing love of his later life, who wanted nothing to do with the offspring of his first marriage. Morrison's first wife Margaret, Mandy's grandmother, had predeceased him by ten years, and their only daughter received nothing.

Speculation then shifted to Mandy's father, Tony, also nicknamed Mandy at the *Jewish Chronicle*, where he worked as advertising director for 30 years. Perhaps he had left a cash mountain? Unfortunately, he enjoyed life rather too much. On his death in 1988, he left an estate of only £57,711 to Peter's mother, his second wife (and her second husband). Most of that was accounted for by the value of the family home in Hampstead Garden Suburb. So his father's wealth does not account for Mandelson's sudden rise up the property ladder.

In its investigation of Mandy's money, *Punch* looked into suggestions that it had been a loan from his close friend Robert Harris, comfortably-off author of the best-selling thrillers *Fatherland*, *Enigma* and *Archangel*. Mandelson had stayed at Harris's home in rural Berkshire while writing his rather less successful book, *The Blair Revolution*, and a property arrangement was indeed once discussed by the pair. 'There was one point two years ago when we were thinking of buying a place in London and Mandy would live in it during the week while we stayed in the countryside,' admitted Harris. 'But then we had another baby and decided not to go ahead with it. That's probably where the rumours started. He has bought his own place without any assistance from me, I can assure you.'[7] Poor Mandy, playing second fiddle to a baby.

In the extraordinary members' club that is Westminster, there is a long tradition of rich MPs and their friends clubbing together to save one of their number from bankruptcy or to tide him over little local financial difficulties. Almost invariably, however, this useful comradely practice is confined to the Tory Party. MPs need not disclose such arrangements, because they are not obliged to declare personal gifts or loans (which it discreetly terms 'relief from indebtedness') in the Register of Members' Interests. The rules state that both the possible motive of the giver, and the use to which the gift is to be put have to be considered. 'If it is clear on both counts that the gift or benefit is entirely unrelated to membership of the House, or would not be reasonably thought by others to be so related, it need not be registered. If there is any doubt, it should be registered.' No such declaration has been made under the name of Peter Mandelson.

The controversial truth about his finances emerged in Christmas week, 1998, drawing Mandelson into his greatest scandal so far. He had borrowed the bulk of the purchase price for 9 Northumberland Place from Geoffrey Robinson, the wealthy Paymaster-General. Robinson, whose financial affairs are under investigation by the DTI Secretary's own civil servants, loaned Mandy £373,000, at preferential interest rates, so he could buy his way up the property ladder.

The loan, made in October 1996 in the run-up to the general election, was advanced at the Midland Bank base rate – substantially lower than the prevailing mortgage rate. This unique arrangement, which allowed Mandelson to borrow much more than his £43,000 a year MP's salary would allow, was kept secret, not only from the Registrar of Members' Interest – who might have had a legitimate interest – but also from Tony Blair. The Prime Minister and top DTI civil servants only learned about the secret loan on 17 December, when Britain was embroiled in a brief but bloody war with Iraq.

Disclosure of the deal in the newspapers on 22 December prompted furious Opposition charges of a conflict of interest between Mandelson's role as a minister supervising the investigation into the Paymaster General's financial affairs.

Mandelson insisted that he had done nothing wrong. 'At all times I have protected the integrity and professionalism of the DTI. Geoffrey Robinson asked for confidentiality and I respected that. I do not believe that accepting a loan from a friend and fellow

Member of Parliament was wrong. There is no conflict of interest in this. The loan was always intended to be a short-term arrangement and I am in the process of repaying the remainder of the loan with the help of my mother.'

The Paymaster-General, under siege from the media for his business activities, concurred. 'Peter Mandelson, a friend of long-standing, asked me for help in 1996. I was in a position to help through a loan and did so with the understanding that it would be repaid in full in due course. That is all there was and there is to it.'

Downing Street weighed in with its support. Blair's office insisted: 'The prime minister is confident that Peter Mandelson has been properly insulated from any decision relating to Geoffrey Robinson.'

But the scandal did not die down. This was one story that Mandelson could not simply spin away. Questioned on BBC2's *Newsnight* on 21 December, he admitted: 'With the benefit of hindsight it would have been better if all the facts of this matter had been got out.' Then the opportunity for the newspapers to 'throw around this sort of mud' would not be there.

The following day, he was back in self confident – if not arrogant – form. He told the Today programme on Radio 4 that the loan was 'an entirely personal, non-political matter between two friends.' All he wanted to do was 'get settled' in the capital. Robinson 'felt it was important for me to have a settled home base in London if I was going to be effective as a minister.'

He omitted to say that he already had a settled home in London, a ground-floor flat in Wilmington Square, in up-and-coming Clerkenwell. He sold this bachelor pad, and repaid £40,624.68 to Robinson before the election, leaving a debt of £332,375.32.

Mandy sought to dismiss charges of conflict of interest. 'In September 1998, the permanent Secretary of the DTI advised me that the department was considering allegations concerning Geoffrey Robinson's business affairs. We agreed that I should not be involved in this process. Since that conversation, I have played no part whatsoever in the Department's consideration of the matter. Because I was satisfied that any conflict of interest had been properly dealt with, I did not disclose the existence of the loan to the Permanent Secretary.' He also denied any requirement for any declaration of the loan in the Register of Members' Interests. Mandy thought his explanation would put an end to the affair. It did not. Even The *Sun*, his hitherto-friendly Murdoch newspaper, was appalled. 'This affair stinks, stinks, stinks,' it thundered. His secrecy, even with the prime minister, was no way for a minister of the crown to behave, The *Sun* called on Blair to take a close look at Mandelson, adding: 'This scandal will cause him massive damage.'

The affair raises a number of critical questions about Mandelson's rule. The media, quoting Mandy's ubiquitous 'friends', said that Mandelson went public on his secret loan because he feared it would be exposed in this biography. And the evidence does point to a preemptive strike. The information was fed out to sympathetic journalists, with the clear intention of limiting the damage to Mandelson, while intensifying the pressure on the Paymaster-General.

Geoffrey Robinson got no political dividend from his generosity. When his ministerial position was under threat in July 1998, and again in the autumn of 1998, Mandelson made no attempt, privately or publicly, to support his benefactor. Christmas offensive was plainly designed to buttress his own position, while further undermining that of the Paymaster-General. Why? As a Senior Treasury Minister, Robinson was closely identified with the power circle around Chancellor Gordon Brown. This group, detested by Downing Street insiders as an 'alternative government', met regularly in Robinson's penthouse suite in Park Lane, overlooking Hyde Park. Mandelson was determined to destroy this second centre of political influence. His deliberate self-exposure of the full details of the secret loan was part of this campaign. Mandelson's initial targets were Robinson, and some key advisers to the Chancellor. But his ulitimate objective is to supplant Gordon Brown at the Treasury, and position himself to succeed Tony Blair as Labour leader. It is a matter of conjecture as to whether he is carrying out the long-term wishes of the Prime Minister himself.

Towards the end of 1998, Mandelson was also swept into the ministerial scandal swirling round Welsh Secretary Ron Davies, who was mugged and robbed of his car at knifepoint on 26 October. The fact that the offence took place late in the evening, in an area of Clapham Common notorious for gay 'cruising', immediately prompted speculation that the minister was a closet homosexual. Davies, twice married and with a teenage daughter, refused to answer probing questions about any gay proclivities. His reticence naturally intensified media interest, which spread like a brush fire to Peter Mandelson simply because he was the best-known homosexual at Westminster who was neither quite 'in' nor 'out'.

Matthew Parris, who came out as gay only after he had ceased to be a Tory MP, mentioned on BBC TV's *Newsnight* that there were at least two gay members of the Cabinet, and when Jeremy Paxman asked him to identify them, he said, 'Well, Chris Smith [the culture secretary] is openly gay, and I think Peter Mandelson is certainly gay.' Paxman, who prides himself on his cool, visibly panicked and changed the subject. But the story was out, if Mandelson was not.

It ran strongly in the *Mirror* and *Sun* and triggered a management meltdown at the BBC. Executives apologised to Mandy, and then vitiated their own efforts by putting out a confidential memorandum to controllers of all radio and television stations instructing them not to repeat the mistake. The memo, from Ms Anne Sloman, chief political adviser (editorial policy) at the BBC, said: 'Please will all programmes note that under no circumstances whatsoever should the allegations about the private life of Peter Mandelson be repeated or referred to on any broadcast.' A copy was sent to Sir John Birt, the BBC director-general and a friend of Mandelson since the early eighties when they both worked on the LWT programme *Weekend World*. The memo was leaked within hours, heightening the political tension and pulling Mandelson further into the scandal. BBC staff were appalled at this naked self-censorship, and threatened revolt.

A BBC spokesman commented lamely that it was not appropriate 'on grounds of personal privacy' to refer to such matters, and said, 'We would take the same action for any individual.' Yet that statement was contradicted even as it was being made. Glyn Mathias, political editor for BBC Wales, demanded of Ron Davies, 'Are you gay?' Political fallout from the BBC gaffe reached Cabinet level, when Mo Mowlam, the outspoken Northern Ireland secretary, described it as 'a serious error' and 'insulting' to broadcasters, viewers and listeners. Her comments, made in a private discussion between *Any Questions?* presenter Jonathan Dimbleby and his panel of guests, were gleefully relayed to the Sunday newspapers, appearing on the front pages of the *Sunday Times*, the *Mail on Sunday* and the *Sunday Telegraph*. From being a passing remark on *Newsnight*, the affair became a full-blown scandal within days. Senior broadcasters demanded an interview with Sir John Birt to get the ban lifted.

Mandy's reaction was to stay shtum in public while working furiously behind the scenes. His constituency agent, Steve Wallace, dismissed the 'allegations' as 'water off a duck's back' and said it was 'just more speculation' – ignoring the uncomfortable fact that it was the truth. Mandelson's constituents were less outraged than he was. Builder Lee Nicholson, 24, said, 'Everybody has heard that Peter Mandelson is supposed to be gay, but nobody knows for sure. It doesn't bother me whether he is or he isn't, he's still a good MP for Hartlepool.' And shop worker Andrea Barker, 26, said, 'I would still vote for him whether he is gay or not. Homosexuality isn't a problem for 90 per cent of people these days. There are loads of openly gay politicians. Nobody cares.'

Some of this intense media interest may be explained by the hostility generated over the last thirteen years by Mandelson, since he became the most manipulative spin-doctor in Labour's history. The job of communications director was traditionally thought of as a low-key one, explaining to the press the latest decisions of the party's National Executive Committee, or, more likely, putting the best gloss on their frequent bouts of internal warfare. In Mandelson's hands, all that changed. He first redirected media prominence to the leader's office and to up-and-coming politicians like Tony Blair and Gordon Brown, and then worked tirelessly to refashion the party's programme away from old-style socialism – bypassing the supposedly policy-making annual conference.

In the process, he not only made many enemies among the ranks of Labour traditionalists, but earned a reputation for rewarding favourites and punishing 'enemies' – that is, those who did not toe his line – in the press, radio and television. He was called 'Svengali', 'the Prince of Darkness', 'Rasputin' and 'the Evil Genius'. Offensive though these nicknames were, he preferred them to being called 'Lord Snooty', after the comic character, because they flattered his reputation rather than subverting it.

But after a decade and a half of this ruthless manipulation, people inside and outside the media were inclined to hit back. And the view began to take hold that Mandy was only the outward and visible sign of a wider network of homosexual men in key positions in public life. Stephen Bayley, the artistic director of the Millennium Dome, who quit in protest at Mandelson's dumbing-down of a great cultural opportunity, wrote a book entitled *Labour Camp*, which took aim at what he called 'the pink mafia' in government and related fields.

Then Richard Littlejohn, in a characteristically trenchant column in the *Sun* headlined 'Mandy, Mandy, Mandy, Out! Out! Out!', asked why the outing of Mandelson by Matthew Parris had been ignored by BBC news, Ceefax and most newspapers. He pointed out that allegations that Ron Davies was forced to resign because of his involvement in a gay sex scandal had been ignored at Question Time in the Commons. Curious – or what? Littlejohn concluded, 'The truth is that there is a virtual freemasonry of homosexuals operating at the highest levels in politics, in the media – especially television – and within Buckingham Palace.'

Lord (Norman) Tebbit, former henchman to Margaret Thatcher, took the scandal one stage further in a characteristically blunt intervention. In a direct reference to the Mandelson saga, he argued that homosexuals should not be allowed to take up sensitive Cabinet posts. In a letter to the *Daily Telegraph*, Tebbit, himself a former trade and industry secretary, said that Mandelson's current post should not be off limits, but the Home Office certainly should. He congratulated Mandelson for keeping his sexuality to himself rather than flaunting it. 'However,' he added, 'in a world where Freemasons are being asked to identify themselves as such in order that the public may judge if they are improperly doing one another favours, surely it is important that homosexuals should not be in a position to do each other favours.'[8]

Tebbit was immediately disowned by the Conservative leader's office, but other ranking Tory politicians began to ask awkward questions about the magic fraternity who were guaranteed discretion on the airwaves. Michael Ancram, the Tory Party chairman, was told by BBC officials before appearing on *Breakfast with Frost* that he could not mention Mandelson or his private life. Ancram protested that he had no intention of doing so, and asked whether any other friends of Sir John Birt were members of 'this new club'. Peter Ainsworth, the Conservative culture spokesman, wondered aloud on the rival GMTV *Sunday Programme* (where the Mandy ban did not operate) whether BBC bosses might not want to upset Mandelson or others in government at a time when the BBC licence fee and its future were under review. In the atmosphere of feverish speculation that followed the Parris outing, virtually any conjecture found currency. Journalist Henry Porter accused Mandelson of engaging in a 'staged spat' with Murdoch's *Sun* over the stories about his sexuality before eventually allowing through Murdoch's bid to buy Manchester United. Mandy was simply 'making it look good' like a crooked security guard in the movies.

Days of farce followed. The BBC apologised to Mandy twice — once in a personal letter from Jeremy Paxman, hand-delivered to his home (Mandelson naturally felt this was inadequate), and then via BBC chairman Sir Christopher Bland. The overall impression was of an establishment scurrying around trying to cover up something nasty in its midst. But the nastiness was not Mandelson's homosexuality. It was the 'new club' of New Labour insiders looking out for each other.

Some observers see the club as a 'pink mafia' or, in the amusing American parlance, the 'homintern' (a skit on the old Soviet Comintern, or Communist International). Stephen Bayley believes that a tiny clique, composed partly of homosexuals, has usurped much of the power of government. 'They have moved government out of Parliament into the media and culture,' he says. 'It strikes me as unhealthy. What is worrying is that people of power and influence are involved in an interest group which just happens to be a sexual one. It is a secretive interest group. It just happens to be about male gay sex. It could be badger baiting, but they have a secret, or they consider it to be a guilty secret.' Therein lies its exclusivity, and its power. The club requires mutual loyalty to its members – rather than to the Blair government, or any other employer or interest group. 'It is both defined by the bonds of secrecy, and strengthened by them. As soon as those bonds are loosened, its powers are diminished,' Bayley suggests. That is why the club demands invisibility. 'Mandelson's power depends on not being seen.'[9] Paradoxically, the more he is seen to be manipulating the levers of power, the more likely his ascendancy is to be endangered.

Speculation about 'Peter's friends' intensified in the wake of the *Sun*–Tebbit intervention. It was pointed out that Lance Price, the new deputy to Alastair Campbell, press secretary to the prime minister, made no secret of his homosexuality. Price is often trusted with the key lobby briefings of Westminster journalists in the absence of his boss. In the wider circle of Mandelsonia, observers identify Mark Boland, Prince Charles's deputy private secretary, as a good friend (Mandy was the only Cabinet minister to attend the Prince's fiftieth birthday party at Highgrove). In the same extended network appears Guy Black, director of the Press Complaints Commission, who is close to Boland and has shown a comradely interest in Mandelson's awkward relationship with the press. At the BBC, Mandelson's pal Howell James, former political secretary to John Major, is now public relations adviser to Sir John Birt, another ally from his days at LWT.

In the febrile days that followed, a fresh scandal surfaced when the news of Mandelson's relationship with a Brazilian student broke in the *Express on Sunday*. The story, innocuous except to those in the know, disclosed that Reinaldo Avila da Silva, currently studying in Tokyo, was a 'good friend'. Mandy's picture appeared on the front page (on 1 November 1998), alongside a 'taster' headline offering the exclusive story on page 7.

On the day before the disclosures appeared, alarm bells rang in the new establishment. Working through his pal the Labour life peer Lord Hollick, chief executive of the *Express* group, Mandelson tried to get the story spiked. Hollick made four telephone calls to the paper's news managers. Mandelson delivered a hand-written protest note to Rosie Boycott, editor-in-chief of the *Express* titles, who lives across the road in fashionable Notting Hill. In the end, the story was scaled down so that it would not be too damaging to his image.

The incident did not end there. Mandelson was said to be 'very upset' and could not understand why disciplinary action had not been taken at the paper. Media commentator Roy Greenslade remarked that 'It will be surprising if the incident doesn't lead to at least one executive being fired.' Almost as he wrote, the job of Amanda Platell, executive editor of the *Express on Sunday*, was offered to an executive on the *Daily Telegraph*, who turned it down. The development prompted serious anxiety, not just among the media chattering classes but at Westminster, where Mandelson's control freakery over the reporting of his love life finally became a political issue.

Peter Bottomley, MP for Worthing and a former Tory minister, put down an Early Day Motion in the Commons demanding an inquiry into whether Mandelson ('or his helpers') had any formal or informal contact concerning the staffing of the *Express on Sunday*. During the investigation, he argued, the trade secretary

should be relieved of his responsibilities relating to the interests
of Lord Hollick and the owners of Express Newspapers to avoid
any confusion of interest. The Motion was plainly mischievous,
but it established a clear political link between Mandy's private
life and his duties as a minister.

Worse was to come. The anti-establishment *Punch* ran a long
article in its 21 November 1998 issue, alleging that Mandelson
had, while on a visit to Brazil as minister without portfolio four
months previously, had a 'wild time' touring the gay bars of Rio
de Janeiro with Martin Dowle, head of the British Council.
Mandelson and Dowle both flatly denied the allegations.

The story was leaked to the parliamentary lobby two days
before the magazine hit the news-stands, but only one newspaper,
the *Daily Telegraph*, had the nerve to run anything about the
'revelations'. Its page 2 lead merely reported that Mandelson faced
new allegations over his private life, which effectively challenged
him to sue for libel or face a media feeding-frenzy over every
aspect of his private life. Mandelson's aides were busy again that
night – 17 November – telephoning newsdesks with dire
warnings if they ran the story. The *Telegraph* article failed to appear
after the first edition.

The word being put out by Mandy's spin-doctors at Westminster the next day was that he denied the allegations, but would
not sue unless they appeared in a mainstream publication. *Punch*
is owned by the immensely rich owner of Harrods, Mohamed al-
Fayed, and is not truly a fringe publication. Its report looked
forward to a second visit that the trade secretary was due to make
to Brazil on 29 November. Within forty-eight hours of the
allegations being published, Mandelson had called off the six-day
trip, citing pressure of parliamentary business. It was the first
political casualty of the allegations about his private life.

The predicted feeding-frenzy is now under way. David Bridle, a
journalist on the gay *Pink Paper*, was only too happy to talk about
his recollections of seeing Mandelson in the sauna at the YMCA
in Tottenham Court Road – 'one of the gayest places you could
find on a weekend afternoon in central London . . . a quiet haven

for gay men trying to stay fit in both mind and body'. In the late eighties, shortly after leaving his post as Labour media chief and before he became an MP, Mandy was a habitué.

'There was one man who stood out from all the others,' recalled Bridle. 'He was in his thirties, had a moustache, was tall and noticeably distinguished, and moved between sauna and restroom with an air of preoccupation. Deep in his thoughts, he rarely spoke to others, but nevertheless seemed to enjoy being around these lively, sporty gay men.'

These men-only sessions in a cosy, wooden sauna and nearby restroom, were a 'social space' for men to meet gay friends, Bridle said. 'The sex, when it happened, was mainly vanilla and un-spectacular.' How 'vanilla'? 'It's true to say there was sex going on, but they didn't start pulling it out and doing things. People maybe got off as a couple but generally that was done where there are not many people around. Or they might drop their towel, get an erection. They might wank . . . no real sex.'

Bridle saw Mandelson several times in the YMCA sauna, but never saw him indulge in sex. 'During that time, and in later years, there must have been stressful times when Mandelson sought the solace of being with other gay men. Maybe at the time, the Y was Mandelson's version of Ron Davies' Clapham Common. A respite from the straight world. Getting in touch with your sexuality and those who share it. But Mandelson didn't use this space for finding sex.' The trade secretary left the Y a few years ago, he added, 'presumably deciding his public profile required it. I don't see that as a rejection of his gayness but, as with any celebrity, it's a protection mechanism.'[10]

Precisely. The country might be able to cope with a gay Cabinet minister – indeed, now, with three – but are voters ready for a gay prime minister? For this is Mandelson's covert agenda: to succeed Tony Blair. His public profile might not survive the damage that widespread knowledge of his sometimes exotic private life might inflict. And the more he tries to keep the lid on, the more vigorously his critics will seek to prise it off. The search for scandal intensifies, rather than diminishes.

2

RED SPOON
_____

If the landed gentry are said to be born with a silver spoon in
their mouth, something similar may be said of Peter Mandelson.
He was born into the aristocracy of the Left, the grandson of
Herbert Morrison, a deputy leader of the Labour Party and holder
of high Cabinet office.

Peter grew up in Hampstead Garden Suburb in north London,
a genteel neighbourhood that was home to high-ranking civil
servants and senior politicians, including Harold Wilson and his
family. The Mandelsons visited them regularly, and were invited
to tea in Downing Street after Labour regained power in 1964. So
it could be said that Peter was born with a red spoon in his mouth.
'He just sort of grew up in a political atmosphere,' recalled his
mother, Mary, years later. 'Peter was quite political at an early age.
He liked talking to politicians.' The future Cabinet minister was
never a shy boy, she added. 'He may have just have waded up and
seen whether he would get a good reception. I don't know what
went on in his mind.'[1]

One of his earliest memories is of watching excitedly as the
veteran American broadcaster Walter Cronkite did a piece to

camera in front of the Wilsons' house during the 1964 general elections. The awestruck 10-year-old Peter was fascinated. It was the beginning of a lifetime preoccupation with politics, television and power. He likes to trace his political genes back to his grandfather. His mother agrees that 'they are sort of similar'.

But for the young Mandelson, the Morrison connection was painful rather than rewarding. The man who served as Labour's home secretary and foreign secretary stonily turned his heart against his daughter and her child, scarcely acknowledging them in later life and completely ignoring them in his self-serving *Autobiography*.

Herbert Morrison, the son of an intensely Conservative authoritarian policeman, was born in Brixton, south London, in 1888. He lost the sight of his right eye when only three days old. He also had a characteristic quiff that made him a butt of the cartoonists down the years. After a series of nondescript jobs, he plunged into labour-movement politics, which occupied the rest of his long life. Like his future son-in-law Tony Mandelson, he worked in newspapers for a time, as circulation manager of the first official Labour paper, the *Daily Citizen*, before the First World War. Thereafter, he became the moving force behind the powerful London Labour Party. He was mayor of Hackney in 1919, and elected to Parliament in 1924 as MP for South Hackney during the period of the first Labour government. He gave Londoners the finest public bus system in the world.

At Westminster, he moved steadily up the ministerial ladder in the thirties and into Churchill's coalition Cabinet during the Second World War as home secretary and minister for home security. In this role, he rallied the morale of Londoners during the Blitz. In 1945, he played a key role in Labour's landslide victory at the polls, and went on to become deputy prime minister, leader of the Commons and, briefly, foreign secretary. But Clement Attlee, the post-war premier, who once objected to Morrison on the grounds that 'Herbert cannot distinguish between big things and little things', clung to office despite illness, to prevent his deputy from becoming leader of the Labour Party in 1956.

Morrison retired from Parliament in 1959, laden with plaudits, and was made one of the first life peers in the dissolution honours list.

It would not be wise to draw too close a parallel between Morrison and his grandson. He was a self-educated working-class boy, not a middle-class aspiring intellectual. However, there are similarities. On Morrison's death, *The Times* noted that 'his concern was entirely with winning elections and carrying out pragmatic reforms'. His bearing was 'a mixture of Cockney brashness and the self-confidence which arises from knowledge, competence and a solidly based political position'.[2] Morrison's biographers, Donoughue and Jones, described him as able, self-confident and enthusiastic, and not one to suffer fools gladly. He possessed a zeal for efficient organisation of 'almost Germanic quality'.[3] Something of these qualities may be observed in Peter Mandelson. 'If he could see Peter today, I think he'd be rather pleased,' his mother says.[4]

But it was Morrison's tortured private life that was to have most bearing on his grandson's emotional development. As a 'political' (as distinct from conscientious) objector to the First World War, Morrison was ordered by a military service tribunal to work on the land. He spent the latter years of the war working as a landscape gardener and nurseryman in Letchworth Garden City, an agreeable spot about 40 miles north of London. There, he met and conceived a passion for Rose Rosenberg, a lively and intelligent woman with a keen interest in politics (she later became the devoted private secretary of Ramsay MacDonald). It seemed a match made by Darwinian political selection. But Morrison confounded his friends by dumping Rose for the village maiden, Margaret 'Daisy' Kent, who shared his love of country dancing.

She was ten years younger than Morrison, and his complete opposite: reserved, to the point of shyness, and handicapped by a serious stammer. She was compared to a painting by Burne-Jones or Rossetti, dressed in trailing skirts that she designed and wove herself. By day, she was a secretary at the Spirella corset factory. By night, she captivated Herbert with her vibrant dancing at the

Skittles Inn, Letchworth. He pursued her relentlessly. They married in 1919, and went to live in Bermondsey.

This was the year of his mayoralty. At its close, Morrison paid tribute to his wife's patience and fortitude, admitting that his home life was tragic. He came home late every night, and was practically a lodger in his own house. His new bride disliked public life, and rarely accompanied him. Besides, she was now pregnant, and endured a painful delivery of the couple's only child, Mary Joyce Morrison, Peter's mother. Daisy had a nervous breakdown, refusing to nurse her baby.

Today, she would almost certainly be diagnosed as suffering from post-natal depression. She also developed a strong aversion to sexual intercourse, and evidently refused marital relations for the rest of their life together – strangely enough, just as her mother-in-law had done, many years previously. Morrison's second wife, Edith, later observed, 'It was one of those marriages that never had a chance. They were seldom seen in public together, and only their closest friends knew the deep unhappiness of both. This long-drawn-out and painful association had a profound effect on Herbert. He made work the whole of his life.'[5] The marriage lasted for 32 years, until Margaret died of stomach cancer. She was, concluded Morrison's biographers, 'a disturbed waif married to the wrong man in the wrong environment'.[6]

Mary Morrison grew up in this disturbed and unhappy household in suburban Eltham, alienated from her father and cared for by a lonely mother subject to nervous collapse. 'I very rarely saw my own father,' Mary recalled many years afterwards. 'I'd see him perhaps at the breakfast table for about five minutes. He was working and would get home well after my bedtime, and then he'd come down to breakfast. That would be the whole week. He might be at home on a Sunday, if I was lucky.'[7]

She also confided that home was 'spartan'. Her father was scarcely to be seen, except at weekends, when he spent most of his time on official papers and responded to her girlish questions with a distant 'Hmmmm'. Occasionally, he took her out, but if she asked for money, she never heard the end of it. Sometimes Mary heard her father return at night, and her mother go downstairs. There would be shouting and her mother would break down sobbing.

On Mary's eighth birthday, which coincided with the general election of 1929, Morrison appealed to the voters of Hackney to put a cross by his name as 'Many Happy Returns for Mary'. She was cross about being involved in 'beastly politics', and Morrison in turn was irritated that she did not support him in his political life, though he did not go out of his way to make politics appealing to her.[8] Plainly, he had little time for his daughter, while she could not wait to escape from this tyrannical, dysfunctional home.

She qualified as a shorthand typist, and while still in her teens met and formed a relationship with Horace Williams, a 26-year-old accountant. They both worked in the civil service: he in the Ministry of Supply, she in the Social Welfare Ministry. More importantly, he was the son of Tom Williams, an under-secretary at the Ministry of Agriculture, whose ministerial ranking went some way towards mollifying the distant home secretary. He disapproved of the match, though he clearly gave his permission as she had not yet reached the age at which she could marry without his consent. The young couple married at Hendon Registry Office on 5 April 1941. Margaret Morrison travelled up from Dawlish, the Devon seaside resort to which she had been evacuated to escape the Blitz, for the ceremony, and Herbert Morrison was present as a witness.

But the relationship was doomed from the start. Mary Morrison was fleeing from an unhappy home into an unwise marriage. It ended as precipitately as it had begun, in divorce. After the war, Mary found a job with Dorland Advertising, one of the largest agencies in the advertising industry. There, she met a handsome, flamboyant account executive, Tony Mandelson, and a mutual attraction quickly flourished. Mandelson (whose real name was George) was known as 'Mandy', the nickname his son would come to hate. Tony's father, Norman, was the financial advertising manager of the *Jewish Chronicle* in the mid-war years when City spending was on a generous scale.

Norman Mandelson lived an adventurous life. He was born in Tumut, New South Wales, a small town in the Snowy Mountains mid-way between Canberra and Wagga Wagga. He served as a 'sometime Reuters agent' in South Africa and Rhodesia, before settling in London. He was a devout Jew, founder and later president of the Harrow (United) Synagogue. The family lived in Pinner, Middlesex, on the north-west outskirts of London, respectable suburbia rather than high-flying, like Hampstead.

By his own account, Tony Mandelson had a 'damn good war', finishing as Major Mandelson of the 1st Royal Dragoons. He claimed to have been the first Allied soldier to enter Denmark in 1945. His service in a cavalry regiment entitled him to membership of the Cavalry Club, which had only one other Jewish member, the Tory MP Sir Henry d'Avigdor-Goldsmid. Mandelson was sceptical of the advertising world, and followed his father to the *Jewish Chronicle*, where he became assistant general manager in 1947; he was to stay there for 30 years. Mandy senior was 'frankly terrible' at his first job on the paper. Routine administration was inimical to him. 'Mandy's world required a soaring imagination and a creative temperament,' recalled staff writer Jenni Frazer years later. 'But he was discovered to have an almost heaven-sent talent – he could sell almost anything to anyone.'[9] He was switched to the post of advertising manager, later becoming advertising director.

A picture of Tony Mandelson at his desk in 1951 shows a slim, handsome, intense-looking man, dark hair slicked back, wearing a serious expression. But this was something of a mask. He was regarded as a larger-than-life character. Indeed, Alan Rubenstein, the *Jewish Chronicle*'s advertising director, who worked with him for many years, said, 'He was a formidable operator. But for years he played the eccentric, until finally he was no longer playing at it – he became that part, totally.' His sense of humour was legendary. On one occasion, Mandelson père helped out on the display advertising desk. A reader rang in with a death notice. Tony asked, 'Name? What? Cohen? Cohen? Spell it.' The grief-stricken caller went on and on, until Mandelson intervened sharply, 'Now you listen to me very carefully. I'm very sorry he's dead, but we're very busy here . . .' On another occasion, he was due to give a brief presidential address to the annual Christmas lunch of the Advertising Managers' Association in the grand ballroom of London's Connaught Rooms. Instead, in the full glare of a spotlight, he emerged in Santa Claus costume and roared, 'Shalom everyone! Merry Christmas from the *Jewish Chronicle*!' Tony Mandelson was not particularly religious, considering that he was the son of a *shul*, but friends noticed that he attended Norrice Lea, the synagogue of Hampstead Garden Suburb, on the Jewish holy day of Yom Kippur – contrary to the assertion in a profile in the *Sunday Times* that both Peter's parents were 'left-wing progressive atheists, as is Mandelson'.

Tony and Mary married at Harrow Registry Office on 24 July 1948. Both gave their address as 18 Meadow Road, Pinner. On the certificate of marriage, she is described as Mary Joyce Williams, formerly Morrison, aged 26, the divorced wife of Horace Williams, with no stated rank or profession. He is described as George Norman Mandelson, aged 27, formerly the husband of Doreen Mandelson, formerly Hennessy, 'from whom he obtained a divorce'.

Even in the post-war years, it was unusual for a man to obtain a divorce from his wife. In the event of a dissolution, the husband normally assumed responsibility for the marriage breakdown, even if it was not his fault. Peter Mandelson's mother's divorce and remarriage are matters of public knowledge. His father's similar misfortune, if so it may be described, is revealed here for the first time. Tony Mandelson had married Doreen Hennessey at Whitby registry office on 10 September 1941, another wartime marriage, contracted less than two months before his future bride wed Horace Williams. On the marriage certificate, he appears under his correct full name of George Norman Mandelson, aged 21, with the rank of 2nd Lieutenant of the 13th Huzzars and the occupation – like his father – of stockbroker. Doreen Hennessy was also only 21, a spinster, of Bournemouth, and the daughter of a civil servant.

From the wreckage of two past liaisons, Tony and Mary Mandelson built a long, successful marriage. Their first child, Miles Anthony, now a clinical psychologist, was born on 16 March 1949, rather less than eight months after the wedding. This indicates that either the baby was dramatically premature, of which there has been no suggestion, or Peter Mandelson's mother was pregnant when she married his father. In the common parlance of the day, they 'had to get married'.

Certainly, the couple seemed in no hurry to give Miles a brother or sister. Peter Benjamin Mandelson did not follow until more than four years later, on 21 October 1953. According to the birth certificate, he was born at home, 3 Eastholm, London NW11. Family myth has it that he was given his first name after Peter Rabbit, the star of Beatrix Potter's books, on the prompting of his elder brother. 'My brother . . . was allowed to choose,' he said later. 'It was out of my control.'

It was a secure and loving childhood. In one photo, Peter is seen sitting on his father's knee on a bench outside their home, aged about 5, busy on a toy telephone, much as he was on the real thing in years to come. He went to the local nursery and primary schools in Hampstead Garden Suburb. 'Peter was very happy at school,' his mother remembers. 'He had a very enjoyable time from nursery school onwards. He was a popular child with lots of friends.'

The Mandelsons were well known around 'the Suburb'. They were both members of the Labour Party. Tony was active in the local Conservation Trust and Residents' Association, ultimately becoming its chairman. Apart from the Wilsons, in the neighbourhood there lived Patrick Gordon-Walker MP, the gaunt political loser and one-time parliamentary private secretary to Herbert Morrison, and eminent civil servants such as Sir Eric Roll, the first permanent secretary at Labour's ill-fated Department of Economic Affairs. Lord Robbins, author of the controversial report on expanding higher education, lived round the corner. And a hundred yards away was the home of the young Charles Clarke, son of a Whitehall mandarin, who was to become Neil

Kinnock's chief of staff and a close friend – then enemy – of Peter Mandelson.

The Mandelsons saw a great deal of the Wilsons. Peter was even given Giles Wilson's cast-off Wolf-Cub jersey. He remembered it as 'very itchy, and too small'. Tony Mandelson and his son Peter were entertained in Downing Street three or four times. By all accounts, Mary did not join them.

But there was little contact with Mary's father, then at the height of his fame. Young Peter was later to cling to an abiding memory of Morrison as an ancient figure who occasionally visited them at weekends. He came for Saturday lunch. 'I remember waiting outside the house for his car to come round the corner. He was a big, dominant man, with a great mop of white hair,' he recollected. 'I treated him with a certain reverence, but he was also very kind – he would put his arm around me. He used to sit down to a good meal with his napkin tucked into his collar – a habit I still have – and have a cigar and a snooze before going home.'[10]

According to Lady Morrison, his second wife, Herbert was virtually estranged from his daughter. 'Herbert never spoke to me about his first marriage, and as little as possible about their only child, his daughter, who I never met,' she related subsequently. 'His relationship with both his wife and daughter had been very painful.' Morrison had given his consent for the first marriage, 'but he hardly ever spoke to her again, not even after the marriage ended.'[11] However, his biographers record that Margaret and Mary did travel with Morrison for a recuperative holiday in Menton on the French Riviera in April 1947. It seems clear that he did not really approve of his daughter's second marriage, either. Certainly, he was not a frequent visitor to 'the Suburb'. Some have attributed this to a latent – and perhaps not so latent – anti-Semitism on the part of Herbert Morrison, though he was converted to Zionism after a visit to a kibbutz in 1935. On that occasion, he was used by militant Zionists. A suitcase full of weapons was brought into Palestine clandestinely among Morrison's luggage; he remained blithely unaware. His biographers record that, even before this experience, Morrison was 'favourably inclined to Jews'.[12] (Since

Jewish identity is passed down the female line, and his mother is a gentile, technically Peter Mandelson is not a Jew.) Lady Morrison, whose views were naturally coloured by the self-interest of a second wife, may still have got it right when she said, 'It may be that unconsciously Herbert's bitter feelings towards his own father somehow got in the way of his relationship with his daughter, blighting it.'[13]

Mandelson later confessed that Morrison severed relations with his daughter after he married. 'After my grandmother died, he married again. His second wife had little time for old friends and family. Then the sight began to go in his one good eye, so he could no longer drive over to see us. I remember coming home from school one day and saying to my mother that I really wanted to see him. She explained that would be very difficult. I was very upset.'[14]

The end came swiftly enough, on 6 March 1965, when Peter was only 11. 'We weren't told how ill he was,' Mandelson related. 'One Saturday evening, when I was watching television, there was a newsflash to say he had died. I ran into the kitchen to tell my mother. It was terrible to learn of it that way.'[15]

Whatever the nature of the Morrison father-daughter relationship, it does seem to have had a damaging impact on young Peter, in more ways than one. He is fiercely protective of his mother, calling her 'the Duchess'. Of her disastrous early foray into marriage, he has remarked, 'My mother's first marriage didn't last long, and she exposed my grandfather to the double embarrassment of marrying very young and then divorcing prematurely.'[16]

Mandelson was close to his father, but there appears to have been some stiffness in the relationship. His mother said, 'Peter always saw eye to eye with his father, but they were slightly different in their attitudes.' Mandelson himself speaks little of his father. 'I wish my father had seen me in these offices,' he said. 'He was such a nice, outward-going man. He loved politics and politicians. He had absolutely no political ambitions of his own. But he would have found my role amusing.'[17]

Mandelson's relationship with his mother was as close as that with her father had been remote. Peter was still taking his laundry back long after he had left home. He describes his mother with restrained passion. 'Quiet, elegant, gracious, soft-spoken but with tremendous steel,' he told one interviewer. 'If you incurred my mother's disapproval, you'd know it.'[18] Yet from a very early age he espoused the 'beastly politics' his mother hated so much. He insists that 'my mother has no love of politics. She offered me no encouragement to go into politics at all.'

Nevertheless, he claims his first political memory goes back to the general election of 1959, shortly before his sixth birthday. In some versions, he is delivering leaflets through letter boxes almost as high as his head. In January 1996, he told Labour women in Wellingborough – like his grandfather, Mandelson is a brilliant handler of ladies *d'un certain age* – that he watched the canvass returns come through in the poll that dashed the premiership hopes of Hugh Gaitskell, the man who supplanted Herbert Morrison. The Mandelsons supported their neighbour Harold Wilson in his bid for the Labour leadership in 1963, after Gaitskell's untimely death. This was yet another source of dispute with Morrison. 'My grandfather had no time for Wilson,' Peter Mandelson said years later. 'He thought he was a bit of a charlatan, and he made little effort to hide his feelings.'

He also retells the story of watching Harold Wilson leave his home in nearby Southway to take up the reins of office in 1964. He remembers 'standing on the pavement absolutely mesmerised as he [Wilson] sped off towards Number Ten', and, later, visiting Downing Street and watching the Changing of the Guard. 'I was doing something special. I was close to power. It was exciting.' The excitement stayed with him.

His mother noticed that young Peter was different from other boys. 'I don't know how, but I always knew Peter would become successful,' she said later. 'He was in control all the time. He knew what he wanted to do and did it. He had his ups and downs. Things got in the way, but apart from that everything went to plan, I think. He's always been active and doing something. He was a very determined child. Quite in control, never messed it up.'[19]

Peter Mandelson went first to the local primary and then, in 1965, to his local grammar school, Hendon County. It was a co-educational school, with around 450 boys and girls drawn from a largely middle-class catchment area of north London. The school had a flourishing sixth form, and the emphasis under its 'fairly autocratic' headmaster E. W. Maynard Potts was firmly on academic achievement. Hendon County had a large Jewish intake – at least half, and perhaps two-thirds according to Mandelson's contemporaries – and each morning there were two assemblies, one Jewish and one for the rest. These were post-11-plus days, so it was a community school, though not yet a true comprehensive. That would come, and soon, involving the radical young Mandelson in his first real political struggle. A form of selection procedure still existed: potential pupils were screened at their primary through academic tests in the classroom. Essentially, they took a form of 11-plus without knowing it.

Young Peter's love affair with politics was soon noticed. In his second year at Hendon County Grammar, he took part in a school geographical field trip to the Shell Tower in Waterloo – then the highest building in London, just downriver from the House of Commons. As the 12-year-olds gazed over a capital substantially rebuilt after the horrors of the Blitz, Mandelson's gaze alighted on the palace of Westminster. He pointed out the seat of government to a girl classmate, and stated confidently: 'That's where I am going to work.'

Hendon County was something of an intellectual powerhouse. Its pupils were privileged, both materially and culturally. Nine out of ten made it to university. From the second year, they were streamed, with the brighter ones put together in a class that was taught Latin. There were, his contemporaries recall, lots of very, very clever children. Peter was not in the top notch. 'He was bright. But not top of the class: maybe fifth or sixth,' said one. 'He was certainly not a swot.' What he lacked in sheer brilliance, he made up for in style. He was not the class clown, but a sharp – acerbic, even – observer of events around him. He is remembered as witty with words, sometimes malicious, laughing at other people's expense. 'Peter had a very mocking sense of humour. It was OK if you were in with him, but it could be quite hurtful if you were on the receiving end of it,' said a former classmate.

Despite signs of rebelliousness, he was popular with the staff. In his first years at Hendon County, his misbehaviour went only so far. Like other boys, he played up to the 'hopeless' Latin teacher, but he moderated his behaviour in front of the sharper teachers. He inherited his father's tallness: in school photographs, he is always the chap in the middle of the back row. In those days, too, he was as friendly with the girls in his class as with the boys. Indeed, one ex-classmate describes him as 'flirtatious with the girls'. To some, he disclosed in the strictest confidence, that he was the grandson of Herbert Morrison, the former foreign secretary. It was only when they inevitably swapped notes that they realised he had 'confided' in others, somewhat diminishing the intended compliment.

Fellow pupil Heather Bell (née Heys), whose father was a Customs and Excise officer living in Edgware, remembers young Peter as 'snobbish, but right from the word go a character'. He was often the centre of attention, but he 'sort of lorded it over his little group'.[20] On an educational school cruise on the *Uganda* in his fourth year, the ship ran into a Mediterranean storm. Virtually all the children were seasick. But 14-year-old Peter braved the November gales and led hymn-singing on the deck to bolster their spirits.

Mandelson quickly showed an interest in the school debating society, sharpening his claws on elder boys who were not so intellectually nimble. He also exhibited early signs of leadership. When, in 1967, the Tory-controlled London borough of Barnet decided that Hendon County should become a comprehensive, its headmaster fought a determined rearguard action against reform. Mandelson was just as determined that the change should go through. He and a couple of friends organised protests, inside the school and without.

Paul Marginson, a close friend at school and now professor of human relations at Leeds University, remembers, 'Peter and one or

two others were among the active supporters of comprehen-
sivisation. Active to the extent of organising kids to go to council
meetings and shout things out from the public balcony.'[21]
Mandelson was also among the ringleaders of a one-day strike at
the school, though the issue on this occasion was not moves
towards becoming a comprehensive.

Like most similar schools, Hendon County had a system of
prefects, modelled on that of the public schools and designed to
instil a sense of responsibility among the older pupils. Prefects
were drawn mainly from the sixth form, but the boys generally
knew by the end of their fifth year if they had been chosen to wield
limited disciplinary powers. They also had their own room, where
they went to smoke.

In his first term in the sixth, Mandelson, already installed as a
prefect, was 'very influential' in leading a revolt against the
system. He argued that it was a 'stooge' operation acting on behalf
of headmaster Maynard Potts, and insisted that it be scrapped in
favour of an elected school committee. His manifesto said that
such an arrangement would be fairer, and better able to represent
the interests of the students. The rebels' first step – a risky one,
despite the rebellious spirit of the decade – was to resign as
prefects. A deputation of about ten of them, hearts beating, went
to the headmaster's study to announce their decision to quit. 'We
got a fairly fearsome tirade for our pains,' recollects Marginson,
'but it didn't dent our resolve. We went ahead, at potential
personal cost.'[22]

When bluster failed, the headmaster resorted to guile. He
interviewed the rebels one by one, pointing out that the school
had a special 'fast track' admission to King's College, Cambridge,
for bright pupils. They could bypass the common entrance
examination, making it a great deal easier to win a place at the
university. Like Mandelson, Marginson was on the list. 'I was told
that because of showing such disloyalty, I would be off the list, and
I wouldn't get to Cambridge. I am sure Peter was given a similar
message,' he said.[23]

By now the rebels were in too deep to extricate themselves. Fired

by teenage militancy, they formed themselves into a Schools'
Action Unit, preaching 'pupil power'. Leaflets appeared, calling on
pupils to rebel against dress codes and rules governing the length
of hair – wearing it long was a commonplace sign of revolt. The
next stage was the formation of a branch of the National Union of
School Students (NUSS), an offshoot of the Left-dominated
National Union of Students. It was widely supported in the school
and formed the basis for a 'day of action' that Mandelson was
instrumental in promoting. The NUSS's political programme
included opening up schools to 'democratic structures' to give
pupils a say in the running of their educational environment.

Some idea of the radical ideas he espoused may be gained from
a manifesto in the Young Communist League (YCL) journal
Challenge, which argued that school students (some old enough to
vote) too often had to put up with 'the dictates of headmasters
who reflect the attitudes of the "thin red line" and "stiff upper lip"
era.' Progressive-minded school students – whether in the YCL or
not – were urged to 'take action' to bring about change. The YCL's
schools organiser, Roger Murray, urged pupils to build a mass
organisation in their schools, demanding the right to organise, a
fully comprehensive educational system, the abolition of public
schools and of corporal punishment, higher spending on education, and community use of school buildings outside teaching
hours. Democracy would come under attack from the Heath
government, the YCL argued, and school students 'must answer
in no uncertain terms' along with parents, teachers and trade
unionists.[24]

Working from a script like that, it is not surprising that to the
headmaster, Peter was a dangerous revolutionary. To his school-
mates, he was an intensely loyal friend who was strong enough to
stand up to an autocratic head and gave others the confidence to
do so. On strike day, an 'enormous number' (Marginson's
estimate) of pupils streamed out of classes and gathered on the
school playing-field. They held an impromptu debate on their
ambitious demands for greater democracy. To their surprise and
delight, there was no punishment.

Some members of the teaching staff were sympathetic, particularly the deputy head, Jack Driver, a 'very warm guy' who believed in keeping open channels of communication with the students. He was also keenly aware that Maynard Potts would resign as soon as the school went comprehensive, which he did in Easter 1971, leaving Driver as acting headmaster. With him went the prefect system, and an elected school committee was set up in its place. The revolution had succeeded.

Mandelson later confessed, 'I was a rebel at school and with the others rebelled against the prefect system. It was a terribly hierarchical sort of old-style grammar school. We got petitions up and led protests. Our old headmaster got up in assembly and denounced me and my chief collaborator as industrial militants who were pulling apart the fabric of the school community.'[25]

Other contemporaries suggest that Mandelson's motives may not have derived solely from a burning sense of social justice, arguing that he was aggrieved at not being made head boy. 'Peter always had an eye for the main chance,' recollects Heather Bell, 'and this was one of those situations where he felt he could shine a bit. He was not as revolutionary as his friend David Shields. I didn't ever see Peter as somebody who would stick his neck out if it was in danger of being chopped off.' Heather became Shields's girlfriend in the sixth form, and his friendship with Mandelson cooled. But there was very little sign of Peter's long-term sexual orientation. 'I seem to remember him having a long-term girlfriend at school,' remembers Heather. 'Certainly, at school that didn't manifest itself. Even though it was the sixties and seventies, sexuality wasn't an issue people were willing to talk about. Nobody was gay. We were all heterosexual, and that was that.'[26]

The pupils' revolt clearly gave Mandelson and his rebel pals a taste for the politics of the hard Left. Initially, Mandelson was attracted to the Young Socialists (YS), formally the youth arm of the Labour Party but in reality heavily infiltrated by ultra-Left Trotskyists. He dallied with them from the age of 15. At this period, and particularly after Labour's unexpected general election defeat in 1970, the Young Socialists fell into the hands of the

Militant Tendency. Bob Labi, a member of the YS National Committee, remembers Mandelson as being one of the three most promising members of the Hendon South Branch.

However, Labi detected a political coolness. 'They were not prepared to debate very much. It was clear that there was a grouping linked to the Young Communist League building up in Hendon that wanted to keep in quarantine from the rest of the YS. They tried to build a *cordon sanitaire*. In those days, it was not unusual to find people in the Labour Party whose allegiance was to the Communist Party (CP), who were de facto members of the CP. There was such a group in the Hendon South YS, who took the line of the CP, particularly on the question of Chile. But they were not able to make much headway influencing the rest of the YS in London. Then, they pulled out and joined the YCL – including Peter Mandelson.'[27]

The key figure in this transfer of political allegiance was Mandelson's close friend at Hendon Grammar, Steve Howell, a handsome, blue-eyed blond who turned the girls' heads. He and Mandelson took several other Young Socialists into the YCL some time in 1971. They sold the Communist paper the *Morning Star* outside Kilburn Tube station (an eminently more proletarian neighbourhood than Hampstead Garden Suburb) on Friday nights. They also circulated *Challenge*, the YCL paper, on the school campus, encouraging other recruits.

In later life, Mandelson sought to play down his time in the Young Communists. 'I wasn't sure if I was technically a member,' he told Andy Beckett in 1996. 'I went to the meetings . . . I really can't remember what led to the YCL. It was short-lived . . . I felt no identification. I spent far more time setting up a tremendous youth club at the Westminster Arms pub in Swiss Cottage. Tearing it apart with my bare hands, then rebuilding it to make it structurally sound.'[28] Attractive though this picture is of Mandy the tough-guy construction worker, it is not quite complete. His role in the Young Communists was sufficiently high-profile to bring him to the attention of MI5, who opened a file on his political activities and maintained it for two decades.

Mandelson has always asserted that he never graduated to the Communist Party proper, which was then in the front rank of the trade-union struggle against the Heath government's incomes policy and industrial relations legislation. However, according to sources active in the Young Communist League at the time, it was usual for all members aged over 18 (the minimum age for CP membership) to be approached about joining the parent party. Rumours that the young revolutionary Peter may have taken out a Party card have never been confirmed and, given the absence of any central membership records in the long-since-fragmented Party, probably never will be.

An investigation for this book by former *Morning Star* journalist Andrew Murray established that Steve Howell thinks it possible that a CP card might have been issued to Mandelson at the end of one particular meeting. Tom Bell, national secretary of the YCL, denies this. 'Peter did make a point of telling me then [in 1978] that he had never joined the Communist Party – it was a bit like Clinton admitting that he took cannabis but didn't inhale,' he told Murray.[29] Nevertheless, Mandelson was involved enough to be appointed a steward at the YCL conference in Scarborough in the spring of 1972 – a job that would only have been given to a 'trusty'.

These days, he strikes an apologetic note about his brief flirtation with communism. 'It was totally off the wall,' he insisted to one profile-writer. 'Here was I, this sober, balanced and mainstream animal, surrounded by all these headbangers.'[30] Surrounded at his own wish, of course. In fact, he stayed with the YCL for a year, before moving on to fresh pastures. Some time later, he wrote to Howell – who remained a communist for many years – explaining his decision to drop out.

Mandelson's youthful adherence to communism would have infuriated his grandfather. Herbert Morrison had been starry-eyed about Soviet Russia in the 1930s, but joined in the Cold War rhetoric with a vigour, declaring in 1946 that the Communist Party of Great Britain was 'not only a political party, it is a conspiracy'.

Peter Mandelson had 'fantastic' energy, according to friends, inside and outside school. Side by side with revolutionary politics, he involved himself deeply in community activity. He took part in the work of a task force set up by the borough that brought young people into contact with the elderly. He did voluntary work for old people, particularly a pensioner couple, Mr and Mrs Bowers. He went out during his school lunch break and did odd jobs for them: fetching in the coal, doing their shopping, or simply sitting with them for a chat over a cup of tea. That led to more serious social work in his immediate post-school days, organising the youth centre in Swiss Cottage for truant pupils and other difficult teenagers. Friends remember that the Winchester Centre was in an old Victorian house in Winchester Mews, just behind the pub.

Alone among his teenage circle, Mandelson also acquired a car, though still only 17. It was a Morris 1100, and he christened it Alice. He gave his pals lifts, often to the family home in Bigwood Road, where they were astounded at his mother's extensive library. 'I'd never seen so many books,' recalled Paul Marginson. 'Mary was a very avid reader. It was a lovely through-room. His house was always open house for all us lot from school. It felt more like upper-middle-class. His father was very extrovert, and great fun. His mother was a real sweetie. God knows why she put up with us, but she did. She was great to discuss things with, suggesting things we might read. My memories are of someone incredibly generous.'[31]

Mandelson left Hendon County Grammar in the summer of 1972 with two 'A' levels in economics and history, plus an 'S' level in history, according to his later job application to the Labour Party. He was already marked down by his contemporaries as the boy who would succeed in politics. 'If there is one thing about him, he is consistent,' said Heather Bell. 'He is exactly the politician that I thought he would be.' Her admiration is tinged with criticism. 'It is one of the supreme ironies that he is MP for Hartlepool . . . he sees the people he represents as he might have looked at viewing figures when he worked in television. He doesn't care about the quality of the programme as long as lots of people are watching it. And he doesn't care about policies as long as people vote for them. That is one of the strongest threads of criticism in him. He is not a revolutionary: never was, and never will be. His views are very firmly couched in the upper-middle-class, fairly privileged background he came from.'[32]

3

DREAMER, CALCULATOR

On leaving school, Mandelson was at a crossroads. He had championed the cause of his fellow school students, and dabbled in the politics of the extreme Left. He had engaged in youth work, and looked after old people. What next for an 18-year-old idealist? His interest in the Third World, particularly Africa, had been awakened by his time in the Young Communists and Young Socialists. Bishop Trevor Huddleston, a hero of the Left for his brave stand against apartheid in South Africa, was the focal point of anti-apartheid politics in Britain at the time, and Mandelson went to talk to him.

The upshot was that he took a year off before University – a step much less common then than it is today – to do voluntary work in Africa. Huddleston arranged for him to go to Tanzania, to work first in a field hospital and then in a missionary school. The experience was profoundly unsettling, and was instrumental in shaping his adult view of the world.

Tanzania in 1972 was a proving-ground for President Julius Nyerere's political programme of 'village socialism'. It was a far cry from the theoretical utopianism espoused by the young

Marxists of north London. In the hot, dusty villages of northern Tanzania, he spent his time teaching, labouring, or assisting in basic hospital operations, holding a bag of ether to anaesthetise the hapless patient. It was not just a formative part of his political education: there was a spiritual dimension, too. Mandelson's friend Brian Appleyard disclosed: 'The proximity of missionaries almost made him a Christian, but not quite.' He has himself admitted, 'The only time I seriously nearly took religion was in my gap year when I worked with missionaries in Tanzania. I very nearly got confirmed.'[1] He certainly returned to Britain in the summer of 1973 a changed person. He had put away childish political things. His socialism was now 'more moral than Marxist'.

His schoolfriend Paul Marginson also noticed a difference. 'I think Tanzania was a profound experience in shaping his views about socialism in practice – what did and didn't work in Nyerere's version of socialism. Certainly, when he came back, politically we were a long way apart. In the intervening year I joined the Communist Party, whereas Peter came back and moved on from the YCL in a different direction. We were not estranged, but by no means as close as in school years.'[2]

Mandelson went up to St Catherine's College, Oxford, in the autumn of 1973 to read politics, philosophy and economics, the classic academic route for a would-be politician. He has acknowledged just how much Tanzania shaped his attitude to his fellow undergraduates. 'I didn't feel I had much in common with all those fresh-faced undergraduates discovering class warfare for the first time.'[3] Nevertheless, he joined the University Labour Club.

In terms of the university's long history, 'Cat's' is a modern institution, being then only ten years old. Its founding Master was the historian Alan Bullock (now Baron Bullock, a crossbench peer). The college was built on the flood plain of the River Cherwell, and Bullock used to say that Cat's was a swamp when he first arrived. The college was constructed on traditional lines, with quadrangles and staircase rooms on the usual Oxford model, but it had a reputation for being different. Among its 300 students, there were more grammar-school boys, more scientists, and fewer classicists. The college did not enjoy a particularly high political profile. Contemporaries remember that there were fewer Labour Party members there than at other colleges – and even fewer Tories.

Even so, Mandelson fell in with a different circle of friends, fellow students at Cat's, highly political, and with a marked social democratic outlook. They were also strongly international, and fiercely pro-EEC, as it then was. One of them, Dick (now Lord) Newby, lived in the room below Mandelson's, and got to know him extremely well: 'I was one of five close friends, and he became almost a younger member of the group. He became close to us all. I got on with him extremely well. I liked him. He was bright, without being exceptionally clever; lively and witty and very interested in politics. He was never hugely studious, in the sense of wanting to immerse himself in books. He was more interested, as we all were, in what was going on, and discussing current politics.'[4]

His new friends were active in the Oxford Committee for Europe, an all-party group, and in the United Nations Students' Association. The latter was the venue for quite substantial meetings. Guest speakers included George McGovern, the defeated Democratic candidate for the US presidency, and Abba Eban, the Israeli foreign minister. Mandelson threw his energies into these bodies, and into an offshoot that rejoiced in the grandiose title of Young European Left, the youth wing of the Labour Committee for Europe. Originally, Mandelson was by no stretch of imagination a Europhile. Indeed, he shared the prevailing left-wing suspicion of the 'capitalist club' of the EEC. 'He changed his mind on Europe,' said Newby. 'He came quite hostile. But he found himself in the middle of all these characters who were very keen on Europe. I don't know how much influence we had on him, but his mind did change.'[5]

Newby and his pals ran Young European Left, which had only a few 'members'. They realised that, small as they were, they could claim affiliation to the publicly funded British Youth Council (BYC), an umbrella body bringing together a wide diversity of organisations for young people from the Boy Scouts to the Young Communist League. Naively, perhaps, it had no bans or pre-scriptions, and was open to all. Young European Left duly affiliated to the BYC, a body of several hundred people on the occasions it met. Then they looked around for someone to act as delegate. 'Those of us older than Peter thought this was a waste of space, and we asked him if he would do it, thinking that nobody in their right mind would want to do it because it was so boring.'[6] But Mandelson was flattered. He took to the job with enthusiasm, eventually rising to become chairman of the Council, though not to his great career advantage.

Mandelson also got involved in the work of the college's junior common room (JCR), the in-house student representative body. In this respect, he earned the disdain of his fellow politicos, who thought the JCR was a place where the scientists went to get drunk. It was, however, a useful outlet for Mandy's administrative energies. His role in the JCR, of which he eventually became chairman (as with Arthur Scargill, it is difficult to conceive of Peter Mandelson being vice-chairman of anything for very long), brought him into close contact with the Master. Bullock took a shine to this personable, hard-working north London grammar-school boy. He enjoyed his company, and began giving him modest research assignments for a book he was working on at the time, the *Oxford Dictionary of Political Thought*. 'He became very close to Bullock,' remembers Newby.

Putting right the problems of Europe and the UN involved regular trips up to London, however, with a predictable impact on his academic work. He failed his first year's examination in politics, a particular embarrassment for a budding politician, particularly as only around two per cent of students performed so badly. It was an inauspicious start, which he put right by swotting through his summer vacation for a retake.

In February 1974, the university Labour Club pitched in to help Evan Luard fight the marginal seat of Oxford in the general election precipitated by the second miners' strike. There appears to be no record of Mandelson ever coming to the aid of the workers in these struggles, or subsequently. In fact, in his 1996 tract *The Blair Revolution*, he sneered at 'the romanticism of the class struggle'. But he did help out in the campaign for Luard's election. He failed to take the seat in the February poll but won with a majority of 1,036 in the second election that year, in October.

St Catherine's also wore another aspect, according to an academic insider who taught Mandelson there in the early seventies. It was 'outrageously gay'. There was a 'very open' group of homosexual — the college was at this time men-only — undergraduates. Yet Mandelson found Cat's a confining place. In his second and third years, his interest was increasingly taken up by outside work, much of it in London. His experience in Africa brought him into the struggle for black freedom. He was active in the movement for Namibian independence, raising enough money to buy the SWAPO freedom fighters a £12,000 jeep. His work continued in the youth arm of the United Nations, and, as we have seen, in the British Youth Council. He began to show real organisational flair, coaxing bodies as diverse as the YCL and the Girl Guides into agreement at Youth Council meetings. His real skill was to make whoever he was speaking to believe they were important and valued. 'He has a real lover's touch,' said a contemporary. Mandelson the calculator was taking over from Mandelson the dreamer.

He began to look round for a job long before he took his finals. In February 1976, he applied to the Trades Union Congress for the post of assistant in the organisation's Economics Department. It was not a predictable direction for him to take. The unions were at the zenith of their powers under Labour, but Mandelson's grandfather Herbert Morrison had not been a friend of the labour movement, certainly not in the post-war period. Indeed, his old rival Ernest Bevin, foreign secretary and former general secretary of the mighty Transport and General Workers' Union, once famously growled, when a Labour MP remarked that Morrison was his own worst enemy: 'Not while I'm alive, he ain't.'

In his application to the TUC, Mandelson made as much as he could of his specialist subjects within his BA course: labour economics and industrial relations. But he admitted that, apart from membership of the National Union of Students and active participation in the Oxford Students' Union, he had 'no direct experience' of the trade-union movement. He was not a member of any union. He had been chairman of the British-Namibia Campaign in 1974 when it was financially supported by the TUC and major affiliated unions. He also insisted, 'I have been a member of the Labour Party for six years, and served on the executive of the general management committee of my constituency Labour Party.' The latter might well have been true. It is difficult to see how the former could have been. It would have meant that he was a member at the age of 17, when he was active in the Young Communist League. He did not mention his YCL background in his application. The TUC was only just emerging from the Cold War years when communists were banned from working in Congress House, as they still were in the electricians' union. He also said he was chairman of the Young Socialists, and an executive member of the Oxford University Labour Club.

In a general statement of support for his application, Mandelson stressed his desire to utilise his education in economics by working in the trade union movement. He claimed to have become acquainted with the work of the TUC through his old communist schoolfriend Paul Marginson, who already held a research post at Congress House, and David Cockroft, a friend at St Catherine's. He also discreetly played the Morrison family card, arguing that he could best combine his 'long-standing family commitment' to the Labour Party with his study of economic organisation and industrial relations by working at the TUC. Mandelson further cited his 'past political experience' of being national chairman of the United Nations Youth and Student Association in 1974, and disclosed that he was currently vice-chairman of the British Youth Council, which conducted international youth work.

This admission was not an obvious help, but Mandelson insisted that he had not divorced his international interests from attention to domestic political and economic affairs, and it was in the sphere of British economic organisation and industrial relations that he wished to work. He suggested that his experience of research, committee work and administration would make him 'useful'.

It was a polished application, and might have got him through the fierce competition for jobs at Congress House, which was then the intellectual powerhouse of the labour movement. He was, observed one senior TUC insider many years later, 'a classic fit: someone who wants to get some experience and put the TUC scalp on his curriculum vitae. It was not an untypical application from someone who has political aspirations, and wants to get a more orientated feel for the labour movement, knowing that it cannot do him any harm in the future.'[7] However, on its own it is unlikely that this application would have succeeded.

But Mandelson the calculator had a secret weapon: the Master of St Catherine's, who thought highly of him. Alan Bullock carried serious clout at Congress House because he was chairman of a commission which, on behalf of the TUC, was conducting a massive investigation into industrial democracy. The Bullock Commission had begun work in August 1975. (Its report, issued in January 1977, recommended a British variant of European-style worker-directors on the boards of private and public companies.)

Bullock wrote twice to the TUC, commending his protégé to the Congress House hierarchy. In one letter, written less than a month after the application, he predicted that Mandelson would not get a first, but argued that he had 'a common sense which compensates for the difference between a 2:1 and a first'. Mandelson was a first-class president of the JCR, 'showing the courage to stand up to his members and to me'.

Above all, he had 'gifts of personality which make it very easy for him to get on with other people and persuade them to work with him'. Bullock added: 'I find particularly attractive his ease of manner and integrity of character and his ability to say no when it is necessary.' He suggested that Mandelson had 'quite a lot of experience in the labour movement' – something that not even Mandelson had claimed – and recommended him 'strongly and with real confidence'. Though this reference might have been written for a would-be entrant to the diplomatic service rather than the hurly-burly of the trade-union world, it did the trick. David Lea, Mandelson's putative head of department, who was also secretary to the Bullock Commission, recommended him for an interview with Lionel (more commonly known as Len) Murray, the TUC general secretary. He sailed through that. He was in, on the inside track.

Mandelson graduated from St Catherine's in the summer of 1976 with an upper second in philosophy, politics and economics. Bullock had been right. He was not first-class honours material, and he would have to rely on his 'common sense' as well as his intellect to make his way through life. Others might find a different expression to describe Mandelson's style: cunning, perhaps. But it was clear that he had more than a beta-plus brain.

At this period, he was very busy on a report on youth unemployment, a pamphlet that would take on the status of a *magnum opus* in the Mandelson myth. This work brought together his twin interests of young people and the labour market. It was chiefly written in late 1976, and published in March 1977 under the auspices of the British Youth Council's Working Party on Youth Employment. In later years, this became the Mandelson report, which was represented to the prime minister, James Callaghan, and so impressed him that the government immediately brought in the Youth Opportunity Programme. Mandelson has often said it was 'the best thing I have ever done'.

In fact, the paper, entitled *Youth Unemployment: Causes and Cures*, was modest in its scope and intentions, and the Labour government was already well aware of the problems posed by the steep rise in the number of young people on the dole. On 1 March 1977, before the BYC report was published, Employment Secretary Albert Booth submitted a paper to the Cabinet

Economic Committee warning of serious trends in the labour market. Unemployment had risen by 300,000 over the previous year, and it was particularly bad among young people and in 'high immigrant' areas. The situation was worsening, and Energy Secretary Tony Benn's permanent secretary, Sir Jack Rampton, even suggested reintroduction of national service to deal with the crisis.[8]

The BYC report was drawn up by a 23-member working-party, which included Mandelson's friends Paul Marginson and David Cockroft, Tom Shebbeare, who later became chairman of the Prince's Trust, and a scattering of young worthies from bodies ranging from the Tory Reform Group to the General Synod of the Church of England. Peter Mandelson was listed as the research secretary.

The report, gathering dust in the TUC archives today, was a classic product of the corporatist thinking of its day, a view of the world that Mandelson has long since abandoned. It had a 'summary of analysis and recommendations for action' running to 13 pages, then 103 pages of dense analysis and proposals to stimulate jobs for the young. In July 1976, the report pointed out, there were 615,000 unemployed people aged under 25. Young men were finding it hardest to get work: jobless under-19 males accounted for almost 22 per cent of the UK labour force, a figure that had more than tripled in five years. 'Unemployment needs special attention because it conditions young people's attitudes towards work for the rest of their lives,' the paper argued. 'It is often the first step towards a pattern of permanent deprivation.'[9]

The report demanded European-wide governmental action 'at the earliest opportunity'. In the UK, there should be an industrial strategy requiring 'a planned approach to the introduction of labour-intensive methods of production', through planning agreements between government and industry. State aid to business should be conditional on a guaranteed level of job creation for every pound of public money. There should be a tougher regional policy, involving 'a stricter regime' of industrial development certificates, and regional planning agencies 'with substantial powers and resources'.[10] Existing job-creation schemes should be expanded, and all school-leavers ought to get maintenance grants until the age of 18 if they were engaged in training. There was much more along the same lines, including a demand that employers introduce early retirement, longer holidays and cut out systematic overtime working. This ambitious programme was not costed, which was perhaps just as well. Chancellor Denis Healey was unwilling to stimulate the economy too much, or to increase public expenditure, as he had made clear to the Cabinet Economic Committee on 1 March.

The report also made a clarion call for young people to be involved – 'given access by right' – in forums and bodies in which planning and policy-making relevant to them took place. It also proposed a form of Youth Parliament: a national structure based on youth councils which would allow young people 'to debate and vocalise their needs' and to help government formulate national social, educational and employment policies. The report concluded, 'The current levels of youth unemployment imperil the future generations of young people. It is vital not only that new policies are introduced to meet this situation but that, also, the opportunity is seized to allow young people to play a greater part in determining their own future lives, in education, employment and leisure.'[11]

None of this ever happened, of course. In due course, a general improvement in the economy coinciding with a falling birth-rate took care of much of the youth unemployment problem, and there was no political appetite for Mandelson's revolutionary manifesto for getting young people into the business of policy-making. It is also unlikely that many young people shared his zeal for sitting on committees and councils, either with those of their own generation or with the middle-aged who took most of their decisions. *Youth Unemployment: Causes and Cures* was a typical product of its time: a plea for more planning, more public spending and more participation.

It was well-meant for all that, and showed that Mandelson could draft a detailed report that would impress his superiors. Yet it was also a curiously stilted document. Despite its strongly worded demands for action, the report did not bring to life the misery of being young and jobless. That was also a developing characteristic of Mandelson's writing: it was well-researched and quite clever, but aloof and unconnected to the sometimes nasty and brutish world of the dole.

Perhaps the most interesting aspect of this contribution to political thinking is Mandelson's own assessment of it. He has often referred to it in interviews, usually overstating its importance. In 1992, he told Megan Tresidder that he wrote the report. In fact, Cockroft was the author of the section on economic analysis, and Tom Shebbeare wrote the middle section comparing the UK with the rest of Europe. Mandelson wrote the conclusions, and used his interpersonal skills to get together a wide-ranging working-party that gave it greater authority. He is immensely proud of its impact. 'We got a call from the Prime Minister saying Mr Callaghan wanted to meet with its authors. So me and three others sat down in front of the Cabinet. We had the Prime Minister across the table from us,' he told Ms Tresidder.[12] He spoke first of the political lift that the report gave him, and only then added how 'enormously proud' he was of having done something really useful that might directly influence government policy. Yet he does not appear to be in any hurry to make copies available to interviewers. He may be conscious that the reality of the document falls short of the hard sell. Three years later, he wrote a pamphlet on *Broadcasting and Youth*, about which he is noticeably less enthusiastic.

4

BROTHERS FALL OUT

Deep in the files of the TUC at Congress House is a single sheet of flimsy blue paper, from August 1978 and headed 'Termination of Employment: Peter Mandelson'. It relates to the end of the sorry saga that was his first foray into working for the labour movement. He was obliged to quit, after working for little more than a year in the heart of what was then widely, if erroneously, regarded as the real seat of power in British politics. James Callaghan's Labour government was in power, co-operating closely with the trade unions through the 'social contract' negotiated by TUC leaders.

Its fruits were many, including a workable incomes policy, legislation to restore the powers of the unions, and a host of social measures desired by trade unionists. These were the heady days of union influence over government, of beer and sandwiches in Downing Street. Some detected a *fin-de-siècle* feeling in the air, as though this was the high point of the TUC's power, and it would all end in tears. According to colleagues at Congress House at the time, Mandelson shared this view, and was privately appalled at the way union leaders spoke to Cabinet ministers as though they were their servants. Others say this is another example of him reasoning after the event, to explain away his failure to build a career at the TUC as other brilliant young men of his generation did.

It had all started so well. Mandelson began work at Congress House on 7 March 1977, nine months after graduating from Oxford, on a salary scale starting at £3,581 a year and rising by annual increments to £4,702. He inherited a desk from Kelvin Hopkins, now a Labour MP, in a long, narrow office overlooking Great Russell Street, close to the British Museum. Buoyed by the personal backing of Alan Bullock, Mandelson could hardly have had a more auspicious beginning to his first real job. He had impressed Len (now Lord) Murray with his intelligence and flair, and David Lea, his immediate head in the Economics Department, recollects, 'We were certainly very happy to employ him.'[1]

He started off in the section servicing the TUC's Industry Committees, which brought together unions within individual industries and public services – coal, steel, printing, building, health, and the like. Much of his time was spent working for the Transport Industry Committee, one of the most active of these bodies, which were a relatively novel feature of the TUC. They were set up in the late sixties and early seventies, in part as a 'modernising' move following Labour's reformist Royal Commission on Trade Unions, which reported in 1968. Essentially, they sought unity among the sometimes competing unions in a single sphere of economic activity, in order to ensure the workers in that industry had a single representative voice.

However, the work, while seen as important within the TUC, was not as glamorous as Mandelson would have liked. Much of it was routine research, and the membership of the Industry Committee could not have been better chosen to test his bourgeois self-importance. It was dominated by officials of the Transport and General Workers' Union, whose general secretary, Jack Jones, was thought by many voters to be more important than the Labour prime minister. The railway unions also had considerable clout, and the ever-constant threat of rail strikes was not to the new official's liking.

Moreover, Mandelson swiftly began to tire of the bureaucratic structure of Congress House. The TUC was deliberately modelled on the civil service, designed to work for the elected union leaders in the same way that Whitehall services the elected politicians at Westminster. At times, TUC general secretaries would also speak of leading the 'general staff' of the labour movement, suggesting a faintly military dimension to their work. Unquestionably, there was a definite hierarchical structure and a civil service way of thinking in the building. In line with the strict view of professional impartiality, staff were required to clear their outside activities with their head of department. They were certainly discouraged from political activity. A previous general secretary, the self-appointed intellectual George Woodcock, invariably asked job applicants one critical question: 'Have you any intention of becoming an MP?' The answer was supposed to be 'No.' There was also a firm line on hard-Left politics. Paul Marginson was sharply criticised by the TUC deputy general secretary, Norman Willis, for having hammer and sickle posters of the Portuguese revolution on the wall of his office.

But Mandelson had already begun his long march to political prominence, and he was irked by what he saw as petty restrictions on his freedom. He was already vice-chairman of the British Youth Council, and in April 1977 – within a month of joining the staff – he was asking his bosses for approval to extend his public role. Could he take up a place on the council of management of Youth Aid, a research and development body concerned with young people? It would, of course, be in his Youth Council capacity, not as a TUC staffer. He did not foresee any conflict of interest. Was this OK? Days later, he asked for permission to meet Prime Minister Callaghan at Number Ten, again in his BYC capacity, to present his report on the young jobless, *Youth Unemployment: Causes and Cures*.

His monumental cheek had the Congress House hierarchy up in arms. The issue of Mandelson's public function was passed right up to Len Murray for a ruling. He was concerned that anyone who participated in such bodies ought to do so on behalf of the ruling General Council of the TUC. Otherwise they were heading for trouble. He also looked at the Youth Council report on unemployment, and agreed that it was written to a high standard. He was keen that Callaghan should take an interest in unemployment among young people, and reluctantly agreed to make an exception in this case. None the less, the incident continued to rankle, and a question mark appeared over Mandelson's future at Congress House.

It was not all tedious research and conflict with authority. Mandelson quickly became a social favourite among the twenty-somethings who worked as assistants in the economic, organisation and press liaison departments. Peta van den Bergh, a press officer at the time, remembers, 'I liked Peter very much. He became a pal. We would sneak out for tea and little gossip sessions. He certainly cheered me up when I worked there, and I missed him when he left.' Although he was by now living in a flat in Kenton Road, Hackney, Mandelson also took his TUC pals Peta van den Bergh and Paul Marginson home to meet his parents in Hampstead Garden Suburb. On her first visit, van den Bergh put her foot in it with Mrs Mandelson by telling her that her father, the journalist Tony van den Bergh, had been introduced to socialism by Herbert Morrison. She later heard from Marginson that 'Mary didn't like to talk about her father', and suspected that the reason may have been Morrison's reputed anti-Semitism, and of course Tony Mandelson was Jewish. 'The impression I got at that time was that the family had been estranged from Morrison and that Peter hadn't seen much of his grandfather.' But it was plainly an engaging social excursion. 'Mary Mandelson was extremely quiet,' recollects van den Bergh. 'She was known as "the Duchess". She was very short, wore her hair up in a bun and seemed eccentric – a bit like the old-world English middle class. The family seemed basically to defer to her. His father Tony was a gregarious, generous character, terribly hospitable and very friendly. I remember being tipsy whenever I left the house.'[2]

Mandelson's position at Congress House worsened as his political profile rose. He was now also engaged in preparations for the eleventh World Festival of Youth and Students, a communist-dominated event due to be held in Havana, Cuba, in the summer of 1978. The 1977 annual report of the British Youth Council records that the council 'played a major part' in the work of the British Preparatory Committee for the festival, and had been chosen to attend the portentously titled Third International Preparatory Meeting, 'which took place in Havana in April 1977 and which Peter Mandelson attended on behalf of the BYC.' As previously disclosed, this was not the council's only contact with the communist bloc. There were delegations to Warsaw, Hungary and the USSR. The BYC exchanged delegations with the Union of Communist Youth of Romania, and gave a dinner in London to honour Nicu Ceauşescu, son of the hated dictator. There was also an exchange with Tito's Yugoslavia, led by David Cockroft. In fairness, it must also be pointed out that relations were also established with the youth councils of Israel and the USA. Mandelson also attended the annual meeting of the Scottish TUC Youth Advisory Committee.

It was a busy year, and Mandelson was rewarded in May 1977 – two months after joining the TUC staff – by being elected chairman of the British Youth Council. He was the nominee of the National Organisation of Labour Students. The promotion did not please his masters at Congress House. If they were unamused at him continuing to act as vice-chairman after becoming a staffer, they were furious at him defying official policy by going for the chairmanship. He sought to appease the hierarchy by spinning his new role in the BYC. His promotion marked a 'significant change' in the council's political direction, he argued. Hitherto, he told the TUC authorities, the Youth Council had been the happy hunting-ground of Tory students and the Boy Scouts. That was true. It was even truer to say that the BYC was coming under the influence of the hard Left, particularly the communists, who realised that here was a hunting-ground from which they were not barred.

Mandelson was sensitive to the charge that he might occasionally find himself at odds with Congress policy, and promised not to embarrass the TUC in his public statements as chairman. His reassurances fell on deaf ears. The appointment had not been cleared with his departmental head, much less with Len Murray. By August 1977, his employers were asking him to get someone else to be the chairman of the BYC. Memos flew back and forth, but Mandelson took no notice. The position was by now exacerbated by a political scandal brewing over the role of the BYC, dragging in the foreign secretary, Dr David Owen. In July 1977, Dr Owen was asked to 'endorse' the appointment of Charles Clarke, the outgoing president of the National Union of Students (later Labour MP for Norwich South) to a one-year posting in Cuba as an organiser of the communist-dominated World Youth Festival.

Clarke, a Tribunite member of the Labour Party, was the unanimous choice of 'a committee' backed by the Foreign Office-financed BYC as Britain's only representative on the permanent body organising the festival in Havana the following summer. His job, said a somewhat naive report in the *Guardian*, was to 'make sure that the festival is not taken over by Soviet-inspired propaganda but becomes a genuine festival representing a wide range of young opinion.'[3] Just how unlikely he was to succeed in this task was clear from the nature of the festival. It was organised by the World Federation of Democratic Youth, based in Budapest, which operated chiefly through Young Communist leagues and their place-men in the student unions. It had only opened its doors to West European groups in 1973, with the aim of winning more converts to communism.

Tory MPs and Conservative student groups urged a boycott of the Marx-fest. Mandelson was quoted in the *Guardian* article, speaking in his capacity as BYC chairman: 'We are meeting Dr Owen to ask for his endorsement because we feel it will strengthen our position to ensure that there is a genuine festival. Charles Clarke was chosen by us because of his wide experience.' His intervention did not go unnoticed. The article went on file at Congress House.

Mandelson went out to Havana on 26 July 1978 as part of a 180-strong delegation (down from the projected 400 participants) armed with a fraternal duty-free bottle of scotch each with which to combat the vast quantities of vodka brought by the Russians and Poles. The British party found themselves rather over-whelmed among the 23,000 young people from 140 countries gathered in Cuba, and very much out on a limb – literally and figuratively. They were billeted with the Icelandic, Irish, Dutch and Belgian delegations in a teachers' training college on the outskirts of the capital. They were also virtually isolated in their firm commitment on human rights. Among the British contin-gent were scions of political life: Margaret Scargill, daughter of the miners' leader (who was also there as a guest of honour of the Cuban government); Kathryn Attlee, grandniece of the post-war Labour premier, and Kath Flannery, daughter of the left-wing MP Martin Flannery. Trevor Phillips, president of the National Union of Students, headed the group. The original ambitions of the British Youth Council had to be scaled down because the Foreign Office rejected appeals for a £5,000 cultural grant. Culturally, Britain was represented by a lone folk group and a couple of film-makers.

David Hencke, who reported the twelve-day jamboree of political debate, folk dancing, pop music and sport – and socialising – for the *Guardian*, recalls that Mandelson played a low-profile role in the proceedings. 'He spent most of his time in smoke filled rooms, trying to get the texts of things changed. He would then come out and give Mandy-style briefings behind the scenes.'[4] He was clearly carving out a role for himself. It was not popular with everyone, not even with his own delegation. The *Guardian* reported that a 'deeply divided' party was returning from Havana after playing 'a controversial and ambiguous role' in the festival. Despite being one of the smallest contingents, the Britons had become 'notorious' for offending against the festival's Marxist orthodoxies, and failing to agree among themselves.

Trevor Philips, an ally of Mandelson, and other leading delegates made speeches and distributed leaflets criticising the trials of Soviet dissidents. The British delegation also used its veto during one of the main debates against a festival communiqué which claimed that capitalist countries were locked in a deepening economic crisis from which the only escape could be profound political and social change. But the delegation was deeply split over a leadership statement on human rights highly critical of the USSR, which had to be rewritten to include breaches of human rights in Northern Ireland and the USA. The final version was only approved by a narrow majority. Hencke observed, 'The stand on human rights – which was bulldozed through by leaders like Mr Peter Mandelson and then effectively undermined by hard-line delegates – caused confusion and prompted the Russians to distribute English language leaflets accusing [Anatoliy] Scharansky (the Soviet Jewish dissident) of being a CIA agent.'[5] The Cuban authorities did not make serious efforts to suppress the activities of Mandelson and his awkward comrades. They knew the festival's underlying commitment to a Marxist view of the world – anti-Zionist, anti-imperialist and pro-communist – was not in serious danger. Mandelson had made his mark, none the less. He was proud of his shuttle diplomacy, and when no-one could be found to march at the head of the British delegation at the closing ceremony in Havana stadium, he strode forward manfully, holding the Union Flag aloft. The comrades noticed that it was flying upside down.

Nearly twenty years later, when the furore over Mandelson's early days in the YCL broke about his ears, Trevor Philips sprang to his aid, insisting that he had played a heroic anti-Soviet role in Havana. 'We made a mess of the Soviet hopes that the festival would end with a paean of praise to Eastern European socialism. The proposition so vigorously propounded . . . that Mandelson was in some way a puppet of Fidel Castro would have caused astonishment amongst those who watched him criss-crossing Havana for ten days and nights, blocking every attempt to bring the Brits into line.'[6]

However, Mandelson's politicking did not endear him to his employers back home. The TUC's patience with their *enfant terrible* was running out. On his return from sunny Cuba, he was asked to give a month's notice of his resignation. Essentially, he was sacked. The final straw was an item in the diary column of the *Guardian* in mid-July, predicting his imminent departure. Mandelson disclaimed all knowledge of or co-operation with the item by Peter Hillimore. He apologised to the general secretary, insisting 'I have said I don't wish to make an issue of leaving the TUC. I strongly regret any embarrassment that might be caused by this piece' (in the *Guardian*). He also said in a note to management that he had originally intended staying at Congress House 'for a number of years'.

In fact, he departed after only eighteen months. He left on 8 September 1978, though he was paid to the end of that month. His verdict was that he had enjoyed the work, and regarded it as a privilege to have worked for the TUC. Its representative work was 'more important than anything else I might have been associated with', he insisted. David Lea says simply, 'We parted company, obviously at our request. He was asked to give a month's notice.'[7]

After leaving the TUC, Mandelson decided to follow in his grandfather's footsteps. He set his sights on London local government. He was an active member of Stockwell ward in the Vauxhall Labour Party. Both the ward and the party were a redoubt of the Bennite hard left – and political destinations beyond. He was in a small but articulate minority on the traditional Right.

He stood up for what he by now regarded as mainstream Labour values and policies, and attended meetings of the Solidarity Group of Labour moderates, led by Roy Hattersley. On one occasion, he was embarrassed to hear Hattersley tell a packed Solidarity meeting in Lambeth Town Hall that it was a particular pleasure to be speaking to such a well-attended gathering, especially as Herbert Morrison's grandson was in the audience. At this stage in his career, Mandelson was keeping quiet about his famous grandfather.

His constituency general management committee, the power-house of the party, was stuffed with hard-liners. 'Some of these people really needed therapy,' recalls an insider; some of Mandelson's friends in the Vauxhall branch, including Roger Liddle and Matthew Oakeshott, were later driven out of the party into the arms of the breakaway Social Democratic Party (SDP). It was a hostile environment, but Mandelson used the tricks of the trade to keep his arguments in play. With fellow-moderate Paul Ormerod, an academic working for the National Institute of Economic and Social Research, he drew up a manifesto calling for one member, one vote in the party – fifteen years before that system was finally adopted – and circulated it among members.

In late 1978, soon after Mandelson's departure from the TUC, a vacancy appeared on Lambeth Borough Council in Stockwell ward, where he lived in a small flat on the Kennington Road. The sitting councillor, Bill Hall, an elderly man who came from Sunderland, managed to get a council flat swap in the West Country – an unheard-of feat – and left the neighbourhood. A by-election in the safe constituency was set for 6 February 1979. The moderates were in some confusion, but Mandelson came to their rescue with an unexpected offer to stand. He won the nomination and the by-election.

Once on the council, Mandelson found himself in the thick of the most hostile and destructive Labour politicking in the capital. He was given a minor role on some committees and sub-committees – the Management Services Committee, the Play Spaces Committee, the Stockwell Housing Committee and the Town Planning Committee. Later, he also served on committees dealing with community affairs, health and consumer affairs, control and licensing. All good municipal stuff, but scarcely Morrisonian in scale.

The real battle was with the hard-Left majority on the council led by 'Red Ted' Knight, which was in fierce conflict with the dying minority Labour administration of James Callaghan, and after the May 1979 general election with the first Thatcher government. No quarter was given in Lambeth politics. Knight had come to power as council leader in 1978 after defeating a moderate, and immediately set about implementing Labour's council election manifesto commitment to expansion — i.e., increased spending — in the borough. He increased rates by 40 per cent in 1979, attracting the wrath of the new environment secretary, Michael Heseltine (later to be lionised by Mandelson), who cut Lambeth's rate support grant by £3 million. The conflict continued for three more years, forcing a threefold rise in the rates.

Mandelson was an assiduous councillor, regularly holding surgeries for his constituents. Their main (sometimes, it seemed, their sole) complaint was housing. Many of them wanted to get off the vast multi-storey estates into which they had been decanted after slum clearances, but there was nowhere else for them to go. It was a dispiriting experience. On the ruling Labour council group, he was usually in a minority of four or five with Roger Liddle, Matthew Oakeshott and fellow Stockwell councillors Paul Ormerod and Patrick Mitchell.

Confidants of Mandelson's at the time argue that once the Gang of Four — Roy Jenkins, David Owen, Shirley Williams, and Bill Rodgers — cut loose from Labour in March 1981, there was a lot of pressure on the beleaguered Lambeth moderates to follow them into the fledgling SDP. 'There was no doubt, especially in the climate at Lambeth when the SDP was formed that almost everybody we knew left to join it,' recalls Paul Ormerod. 'We were clearly under a lot of pressure. All our mates had gone. The SDP won two by-elections in what formerly had been very strong Labour wards in July 1981.'[8] Roger Liddle, later to be Mandelson's co-author and a key adviser in the prime minister's Downing Street office, was one of the first to decamp.

Mandelson initially stood out against the tide. Indeed, he has always claimed that there was never any question of him jumping ship. 'For the record I did not and would not ever contemplate joining the SDP and was never offered an enrolment form,' he insisted some years afterwards.[9] On another occasion, he claimed that his mother would never have spoken to him again had he quit Labour.

Close party friends at the time remember it a little differently.

They say he had a secret pact with like-minded moderates that they would stay in the Labour Party. But if Tony Benn emerged the victor in his battle to oust Denis Healey as deputy leader of the party in the autumn of 1981, they would quit and join the SDP. His party friends further insist that he had 'psychologically said "Yes" we are prepared to'. One confidant very close to Mandelson recollects, 'We had long conversations about this, one to one, and on the telephone. Once you are in that frame of mind, the next six months were crucial.'

Healey triumphed by the smallest possible margin – 0.8 per cent – at the Brighton conference in late September, but the pressures on Mandelson continued unabated. 'Things went from bad to worse,' says the confidant. 'We finally agreed we would leave.' The informant told John Lyttle, a former Transport House staffer working for Shirley Williams. By the same account, Mandelson is said to have told Roger Liddle that he had already arranged a drinks party at his Kennington flat. 'We would turn up and our conversion would be announced,' said the informant. 'But in the meantime, we both decided against, and it never came up again.'

Lyttle was furious, arguing to SDP colleagues, 'We should have told the Press' – that is, left the pair with nowhere to retreat after announcing their departure from Labour. Fellow moderates agree that it would have been 'impossible' for those on the right of the party *not* to have thought about joining the SDP. 'Living in Lambeth it was impossible not to think about it,' said one.[10]

The interesting dimension to this minor political drama is Mandelson's insistence that he was never attracted to the SDP. No disgrace attaches to former membership of the SDP – quite the contrary. Apart from Liddle, Number 10 also employs Derek Scott, a Labour turncoat who stood as parliamentary candidate for Swindon (thereby losing the seat for Labour), as the prime minister's economics adviser. In Mandelson's 'inclusive' political world, it is not shameful to have been a Conservative, or even to continue to be one, as his celebrity treatment of Michael Heseltine has demonstrated. So it cannot be a sense of undue modesty about his past that motivates Peter Mandelson. Perhaps it is a desire to ensure that history is written to his taste.

On Lambeth Council, Mandelson was plainly not as effective a municipal figure as his famous grandfather. Ted Knight has 'great difficulty in recalling him, other than he was around'. The hard Left was in a substantial majority, 'so he wasn't able to do very much. . . . We thought he was going to stand as a candidate for the SDP. But he didn't appear as a Labour candidate, either.'[11]

People like 'Red Ted' put Mandelson off the adversarial chores of town hall politics. In the aftermath of the Brixton riots of April 1981, Mandelson was sharply critical of the council leader, who described the police presence in Lambeth as 'an army of occupation' and demanded their removal. By then, Mandelson had decided not to run in the May 1982 council elections, and from this safe vantage point he argued, 'Given the choice between having the Labour Party and Ted Knight in the borough and the police, 99 per cent of the population would vote for the police.'

Mandelson shared some of Knight's opposition to the methods of policing – Brixton police had been placed under the direct control of the home secretary. But he declared that 'screaming and raging' would not help. 'I really do fear for the reaction of Labour voters at the Greater London Council elections. We hoped for a better understanding with the police when there was a change of the divisional commander, but Ted went to see him, shouted and raved and the result was that the police dug their heels in and were even more determined not to change anything.'

Mandelson insisted that he was 'basically a supporter' of much that Knight stood for – 'after all he's given me an important position within the council'. At the time, Mandelson was vice-chairman of the Planning Committee. This may have seemed important to him, but he had no qualms about giving it up at the end of his first term. Moreover, his fears of a Labour pasting at the polls were confirmed. In Lambeth, the party lost 14 percentage points, compared with a London-wide average of only 8 per cent. It was time to move on.

5

FIXER, SPINNER

Leaving the TUC in the way that he did, did not do wonders for Mandelson's curriculum vitae. Less ambitious young men would have abandoned the labour movement for something less exacting. But he refused to give up, and cast his net widely in the search for a new job that would get him closer to the heart of politics.

It was an inauspicious time. After Mandelson's departure, the TUC had been treated to a tragic-comic display of over-confidence by Callaghan at its autumn congress in Brighton. The prime minister's address to the unions turned into a farcical guessing-game about the prospects of a general election, culminating in singing 'There was I, Waiting at the Church'. When it finally sank in that he was deferring the date of the poll, oblivious of pressures building up on the industrial front, union leaders were besides themselves with rage and frustration. They knew they could not hold the line over Chancellor Healey's imposed 5 per cent pay-rise limit. 'There *will* now be a Winter of Discontent,' predicted Moss Evans, general secretary of the then-mighty Transport and General Workers' Union. His own members, beginning with the oil tanker drivers, ensured that it was a self-fulfilling prophecy.

The unprecedented bout of industrial action afflicting both private and public sectors – but graven on the public mind as the 'Now we can't bury our dead' strike – contributed substantially to Labour's crushing defeat at the polls on 3 May 1979. Thatcherism was born, and Peter Mandelson was still scouting for a way back to political activity.

His opportunity came later that year, when Albert Booth, who had been secretary of state for employment in the Callaghan government, looked around for a researcher. Booth, a tall, erect, undemonstrative man, reckoned to be one of the most principled politicians in the party hierarchy, was now shadow transport secretary. In the spectrum of party opinion, he was decidedly of the Left: a solid member of CND who at the next election would pay for his opposition to nuclear weapons with the loss of his seat at Barrow-in-Furness – where the Trident nuclear submarines are built. Booth took over the transport portfolio at Callaghan's request after the autumn shadow Cabinet elections. It was perceived to be a big job, requiring a safe pair of hands. Labour's transport policy was to be completely restructured.

Agreement was reached with the Tories on how much 'Short' money would be available for Opposition frontbenchers. The grant, named after its originator, Labour deputy leader Ted Short (now Lord Glenamara), ensured that shadow ministers had some resources to employ full-time research staff. Booth was awarded his share, and advertised the post in the *Guardian*, *New Statesman*, *Tribune* and now-defunct (Mandelson was in at the death) *Labour Weekly*. Mandelson was one of six applicants. He was a clear front-runner, having already worked for the TUC Transport Industry Committee. He knew his way around the policy, and, importantly for Booth, he knew the people, the union officials and leaders whose active co-operation in revamping the policy was sought. 'He knew where the union contacts were, and how to set up meetings with them,' remembers Booth. 'He learned a lot at the TUC, and he could put it to good use.'[1] He got the job, which involved research, liaison with the trade unions, the metropolitan councils and other local authorities, and some policy-paper-drafting. His salary is not known, though Booth recollects that 'We used the whole amount we had'.[2]

The transport team was completed by John Prescott, MP for Hull East, the gruff but wily ex-merchant-navy seaman, and Roger Stott, MP for Westhoughton, a former Post Office engineer, who had been Callaghan's PPS until the dissolution. Together, they were charged with completely reorganising Labour's transport strategy, in the teeth of Mrs Thatcher's drive towards privatisation. There was no great hurry. The new policy was designed to go to the Trades Union Congress and the Labour Party conference in 1982. Mandelson, with a House of Commons research pass, worked from Booth's ample office overlooking Star Chamber Court at Westminster. The former shadow transport secretary recalls him as 'a very friendly, sociable guy', who put in high-quality work. 'Peter took a pride in doing that job particularly well. In terms of the job, we never had a wrong word. He knew exactly what was delegated to him.' Mandelson the fixer managed to get 98 per cent support for the policy document from the disparate – warring, even – transport unions, something practically unheard of before.

In the summer of 1982, with Labour's transport strategy review complete, Mandelson felt it was time for a change. The party of his grandfather and Roy Hattersley was in turmoil, with the hard Left gaining the upper hand. He had quit Lambeth Council in disgust at the antics of Ted Knight and his comrades. He felt disillusioned, but not terminally so. He decided the best thing to do was to strike out of the Westminster village into new territory: television. His decision was 'not entirely a surprise' to Albert Booth, who put it down to the difficulties of making transport a relevant issue on the doorstep. 'Voters knew all about arguments in the Labour Party, but nothing about the constructive policy work we had done,' he admitted.[3]

Frustrating though that may have been, it does not explain why he should decide to break into television. Mandelson consulted Bryan Gould, a rising star in the Labour Party who had gone to work as a documentary film-maker at Thames TV after losing his seat in the general election. The two men had become friends after meetings at Jenni Jaeger's salon in Putney, but they were not particularly close. 'He thought I would be a very good referee for a job at London Weekend Television,' Gould remembered. 'I didn't know him particularly well. It's a familiar dilemma . . . I didn't want to offend him, so I agreed to give him a reference. I was helpful but not very informative. I was quite surprised. I didn't see him in any way remarkable. I thought he was just a pleasant young man with appropriate political instincts.'[4]

Mandelson kept his media ambitions to himself, declining to tell even his close friend David Aaronovitch, a fellow-traveller on the Cuban expedition. 'Peter was a pretty regular visitor to our house,' Aaronovitch remembered later. 'Yet I didn't know we were both applying for the same job on the same day.'[5] The position was that of researcher for the prestigious London Weekend Television programme *Weekend World*, presented by the egghead former Labour MP, Brian Walden. At the time, LWT was an intellectual blue-chip television company, employing Melvyn Bragg, John Birt (now director-general of the BBC), Christopher Bland, Barry Cox, Robin Paxton and Greg Dyke. To get an interview was no mean feat. To get a job would be a mark of brilliance.

On the day of the interview, Aaronovitch triumphed. One story suggests that Mandelson was rejected at the interview because he was 'considered too emotionally biased in favour of Palestine'. This seems most unlikely. The station was sufficiently impressed with him to offer him a less glamorous job, as a researcher with *The London Programme*, the weekly current-affairs programme dealing with events in the capital. He took it without hesitation. South Bank was an exciting place to be for a young man on the make in the media. Mandelson made the most of his opportunity. With his experience at the TUC and work for Labour's shadow Cabinet, he proved to be a first-rate researcher. Following assessment reports at the end of his first year he was promoted – like Aaronovitch – to the role of producer with *Weekend World*.

It was a remarkable step up, but friends at South Bank could not quite understand what he was doing there. He was making programmes, particularly on Northern Ireland. But he was also making contacts in preparation for the next big move. Colleagues saw him as a trainee politician, rather than a trainee producer: a man who seldom gossiped, but knew everything that was going on. 'Peter was not interested in any way in television,'[6] says Aaronovitch. Another colleague remarked, 'I wouldn't have said he was a brilliant TV practitioner. But *Weekend World* was more about contacts. And he had a wonderful combination of charm and ruthlessness.' Brian Walden was more complimentary, arguing that Mandelson is highly intelligent, lucid and possessed of guts. 'He would have gone right to the top in television,' he insisted. The two spent many hours talking about the machinations of politics, discussing arcane topics such as the election-winning techniques of Franklin D. Roosevelt. 'Peter's a tactician,' concluded Walden, 'not an idealogue. He's very much his grandfather's grandson.'[7] Mandelson himself echoes the assessment of his colleagues. Asked about his time at LWT, he didn't mention television. 'I loved the immersion in policy analysis,' he said. 'Sorting out views; explaining and identifying options. It was wonderful to have the most tremendous resources; the opportunity to go into any area of policy and see anyone you like.'[8] The meddling minister without portfolio is already discernible.

Yet television was not always the glamorous business it was cracked up to be. At one Labour Party conference, Mandelson was having lunch with his LWT boss, Bruce Anderson, and Terry Duffy, the notably plebeian president of the engineering workers' union. The latter suddenly picked up his plate and instructed the young television staffer, ''Ere, lad, get me another 'elpin of puddin', would you?' Mandelson meekly obliged. A Labour wannabe was in no position to offend a union leader with a million block votes in his pocket. But Anderson could tell from his manner that he was not happy. 'If Mr Duffy or his successors thought that such pudding-servitude would be a paradigm for the relationship between the industrial and the political wings of the

Labour movement, they would have to think again,' he later observed. For Mandelson, this was essentially another taste of the unappetising side of trade-union power. At the TUC, in the final years of the Labour government, he had seen and heard at first hand how union bosses like Duffy could ring up Cabinet ministers at home or in the office and tell them what to do. This experience was so deeply burned into him that it re-emerged more than a decade later, in his vision of a Blair government, as a shame on the party that must never be repeated.

At LWT, Mandelson also demonstrated his powers of flexible loyalty. In the hothouse atmosphere of the studio, passions were easily stirred. Mandelson formed a close professional friendship with Robin Paxton, the programme executive. Paxton was anxious to get his own programme, and junior producers rebelled at the changes further down the management chain that his departure would cause. They got up a petition to stop the changes. Mandelson was the only one of the group who didn't sign, according to Aaronovitch. 'It was an act of disloyalty to the collective on the one hand, or to the friend on the other,' he mused. Clearly, he was seriously into playing work-politics, even if he was somewhat disillusioned with the real thing.

In the summer of 1982, Mandelson was gadding about in the southern reaches of the Welsh marches, north of Ross-on-Wye, in a great curve of that beautiful Wye river, when he virtually stumbled over the tiny parish of Foy, just inside Herefordshire. There, he saw the country home of his dreams: a farmworker's semi-detached cottage. Number 1 Brick End, was solidly con-structed from local sandstone. It had two bedrooms, two rooms downstairs and a ground-floor bathroom. Behind the cottage, a country garden with an apple tree backed on to open farmland, ploughed in dark-red sandy soil. A disused stone piggery stood in the corner. At the front, Brick End Fields shelved down to the meandering Wye, at a point where Foy footbridge crosses the river to steep hills on the other side. It is an idyllic spot. The hamlet is at the end of a dead-end road, past the fourteenth-century church of St Mary the Virgin.

The property, owned by the big local farm, Carthage, had been on the market. Now, alas, it had a SOLD sign outside. He reluctantly retraced his steps to Monmouth, but a couple of months later the sale fell through and he bought the property for £31,000. It was to be both principal home and bolt-hole for the next seven years. He shuttled between the capital and, at the weekends, Herefordshire, confessing later, 'With every mile I drive from London, my mood lifts.' In the garden, he cultivated red roses. They are still there, grown woody with age. In his faintly chintzy sitting-room, red roses stood in a vase on the television set, next to his favourite deep-blue armchair.

Brick End was not primitive, but it was not Bloomsbury either. There was no central heating, and every Friday night Mandelson would telephone his new next-door neighbour, Pearl Bevis, asking her to light the fire in readiness for his arrival. 'He always liked the wood fire lit in the winter to come home to, and also the lights on, because he used to like the house lit up when he was coming down the road.' Mandelson would nip round to his neighbours and say hello as soon as he arrived. 'He was very, very nice,' said Mrs Bevis. 'And he loved it here. He really did.'⁹

Alongside the Wye are magnificent walks, and Mandelson was sometimes seen out walking, occasionally with his lover, Peter Ashby. But much of the weekend he was on the phone. 'He lived on the telephone,' said Pearl Bevis. When he went into *Who's Who*, Mandelson proudly listed his home as 1 Brick End, and one of his recreations as country walking – the other being swimming.

Television was engaging enough, but Mandelson felt it wasn't the real thing. That was politics. He was marking time at LWT, making contacts and extending his network; he was now in his thirties and he was going nowhere. In the summer of 1985, when the Labour Party was still gripped by the backwash of the year-long miners' strike that had ended only a few months previously, Mandelson met Charles Clarke, Kinnock's chief of staff, for one of their periodic lunches. Over the meal in a basement restaurant in Pimlico, Mandelson confided that he was seriously considering how to get back into politics. Clarke mentioned that a closely fought by-election was in the offing in central Wales. Tom Hooson, the genial Conservative MP for Brecon and Radnor, had died, bequeathing a majority in excess of 9,000 votes. But given Thatcher's current unpopularity, particularly in a constituency so close to the Welsh mining valleys that had been solid for the pit strike, the seat might just be winnable for Labour.

Clarke suggested that Mandelson might take some leave from LWT and go down to Wales to help in the campaign. He did not need a second bidding. Mandy already had his cottage in Foy, close to the constituency, and while he was not politically active in the locality, he saw the potential of the coming contest. He took three weeks off and went down to mid-Wales. Brecon and Radnor, geographically the largest of the Welsh seats, was well known for its exciting three-way fights. It had been Labour from 1931 to 1979, when the Tories under Margaret Thatcher regained it by 3,027 votes on a 6.5 per cent swing. The mining influence was on the wane. Agriculture was the main economic activity, together with tourism in the little spa towns of Builth Wells and Llandrindod Wells, the book town of Hay-on-Wye and the county town of Brecon. Six out of ten people owned their own homes, and the middle and professional classes were well presented.

Labour's candidate was Richard Willey, the son of Fred Willey, a former Labour Cabinet minister who had also been chairman of the parliamentary Labour Party. Mandelson became his 'minder' for the duration of the summer campaign, steering him towards media opportunities and away from potential banana-skins. 'He just rolled up his sleeves and got on with it,' said a party official. 'When he gets stuck into something, he is a hard worker, and very committed.'

Brecon and Radnor was the first of Mandelson's glorious failures. His man did not win (in fact, Richard Willey later committed suicide) but he lost by a mere 559 votes to the Liberal–SDP Alliance's Richard Livsey, while the Tories ran a poor third. The vigorous, professional performance turned in by Mandelson enabled him to re-establish contact with Labour's campaign people. And at a critical juncture. Mandelson knew that the party's high command under Neil Kinnock, party leader since 1983, had set in train a thoroughgoing reconstruction of its Walworth Road headquarters.

The number of departmental heads was to be slashed from twelve to four. One of these would be a new media supremo, bringing together campaigns and communications. It would be a high-profile post, bringing the party into a new era of media relations and advertising. Labour leaders had just disencumbered themselves of the party's head of press relations, Nick Grant, a former health-union media officer who had failed to meet their expectations. Robert Maxwell, the maverick multi-millionaire owner of the Labour-supporting *Daily Mirror* (and, it subsequently emerged, a crook) took Grant off their hands and gave him a job. A Labour insider at the time commented later, 'It was the only promise Maxwell ever delivered on.'

There was bound to be strong competition for the post of media spokesman, notably from the trade unions and the Left, whose champion Larry Whitty, head of research for the general union GMB had recently been appointed party general secretary. There was also pressure to appoint a woman. Nita Clarke, formerly press officer for Ken Livingstone at the Greater London Council, fitted the bill admirably and had much support. Another front-runner was David Gow, a *Guardian* journalist with a number of well-placed friends in the party hierarchy.

According to the political journalist, Andy McSmith, who worked in Labour's press office in the late eighties, Mandelson used the opportunity to sound out Charles Clarke in Brecon. But Clarke himself insists that Mandelson's role in the by-election was 'a statement of actuality that he had decided to get back in the political process'. It was 'certainly not done with the directorship of communications in mind.'[10] It must surely have been both. Mandelson was too smart not to realise where a good by-election campaign might take him, and he was off the starting-blocks as soon as he got back to London. The post of director of communications was publicly advertised, at a salary of £28,000 a year. He applied.

His 'private and confidential' application form was a fine example of Mandelsonian self-publicising. Asked about management experience, he said that as a TV producer he had managed a team of researchers, director, production assistants and graphics (*sic*) artists for 'my' programme. And while at the British Youth Council, he had been responsible for the 'complete overhaul' of the organisation, involving thirty affiliated organisations (there were many more) and managing ten members of staff. While admitting that his primary media experience was in broadcasting, he added, 'I am familiar with news and current affairs operations and I have daily contact with a wide range of political and economic newspaper journalists.'

Answering a question about public relations and promotion, he admitted, 'I am not an advertising or PR professional but I have developed good judgement about dependable promotion methods and advice that can be trusted.' He also invoked his experience of working for Albert Booth. On the campaign front, he cited his experience as a ward organiser, councillor and most recently as 'the candidate's aide' at Brecon and Radnor, which sounded as if he was the only one. Mandelson made much of his time at LWT, saying that as a *Weekend World* producer he had commissioned substantial opinion polls from MORI and Harris 'which have constituted the core of our programmes'. This gave him 'a high degree of expertise in organising and analysing polls'. Finally, he stressed his considerable experience at the TUC of working to committees and preparing reports and agenda items: a clear pitch at the Executive Committee.

He also wrote: 'I have written substantial documents on Unemployment (1977 and 1979), Broadcasting and Youth (1980) and Transport Policy (1982) for the TUC–Labour Party Liaison Committee.' This body brought together the barons of the trade-union movement and the shadow Cabinet, including the leader. It discussed policy, but did not publish policy papers. And the politicians might dispute his sole authorship of Labour's transport policy.

Mandelson was required to give two referees, one from the party and one from outside. John Prescott MP, Booth's number two at Westminster, was his party referee, and his second referee was supplied by Geoffrey Goodman, the respected industrial editor of the *Daily Mirror*. Goodman, who had worked at Downing Street, heading the Labour government's Counter-inflation Unit, was a surprising catch. Not only was he highly regarded in the labour movement – particularly the influential TGWU – but he also had television experience. He appeared regularly on *Weekend World*, where he got to know Mandelson as one of the packaging merchants who put together soundbites for the show. Every week, the programme sought to buttress its arguments with brief clips – counted in tens of seconds – from independent sources. The more commanding the better, and they did not come more authoritative than snow-haired Geoffrey Goodman. Mandelson went to see Goodman in his office at MGN headquarters on Holborn, asking for his support. The *Mirror* man, by this time tiring of the way his observations on industry and politics were squeezed into 'plastic parcels', was friendly, if taken aback. 'I didn't know him well, but we were on reasonably good terms,' he remembered. 'He wanted to apply for the Labour Party job, and would I support his application. I said I was surprised. He said he was very much in favour of what Neil Kinnock was doing, and he knew I knew Neil Kinnock. I said OK, and much to my amazement he got the job.' The favour was not returned. 'Now, when I stumble across him by accident, he looks the other way. I am full of remorse [for backing him] now.'[11] John Prescott also had later second thoughts. 'There are times when I have wondered about that, but I can't doubt his skills.'[12]

However, it was an impressive-sounding application. At this stage in the game he was not the front-runner, nor initially had he much support from Neil Kinnock. Whitty and Kinnock both favoured Gow, a cheerful, chubby man whose engaging nature concealed a sharp brain. But Gow had theological-style doubts. He wasn't sure that he could expose his family to the kind of pressure that the job would bring: the endless demands on his time, the probable invasion of domestic privacy. And as a journalist with a sceptical view of the world, he felt that Kinnock might demand too much blind loyalty to the leader, whereas the post – technically, at least – was as the party's chief spokesman, not the leader's.

Gow pulled out of the race a few days before the National Executive Committee (NEC) began whittling down the shortlist. Mandelson had been very busy. His contacts on the trade union side were virtually non-existent, but he milked his high-profile friends, in the television world and in Parliament, for all they were worth. John Prescott, who had a lot of clout on the NEC, had agreed to be a referee. Roy Hattersley, the deputy leader, also promised his backing, saying Mandelson would be 'a very strong candidate'. This support was later magnified into a Hattersley fix by his own personal spin-doctor, David Hill, who claimed, 'It's down to Roy and I that Peter became director of communications. Neil was uncertain about it, but I knew Peter because he had worked on the shadow cabinet corridor as an assistant to Albert Booth. Roy and I insisted he was by far the best candidate for the job.'[13]

Media contacts also weighed in privately. Kinnock, who had had dealings with Mandelson while preparing for appearances on *On the Record*, took 'quite positively' to him. Whitty still favoured Nita Clarke, partly because he knew her and he didn't know Mandy. He thought he could work with her, but not with this gimlet-eyed television man.

In the days before the crucial NEC meeting on 24 September 1985, a coalition was put together around Mandelson, while supporters of Ms Clarke – who was later to marry Tony Benn's son Stephen – frantically tried to stop her support haemorrhaging away. There were even unsubstantiated rumours of people contacting the press to denounce Mandelson as a homosexual. On the day, Kinnock actually asked Whitty 'if he had a problem with Mandelson being gay'. The general secretary replied that he was not aware of his sexual orientation, but friends on the Left had described Mandelson has a complete conspirator. John Prescott urged Whitty to back the man who was now Kinnock's privately declared choice, arguing that he would 'do good things' for Labour.

The atmosphere at the NEC meeting was tense. Nita Clarke was still thought to have the edge. But Kinnock had been on the telephone the night before, seeking to turn key votes in favour of Mandelson; those he rang included Eddie Haigh of the TGWU (Textile Section) and Tom Sawyer of the National Union of Public Employees (NUPE).

Mandelson gave a bravura performance at his interview. He impressed those present with his arguments that there was a new mood among the electorate. Thatcher's promotion of individual enterprise had struck a chord with voters, though they wanted a 'caring' government and prized the NHS highly. He suggested that they wanted a socially just society, more on the lines of Sweden than of the freebooting USA (though America was later to become *his* model). Labour, he suggested, had concentrated too much on internal dialogue, and had failed to communicate with the public at large. He would strive to close this 'credibility gap', which had its roots in the party's splits and the voters' lack of trust in Labour on economic policy.

It was a courageous manifesto, pulling no punches and delivered to the very people who could be blamed for contributing to Labour's dismal electoral performance. Insofar as the vote was a free one (some felt mandated by the people who sent them there), the NEC was finely balanced between the merits of Clarke and Mandelson. Sawyer actually passed a note across the table to Kinnock, asking, 'Who do you want?' The Labour leader told him to back Mandy against Clarke, despite her being closer to NUPE's brand of politics. Sawyer, later promoted to the general secretaryship of the party by Tony Blair – and subsequently ennobled – did the leader's bidding. Eddie Haigh followed suit. Mandelson would not have got the job without these two key defections. The decision to appoint him was carried by a majority of only four. Without the defectors, it would have been a tied vote.

Mandelson was the only outsider to be appointed to the newly refashioned departmental headships. It was a remarkable achievement. Tony Benn, who had voted for his future daughter-in-law, noted the appointment in his diary laconically. He was soon to be very much more voluble on the subject.

6

ROSES ALL THE WAY

Labour's media performance when Mandelson took over at Walworth Road HQ was admittedly a shambles. But it was a good time to take on the job. He started with a clean sheet and the whole-hearted support of the party leader, if not of the ruling national executive. Even those who had doubts about his politics conceded that it was time for a change. He might just be the right man.

Mandelson took over on his thirty-second birthday, shortly after the annual conference in Bournemouth. Though not yet in post, he was present at the conference when Neil Kinnock launched his famous attack on Militant, the hard-Left faction running Liverpool council. Kinnock lambasted Militant for the 'grotesque chaos' of a Labour council hiring taxis to scuttle round the city handing out redundancy notices to its own workers. To thunderous applause, he told delegates, 'You can't play politics with people's jobs.' The speech brought huge plaudits from a usually hostile press, and Mandelson was in raptures. 'He was ecstatic,' observed one of his new colleagues. 'Charged up. He rushed around telling everybody it was a turning-point.'

It was. Tony Benn noted in his diary that 1 October 1985 had been 'a historic day in the party'. What Hugh Gaitskell had attempted in 1960 had been tried again – the destruction of the Left, the conference and the unions. Behind the violent public attack on Militant, Benn noted an important shift in policy-making, away from the conference towards the shadow Cabinet – that is, the leader's office. It was a development that Mandelson welcomed and was determined to promote as rapidly as possible.

Kinnock's Militant speech did much to halt the slide in the opinion polls to the Liberal–SDP Alliance, and the Westland affair, which broke in January 1986, was a godsend for Labour's media machine. Margaret Thatcher appeared to be consumed by a political death-wish over the future of a small West Country helicopter firm that was in financial difficulties. She favoured a sale to the American firm Sikorsky, while her defence secretary (and long-term rival), Michael Heseltine, wanted a European consortium to take over. Before the affair subsided, Heseltine had walked out of the Cabinet, and Trade Secretary Leon Brittan was forced to resign over damaging leaks to the press assumed to have been authorised by the prime minister. Thatcher herself told close friends that Westland could have toppled her.

Not for the first time, events were moving Mandelson's way, and he was growing in confidence. Still only four months in the job, he felt strong enough to try to stop Tony Benn appearing on BBC TV's *Question Time* on 27 February 1986. The party's national executive had just voted to begin proceedings against Militant supporters in Liverpool. Benn was an articulate opponent of expulsion, and Mandelson did not want the Left's veteran standard-bearer questioning Kinnock's purge of Militant on prime-time television. But Benn was far too big a figure in the party to approach directly. Instead, Mandelson telephoned BBC bosses and suggested they drop Benn. Since the programme had invited him specifically to answer questions on Militant, they refused, and Benn duly appeared. This was the first reported occasion when Mandelson tried to influence programme-makers. The practice was to become commonplace.

Another stroke of good fortune presented itself in February in a by-election in the marginal Conservative seat of Fulham, occasioned by the death of Tory MP Martin Stevens. During the preceding weeks, the Westland affair had sent the Tories plummeting in the polls. The Liberal–SDP Alliance was ahead of the two major parties, and its spokesman talked up the chances of capturing a key west London constituency. The Alliance candidate was none other than Mandelson's long-standing friend, Roger Liddle, former Lambeth councillor and special adviser to Bill Rodgers, one of the original 'Gang of Four'.

Liddle had defected with his political mentor to the SDP. In Fulham, he stood on a virulently anti-Kinnock ticket, telling voters in his election address that they had to say 'NO' to Labour because 'there are tens of thousands of militant extremists, not just a dozen or so. Nothing will be done about them. The chaos and the wrangling will go on and on. . . . Labour is a shambles. It is weak and divided. It will never govern the country again. It has let everybody down.'

Labour fielded Nick Raynsford, an energetic local man, a former member of the borough council and currently director of SHAC, a London housing aid centre. Mandelson promoted him under the simple banner of 'Nick Raynsford Lives Here'. It was a short, hard-fought campaign. The Alliance noted that Labour poured in money and people, and used lavish, colour-printed election literature for the first time. This was to become a hallmark of Mandelson's campaign style, whether for the party or for himself: throw in everything against the enemy, and then some more.

It worked. Labour won, with Raynsford storming to the front to take 44.4 per cent of the vote, a majority of 3,503 over the Tories' Matthew Carrington, who ran a poor second, polling 34.9 per cent. Roger Liddle, great white hope of the Liberal–SDP Alliance, and future co-author with Mandelson, was humiliated in third place, with less than 19 per cent. Raynsford was appointed parliamentary private secretary to Roy Hattersley, Mandelson's mentor. (Labour's success was to prove short-lived though. Little

over a year later, Carrington regained the seat for the Conservatives in the 1987 general election, doubling Raynsford's
majority; the Mandelson magic had not lasted.) For the moment,
Mandelson's reputation soared. As the SDP leader David Owen
noted later, 'Labour under Neil Kinnock had thrown off the old
[Michael] Foot style and was now capable of effective
campaigning.'[1]

Everyone at Walworth Road noticed his Stakhanovite working
habits. He was in his office by 8 a.m., and often worked until late
into the evening. He was never off the phone to big-name
journalists. Colleagues also noticed a shift in professional emphasis.
Previous Labour media chiefs had regarded themselves as
representatives of the whole party, embracing the national
executive, the parliamentary party and the leader's office.
Mandelson never made that mistake. With an unerring nose for the
fresh direction of power, Mandelson attached himself closely to
Neil Kinnock. He was often to be found in the Commons, or in the
leader's office. He was always on Kinnock's side in any argument.
Photographs of the leader appeared on the walls of Mandelson's
second-floor office in Walworth Road, and tension began to creep
into office relationships. 'What had been a happy office ceased to be
so,' recollects Andy McSmith, a press officer there at the time.[2] The
feeling was mutual. A source close to Kinnock disclosed that
'Mandelson regarded Walworth Road as a nest of vipers. Quite
rightly. He had an ambiguous relationship with it. We felt, the
modernising Neil Kinnock felt, that Walworth Road was not an
efficient operation. We needed to get some vitality into it.
Mandelson was a very important vehicle for that.'

Mandelson's first hiring was Rex Osborne, a contemporary at
the British Youth Council who was now an analyst, who came in
as political intelligence officer. He also headhunted John Booth, a
journalist he had met during the Brecon and Radnor by-election,
as his chief press officer. Booth, who had worked on the *Washington
Post* and the *Guardian*, and headed the media office of the National
Union of Teachers, was a former Labour parliamentary candidate.
He seemed ideal for the £13,450-a-year post, and began work at

Walworth Road in January 1986. But the arrangement was to end in tears, chiefly Booth's.

As time went by, Booth noticed that Mandelson spent less and less time at Walworth Road, and more and more in Kinnock's Westminster office: 'I didn't know what he was doing a lot of the time, and I found that quite difficult.'[3] He was also puzzled by an invitation, in place of Mandelson, to a meeting of something called the Shadow Journalists' Group. Among its members were Alastair Campbell, Philip Whitehead, Keith Harper of the *Guardian*, John Lloyd of the *Financial Times* and Steve Vines of the *Observer*, none of whom would quarrel with the label 'Labour moderate'. At the time, Mandelson was on holiday in Sardinia with his boyfriend, Peter Ashby. Booth was intrigued by the existence of this body, which had no place in the formal structure of the party. He was never invited again. 'I had stumbled across something I should not have known about,' he now believes. 'This was what became part of the Shadow Communications Group.'[4]

He was right to suspect that something was going on in the background, but wrong about its origins. In fact, the Shadow Communications Group, soon to break cover, had its origins in a breakfast group set up by Kinnock's press secretary, Patricia Hewitt, in 1983. She brought the party into contact with Bob Worcester, head of the MORI polling agency, and Chris Powell, head of the advertising agency Boase, Massimi Pollitt, which Labour had used. This embryo group brought in John Gau, a BBC television producer, to revamp Labour's political broadcasts so they looked more like a current-affairs show. The group also dreamed up the idea of a party theme tune – a Brahms melody – to give a sense of identity to Kinnock's public appearances.

However, it was the arrival of Mandelson that put this process of using outside sympathisers to greatest effect, both for the party and for his own burgeoning role in it. First, he persuaded the Walworth Road chiefs that they had no alternative but to 'structure something from scratch'. According to a top-level party insider, Mandelson got his way by claiming that none of the established advertising agencies would take on Labour after the

1983 election debacle. 'Peter was able to get on board, through the network, producers and writers,' the source added. 'But it was very much by default. That was the only way he could do it.'

The Shadow Communications Agency was formally established at the February 1986 NEC meeting. Mandelson was made co-ordinator, and ensured that it reported to him rather than the general secretary, Larry Whitty. He brought in, recalls Andy McSmith, 'a small army of advertising copywriters, psephologists, market researchers, graphic artists and others', all unpaid, whose labour would have cost millions of pounds in the marketplace.[5] Mandelson also secured the services of his friend Philip Gould, an advertising executive who was to become central to the rebranding of the Labour Party. The two met at a dinner party in 1985, and the importance of their political partnership cannot be over-estimated. Gould, joint chief of Gould Mattinson Associates and married to millionaire publisher Gail Rebuck, took over the leadership of the Shadow Communications Agency. Gould had already cleared his role with Kinnock's office, via the leader's chief of staff Charles Clarke.

According to the contemporary hymnal for New Labour, written by sympathetic journalists Patrick Wintour and Colin Hughes, Gould was commissioned by Mandelson and reported directly back to him. They were in daily contact 'and so fused their operations that they often found it hard to distinguish who proposed what. But their division of responsibility was clear: Gould diagnosed and evaluated, Mandelson carried out the surgery . . . often taking enormous political risks with his own position in order to do so.'[6]

The agency's first outing was not exactly a runaway success. On 25 March 1986 – the eve of Militant's 'trial' by the NEC – it made a presentation entitled 'Society and Self' to Labour's Campaign Strategy Committee. Mandelson was present. It was offered as a qualitative survey of thirty groups, each comprising eight people – for the most part uncommitted Labour voters. They had been interviewed for ninety minutes on issues thought to be close to their hearts. Members of the national executive attending the presentation were told that the exercise was to understand the nature of the target vote.

Some, like Tony Benn, were horrified by what they saw. On to the screen flashed messages such as 'It's nice to have a social conscience, but it's your family that counts' and 'If I had a brick, I would throw it in Arthur Scargill's face.' Gould and Mandelson argued that voters were more interested in people than in ideas. 'What was required in the party leadership was decisiveness, toughness and direction: people wanted a tough person at the helm,' noted Benn.[7] He left the meeting feeling physically sick at what he saw as the Tory argument that 'you had better be more like Thatcher if you want to win'. What he had witnessed was the first use of focus groups by spin-doctors (though they were not yet called by that name) in British political history: the structured exploitation of small numbers of people to achieve a political objective. In this case, it was to redirect Labour away from its traditional fascination with policies and decision-making annual conferences towards a presidential style of party leadership, with image and policy determined by the leader and a small coterie around him. It was nothing short of a revolution, even if that evening's presentation was only the first beginnings.

One outcome of the new stress on image was the adoption of the red rose as Labour's symbol instead of the red flag. Labour has always set great store by symbolism: 'The Red Flag' is still sung at the end of annual conference. Mandelson was determined to get rid of the party symbol. It was too reminiscent of workers marching Soviet-style behind red banners: old-fashioned, and not voter-friendly – not, at any rate, to the voters of Middle England he wanted to attract.

This was not a new idea. Labour candidate Leigh Hatts wore a red rose years before. Nor was it Mandelson's idea. Neil Kinnock had been privately expressing dissatisfaction with the red flag. He was attracted to the red rose used by European socialist parties and the Socialist International – though not to the socialist-realist fist in which it was clenched. Graphic designers from the Shadow Agency worked on dozens of variants until they came up with the emblem that remains in use today. Mandelson was initially anxious about the new symbol. He took the design to Larry Whitty in great trepidation, saying, 'I want to show you something.' Whitty acclaimed it as a brilliant design and major breakthrough. Mandelson feared that he would not get it through the executive – a well-founded fear, for the traditionalists fought an unsuccessful rearguard action to save the red flag.

The red rose may have been Kinnock's idea, but Mandelson got the credit for it. When the new symbol got top billing at his first conference as communications director in Blackpool that year, it aroused immense media interest, more than the debates at what was essentially a publicity rally on the eve of a general election (which was expected within months). At the close of proceedings, Neil and Glenys Kinnock threw an immense bouquet of roses from the platform into the arms of cheering delegates. Tony Benn fled from the hall in disgust, which no doubt convinced Mandelson that he had got it right.

Not everything was going well, however. Mandelson had decided to sack his chief press officer, John Booth, the man he had virtually hired in the Museum Tavern, which was close to the TUC headquarters, with a promise that the job interview would be a formality. The two did not get on, and Mandy told Booth that he intended to terminate his contract of employment. Furthermore, as a 'probationary' member of staff until 31 July, he was not entitled to union representation. Booth sought advice from the National Union of Journalists, which came to his aid and insisted that Mandelson would have to follow correct procedures.

A gap had been opening up between the director of communications and his press officer almost from the beginning, largely occasioned by Booth's perception that his main duty was to the party, whereas Mandelson oriented himself towards the leader. The split was exacerbated by the Wapping dispute, which broke out in late January and set several thousand striking print workers against Rupert Murdoch's News International. Labour's NEC was divided over a boycott of the four Wapping titles – *The Times, Sunday Times, News of the World* and *Sun* – and finally agreed a compromise: the party would not engage in normal dealings with News International journalists, but – with the Fulham poll pending – would make an exception for by-elections.

Booth carried out the edict, but was surprised, when Mandelson went on holiday, to get a telephone call from Robin Oakley, political editor of *The Times*. Oakley invited him out to lunch, and at the end of the meal asked Booth if he would keep up the relationship that Mandelson had with *The Times*, while the communications director was on holiday. A mystified Booth said he wasn't aware of any relationship. Oakley explained that Mandelson could not be seen to be talking to *The Times*, 'but obviously we have been kept informed of what is going on'. Booth replied that that was not his understanding of the NEC decision, and he would not operate Mandelson's 'relationship'. Oakley did not press the point. 'I got the impression that relations continued, but discreetly, rather than publicly,' Booth said later.[8]

Professional relations between the two men continued to deteriorate during the summer, culminating in a verbal warning from Mandelson on 17 July that, while he had no wish to mount a case against his competence, Booth 'had not fitted in'. In a formal letter on 25 July, Mandelson complained of Booth's 'high handed, insensitive and insular approach', displayed during the Fulham, Ryedale and West Derbyshire by-elections. 'As you recall when you returned I expressed my disapproval of the way in which you failed to consult me on your own role in those by-elections, failed to liaise with me throughout the period and adopted an insensitive style.'[9] Mandelson agreed to extend his probationary period for a further three months, warning Booth that if his performance did not improve he would then be dismissed.

Not everyone in Labour's high command echoed Mandelson's snooty tone. Denis Healey, the former deputy leader, wrote to Booth that same week praising him for the media job he had done during a trip by the shadow foreign secretary. 'I should like to thank you for the excellent work you did for us on our visit to South Africa, and to say how sorry I am that there is some question of you leaving Walworth Road.'

The next day, Mandelson told Booth – a trained journalist who took a note of the meeting – 'If we have to terminate your contract I will make any fabrication of the truth and stick by it faithfully.' Booth was dumbfounded. 'Nobody had ever said anything to me like that in my life. I didn't think anybody in the Labour Party could say things like that.'[10] He soon learned what life in the Labour Party could be like.

Booth was banned by Larry Whitty from attending the Blackpool conference, making it virtually impossible to 'prove' that his work had improved. Mandelson dismissed the ban as not a matter for discussion with the NUJ, and urged the union to 'bring this matter to a conclusion with the minimum harm to either side'. The story was picked up by the public relations press, with *PR Week* reporting that in Booth's absence 'an understaffed press office worked day and night to cope with the biggest influx of journalists to attend a Labour conference in recent years'.[11]

Inevitably, Booth's appeal to party bosses to reject Mandelson's dismissal moves failed. He was sacked by the NEC on 17 November, though the party acknowledged its share of the blame by giving him a pay-off of almost £5,000. Nobody could be in any doubt how powerful Peter Mandelson had now become. Not even Lynne Franks, the undisputed queen of the public relations world, who was hired to be Labour's consultant on youth. That relationship did not last either. In the autumn of 1986, Ms Franks revealed that she was no longer working for the party on a permanent basis. She denied having been sacked. Andy McSmith recorded that for Mandelson, the episode was a huge embarrassment. 'Her contract with the Labour Party having come to an ill-tempered end, Lynne Franks later said that the red rose logo reminded her of lavatory paper.'[12]

Labour's national executive was useful to Mandelson when he wanted to sack someone, but top-level party sources say that for the most part he found NEC meetings 'a complete waste of time'. Nor did he seek to hide his contempt for this motley collection of trade-union barons, left-wing darlings of the constituencies and politicians on the make. Larry Whitty was obliged to defend him against complaints from widely different parts of the political spectrum, including veteran right-wingers who thought he was riding roughshod over them.

Furthermore, there was an increasing chorus of complaint from senior party figures that they were being marginalised by Mandelson, who personally controlled television appearances by members of the shadow Cabinet. John Prescott, who had acted as his referee for the Labour Party job, was one of his victims, along with Michael Meacher, who had contested the party deputy leadership in 1983. Prescott, not a man to take such an offence lying down, began referring to him in public as 'Mendelson' too many times for it to be a coincidence.

In the office at Walworth Road, he was like a breath of fresh air to many of the staff. Carole Boardman, who worked as a press assistant for Mandelson in the run-up to the election, praised him as 'brilliant', and said, 'He knew what he wanted. He knew where he was going. He had the money, and his campaigns like Putting People First were truly breathtaking. He was a force for good in those days. He hadn't lost his sense of humour then. It was an exciting place to be.'[13]

As the election deadline neared, Kinnock made some critical changes in the political hierarchy. Robin Cook, the campaigns co-ordinator, had lost his seat in the 1986 shadow Cabinet elections, and Bryan Gould was brought in to replace him. Gould, Mandelson's referee for the LWT job, inherited his protégé as part of a Campaign Management Committee, along with Charles Clarke, Larry Whitty and Patricia Hewitt, the leader's personal press secretary.

This group took over the detailed planning of the election, drawing up the programme of events, the press conferences and the campaign framework. Mandelson played a key part in the work of the committee, but some sources in the party hierarchy argue that his role was less important than those of Clarke and Patricia Hewitt.

Gould recalls, 'At the time I arrived, Mandelson had no great reputation. He was thought generally speaking to be a good thing, a bright young man. It was recognised that he was unpopular in some parts in Walworth Road, and some of his staff didn't like him. That was the perception, but by and large he was thought to be doing fairly well. The Mandelson myth had not really got under way at that point. He was simply seen as a bright and creative member of the team. I found him interesting and good to work with, although he was prone to get a little detached if he was bored, or didn't agree with what was being said or done, whereas if he liked it, he would become very effective.'[14]

Mandelson's influence extended well beyond the media and campaigning remit. With expectations rising of an early poll, he was clearly established as a key operator in Labour's high command. He choreographed a presentation by Bryan Gould on Labour's prospects given to a shadow Cabinet gathering in early January 1987. But Mandelson's increasing self-confidence was becoming irksome to more traditional Labour figures. On 16 February, Kinnock took the chair at a joint meeting of the shadow Cabinet and the NEC, the first since he had become leader. It was a rehearsal for the Clause Five meeting that would determine the shape of Labour's manifesto. Kinnock identified Thatcher as the Tories greatest weakness, a 'hateful' figure but thought to be strong. Labour must attack her as weak and wrong. Tony Benn, for one, found the emphasis on leadership personality depressing, and Kinnock's performance – like 'a very insecure chairman of a company addressing shareholders, or rather sales representatives in the field'[15] – unconvincing. Mandelson's influence clearly lay behind the stress on personality. The Shadow Communications Agency reinforced this image with their assessment of Labour's poor position in the polls, arguing that while the voters were afraid of the 'loony Left', and the party's inexperience, they did like the fact that Labour had 'a leader in control'.

Mandelson was at the meeting, and gave a presentation on polling. Benn noted in his diary, 'I find Mandelson a threatening figure for the future of the party . . . he has taken over, and he and Kinnock now work closely together.'[16] Larry Whitty, he decided, had been reduced to a figurehead, while Geoff Bish, the director of research, had been pushed into the background.

Bryan Gould, who was also present, found Mandelson a curious mixture of strengths and weaknesses: a charmer and the most effective manipulator of people he had ever met. 'He was a brilliant strategist,' Gould wrote later, 'in the sense of securing goals of a personal nature, but he was a limited political thinker who was surprisingly wooden when it came to articulating ideas.' The briefings he gave to the campaign committee and the shadow Cabinet on the political outlook were accurate and well-focused, but 'surprisingly banal'.[17]

The Walworth Road campaign team had only a few months to prepare for Kinnock's first assault on Downing Street. According to one insider, Mandelson took over the nuts and bolts of the campaign, drawing up an elaborate 'grid'. This procrustean bed, into which all electioneering activity had to be slotted, laid down what shadow ministers would do in the four weeks before polling-day. Mandelson had lots of charts and plans, and had even decided that, seven days before voters went to the polls, the government would be rocked by an NHS scare story. This version is disputed by Bryan Gould, who insists that the credit for this 'grid' rightly belongs to him. In all likelihood it was a team effort, aimed at avoiding the shambles of 1983 when the shadow Cabinet was dispersed around the country like a flock of chickens, each one ignorant of the others' message and whereabouts. This time, fifty Labour prima donnas were locked into a tight framework of who said what, on which radio or television programme, and where and when they did so. It was one of the genuinely successful organisational elements of the campaign, and became the model for future Labour election efforts.

But before any of this behind-the-scenes activity could bear fruit, Mandelson had a public-relations disaster on his hands. The death of Guy Barnett, Labour MP for Greenwich, on Christmas Eve 1986 triggered an unwanted by-election in south London. Labour's candidate, Deirdre Wood, was an unreconstructed left-winger, unremittingly hostile to the 'capitalist press' (which is invariably a difficulty, there being almost no other) and facing a strong challenge from a local SDP stalwart, Rosie Barnes, a media-friendly mother of three who 'seemed nice because she was nice'. The tabloids seized on Wood's record as a 'loony Left' councillor on the GLC and the Inner London Education Authority, sapping support for Labour, who should have started the campaign as front-runner.

Nothing Mandelson could do, or fail to do, was sufficient to prevent the SDP landslide. Tactical voting took place on a massive scale, with huge desertions from the Tories and on a smaller scale from Labour. On polling day, 26 February 1987, Ms Barnes romped home with 53 per cent of the vote. Her sensational victory put the Liberal–SDP Alliance back into second place in many polls, while Labour languished at below 30 per cent. Greenwich renewed speculation that Thatcher might call an early general election to choke off a political revival by the Alliance, particularly when the Liberals easily retained Truro a fortnight later. The Tories were not obliged to go to the country before the spring of 1988, but Labour's weak by-election showing and poor performance in the polls increased the temptation to call a summer election.

More misery was in store. In late March, Mandelson accompanied Kinnock and Healey to Washington for a summit with President Ronald Reagan. The trip was a public-relations fiasco. In the Oval Office, Reagan 'mistook' Healey for the British ambassador, and proceeded to berate the Labour leader for his party's policy on unilateral nuclear disarmament. The meeting came to a summary close, leaving the Labour leaders humiliated and furious. Naturally, the press had a field day, while Mandelson shared the discomfiture.

The experience encouraged him to play a more overt role in the policy field. A very senior source disclosed, 'His interference in policy was much less marked to begin with. It only manifested itself just before the 1987 election, particularly on defence.' A new policy statement, *Britain and the World*, gave a 'seriously different view' of the party's defence strategy from the line agreed at Labour's conference. Mandelson was beginning to move from policy-presenter to policy-maker. He visited Bryan Gould and his family in the Essex village of Westcourt Barton with boyfriend Peter Ashby on May Day 1987, conscious that the election fever gripping the country would be cured only one way. Thatcher duly obliged on 11 May, announcing the date of the general election for 11 June.

Labour's Campaign Committee swung into action immediately, meeting every morning at Walworth Road at seven o'clock. Bryan Gould, Mandelson and the others conducted a daily inquest on media coverage, examined the party's polling and reports from constituency agents round the country. They then moved camp to Transport House, Smith Square, a couple of miles away across the river to discuss progress with Neil Kinnock, if he was in the capital, or with other senior Labour figures if he was on tour. They confirmed the day's theme, and briefed candidates accordingly. Emergencies were also dealt with as they arose. Mandelson, Bryan Gould and Philip Gould then had a second session to assess the advertising side of the campaign. Mandelson and Gould also met to assess how the day was going, and to put the finishing touches to the next day's slot in the 'grid'. Since Kinnock was out campaigning in the country most mornings, the daily London press briefings were normally taken by Bryan Gould, with Mandelson in the wings. Gould was delighted with the 'verve and elan' of the press conferences, believing that the 'revelation' that Labour was doing well had become the story of the campaign.

Mandelson got his way on defence when the shadow Cabinet and NEC met for the Clause Five manifesto-writing conference on 12 May. Labour's unilateralist policy was watered down, over-turning conference policy on the US weapons and bases in Britain. A Kinnock administration would negotiate with the Americans for their removal. If talks failed, Labour would consult with the Americans and 'inform them that we wished to remove their mis-siles'. Hardly the ringing declaration of unilateralism approved by conference, but closer to Mandelson's multilateralist approach. However, he had reckoned without the inventiveness of the media, particularly the tabloid press. Clear, and noisy, differences on defence emerged between the party hierarchy and leading figures from the recent past, including James Callaghan. They were exploited mercilessly.

Labour also had great difficulty in dominating the news agenda. Gould admitted later that, whereas his Tory opponent Norman Tebbit could simply pick up the telephone and launch a story on every front page, Labour had to struggle to get its themes established. Three times, Gould and Mandelson tried to launch the hated poll tax as a story, and three times they failed. The press were more interested in Labour's divisions over defence, and the unpopularity of Neil Kinnock as leader.

One aspect of the campaign did have a significant impact, and it came from an unlikely quarter. On 21 May, Labour screened its now-celebrated party political broadcast made by Hugh Hudson, director of the Oscar-winning *Chariots of Fire*. Essentially, it was a video biography of Neil Kinnock, opening with soft-focus film of him walking the clifftops of the West Country with Glenys while gulls circled overhead. It moved on to his conference attack on the Militant Tendency in Liverpool, and closed with his memorable speech about being the first Kinnock in a thousand generations to go to university. The broadcast, still regarded as the best of its genre, had the desired effect of improving the leader's standing in the polls, but the benefit proved fleeting. Within the party, there were mixed feelings. The broadcast, pandering to Mandelson's view that the leader was more important than many of Labour's policies, made Tony Benn's blood run cold.

For most political observers, Kinnock the Video (it was repeated a week later), proved the high point of the campaign. It demonstrated that Labour had come to terms with television democracy, and much credit is due to Mandelson on that score. But it did not turn round the campaign. Apart from one freak poll, the Tories stayed solidly ahead in public opinion. Worse still, the much-vaunted 'grid' broke down in the last week. Labour's leaders were all, by Bryan Gould's admission, 'very tired'.

They had left the last square of the graph blank to inject a dramatic last-minute initiative based on how the campaign was going. Unfortunately they were all – Mandelson in particular – too exhausted to dream up a new theme. The Tories seized their opportunity and piled in everything behind a weekend attack by Chancellor Nigel Lawson on Labour's tax plans, focusing on proposals to increase national insurance. 'It fell apart on the Saturday before polling day,' Bryan Gould confessed subsequently. 'For the first time we had nothing planned, and rack our brains as we could, nothing materialised.'[18] Labour was caught on the back foot the next day. Kinnock and his deputy, Roy Hattersley, seemed to be reading from different scripts on the tax issue, and the media once more headlined divisions at the top. Mandelson's skilful influence over the press was conspicuous by its absence. He had his own story to sort out, as shall be seen.

In the last few days of the campaign, Kinnock was privately admitting to close colleagues that Labour would lose. The steam went out of the campaign. In Gould's words, it 'lacked focus, and just drifted away from us'.[19] The campaign team engaged in inconclusive and tired debates about the wisdom of persuading Kinnock to make a direct appeal to Liberal–SDP voters to support Labour as the only way to get the Tories out. Kinnock was reluctant to take this make-or-break move, largely because the Walworth Road campaigners agreed among themselves that the leader would have to live to fight another day. Kinnock himself did not want to appear 'vainglorious', and so did nothing. The campaign petered out, and on 11 June Mrs Thatcher was returned with an overall majority of 101 seats. Gould admitted later, 'In retrospect, there was never any saving the campaign. We were wrongly positioned, and Neil Kinnock, despite all his great strengths, was not trusted by an important part of the electorate. Neil himself had been very much cast down, and even offered to resign. Not seriously, I think. He was really trying to seek reassurance, but he did offer to resign.'[20]

Yet a BBC–Gallup survey after the election found that 47 per cent of voters placed Labour first in the television campaign contest, and other polls put Neil Kinnock ahead of Thatcher in presentation terms. The experts' verdict was that the Tory campaign had been faulty, while Labour's discipline, forward planning and emphasis on communications had paid off. Doubts about the value of Labour's 'glitznost' were not confined to Conservative ranks, however: some of Kinnock's professional media backers argued that the glitter was counter-productive, pointing up the weakness of Labour's policies on the economy.

With the benefit of hindsight, the campaign was not quite as professional as instant history made it. Yet it is most often cited as Mandelson's greatest triumph. In the mythology of his political career, it was the best campaign that Labour had ever fought. The fact that Labour did not win is usually relegated to a jocular footnote. He claimed the credit for the positive side of the campaign, while off-loading the blame for losing. He is uncompromising about image and presentation. 'Both are important because there is no point in having a good message and throwing it away on bad presentation,' he said later. 'If what comes across is scruffy, incoherent or ugly, then people are going to be put off the case you are making. The point is to catch people's attention. We have to behave ourselves in a way, to present and project ourselves and our message in a variety of ways that make people think of us in a favourable light, trust us and make them more amenable to voting for us.'[21] Much of that is common sense, and does not require a spin-doctor to spell it out. His use of the terms 'scruffy' and 'ugly' is interesting, however. It suggests a Wildean view that the image has to be beautiful, as well as meaningful.

Mandelson has always claimed a victory, of sorts. 'We won the battle for the opposition in 1987. We didn't succeed in displacing the government. In the run-up to the election, the opposition parties were still competing with one another, almost level-pegging in the opinion polls as the campaign began,' he argued. 'Many people still regarded the Alliance as quite a potent force. That was a problem for us, because naturally we wanted to be seen as the only alternative to the Conservatives. We succeeded in seeing off the Alliance, who were smashed into smithereens as much as anything by the strength of our campaign.'[22] This was only partly true. The polls marked the Alliance down to 21 per cent in the early stages of the campaign. I was with the Paddy Ashdown campaign team when the figures came out, and it was clear that the Alliance was fading from the start. Mandelson built them up as a strong rival for second place, which they never really were, in order to divert attention from the real failure of the campaign, to take seats from the Tories. He concluded to *Blitz* magazine that both the party and the voters were very impressed by Labour's 'tremendous sense of vigour and confidence' imparted by the 1987 campaign. If so, it did not show in the polling-booth. Labour's vote was up by less than 4 per cent on the cataclysmic defeat of 1983.

It may be argued that Mandelson had been in post for less than two years: not nearly enough time to turn the party round in the eyes of the voters, particularly if they remained suspicious of Labour's policies. And that is indeed Mandelson's second line of defence. It was not the campaign that lost the election, and certainly not the leader. So it must have been the policies. In the aftermath of defeat, he perfected the formula that 'substance has now caught up with style' to explain how the wholesale review of party policy was beginning to match his presentational skills. He said, 'Journalists had to find ways of explaining why we had this brilliant campaign yet we lost so badly. So people explained it presentationally. Perhaps what was wrong was the policies.'[23] In fact, it was Mandelson rather than the commentators who had to construct this *ex post facto* argument. The journalists did not need to explain anything to anybody. Mandelson did. It was his campaign, as much as anybody's.

Labour's concentration on Kinnock the leader, insisted Philip Gould, worked. 'We have shaken the great dam against voting Labour. Labour is now a serious contender and Neil Kinnock a credible leader of the nation,' he claimed. Historians would see 1987 as the campaign that saved the Labour Party. But the experts' view was scathing. David Butler and Denis Kavanagh, authors of the standard work on the election, observed, 'A well-crafted campaign failed totally to dent Conservative support.'[24]

Yet the Conservatives were among the first to buy the Mandy myth. They 'mourned the absence of a Peter Mandelson-type figure, somebody experienced in television and able to act authoritatively in communications'.[25]

The fact that the campaign had been built around Neil Kinnock, almost as a personality cult, yet had still failed to rouse the passionate support of the people, made Mandelson think twice about his political direction. He was generally, if in some respects erroneously, held to have had a good war. If he stayed on, he might have to wait until 1992 for the next general election, and with Kinnock at the helm there was still no guarantee that Labour would oust the Tories. Their grip on power had proved vice-like. The government, rather than Labour, had seen off the Alliance.

He began to turn his thoughts towards following his grandfather into Parliament. It was an ambition that dared not speak its name, because party apparatchiks were supposed to be just that: staff officers, not out in the field. But an unwelcome new development during the campaign had made Mandelson, not the people he was projecting, the story.

7

OUTED!

Shortly before nine in the evening of Saturday, 16 May 1987, Nigel Nelson, political editor of the *People*, tracked down Mandelson in the office of Mike Molloy, editor of his sister Mirror Group paper, the *Sunday Mirror*. Nelson had been searching for him since rumours began to surface earlier that day that the rival tabloid *News of the World* intended to 'out' Mandelson. He found him poring over the first edition of the paper.

The *'News of the Screws'* is not known for pulling its punches, and in the heat of a dirty-tricks general election, the paper did not mess about. On the front page, a basement taster yelled, 'Kinnock's No 1 Man in Gay Sensation!' On two and three, the main news pages, Mandelson's relationship with Peter Ashby – and Ashby's with Kay Carbery – was splashed as an exclusive under the headline 'My Love for Gay Labour Boss'.

Nelson found Mandelson with his head in his hands, the paper thrown on a table in front of him. 'He was totally devastated about the story,' recollects the man from the *People*. The report was clearly designed to damage. The *NoW* reported that Labour's £21,000-a-year election-campaign supremo was at the centre of a 'bizarre gay love triangle'. Mandelson and his 'live-in lover', Peter Ashby, shared a terrace house a few hundred yards from Ashby's ex-girlfriend, the mother of his 4-year-old son, Joe. She was identified as Kay Carbery, a 36-year-old secretary at the TUC, who had 'given her old flame's strange relationship her blessing'. The two Peters often called at her home in Hackney, east London, to take Joe out for walks in the park.

Anxious to drag the Labour leader's name into the frame, the report continued: 'Mr Kinnock is also said to know and approve of his top aide's strange domestic set-up.' Ms Carbery had fallen for the tall, handsome Ashby, unaware of his love for Mandelson, and the two had had a brief affair. They went on holiday to Morocco, and Joe was born nine months later. Ashby, 35, a writer, spoke openly to the *NoW* about his 'deep love' for 33-year-old Mandelson. 'We love each other, and we love Joe. Kay approves, so what's the problem? It's a very adult relationship, but we get on great. Peter Mandelson is like an uncle to little Joe. They are very fond of each other. At weekends, we pop round to Kay's house and then we all go out together. Neil Kinnock is aware of the situation, and doesn't mind. Peter told him everything. He even introduced me to Neil.' Ms Carbery was equally forthcoming. 'Peter Ashby and I have a deep affection for each other – but we would never have married. I don't know if Mandelson resented our fling – but he's been marvellous to Joe. He's like a second father.' She spoke of the pair as Daddy Peter and Uncle Peter. 'People might think it's a weird set-up. But I think it's great,' she added. 'I live here with another woman, and we get on famously. Obviously, Joe doesn't know that his father is a homosexual. He thinks the two men are just good friends.'

Kay Carbery also spoke about Aids – presumably in response to questioning from John Chapman, the 'man from the *Screws*'. She insisted: 'I'm not worried about Joe catching AIDS off them. After all, they have a long, stable relationship and are unlikely to catch the disease.' In 1987, Aids was still a relatively new medical phenomenon. It was talked of as a 'gay plague', and public fears were easily aroused. Mandelson was stunned that his relationship with Ashby could be construed as an Aids risk to Joe, for whom he clearly had a genuine, quasi-parental affection. 'That was the thing that most upset him,' remembers Nelson. 'He wasn't crying, or anything like that. But he was very shaken. He said, "This is terrible. This is awful".'

The *News of the World* made as much political capital out of the story as it could, claiming that Mandelson's appointment – then two years old – 'was bound to be seen as an embarrassment on the eve of the General Election campaign.' The paper linked its 'outing' of Mandelson to Tory attempts to make 'Gay Rights education in schools in Loony Left boroughs' a key election issue. It dragged in a mention of books like *Jenny Lives with Eric and Martin*, issued by the Inner London Education Authority, in which one picture showed a 5-year-old girl naked on a bed with two homosexual men, and argued that Kinnock had tried to distance himself from militant Labour councils who backed gays wanting to adopt children. It was a comprehensive smear operation, topped off by a leading article headlined 'The Hidden Menace', which warned of 'the iceberg of socialism' beneath Neil Kinnock's election policies and opined: 'Pity Kinnock, too, over our exclusive revelation today about the life-style of his right-hand man. Publicly, Kinnock tries to distance himself from the loonies and the gays. Can he not see that proximity to the likes of Peter Mandelson is bound to bring embarrassment?'

The full hypocrisy of the *News of the World*'s fake horror was readily visible from an advertisement on the same page as the Mandelson story. It showed a muscular man in an erotic pose, with the message 'stripped for action', and offered 'exciting exotic sun & swimwear to erotic thongs, backless and see-throughs. Luxurious and supremely comfortable apparel for the virile male.' The advertisement was plainly directed at homosexual men. In other words, it was fine for the tabloid *NoW* to make money out of the pink pound, but shocking for politicians to be gay.

The story had no discernible impact on the general election. It was not widely followed up, even in the rival tabloids. In a dirty-tricks election, it was just another piece of dirt. Mandelson refused to make any comment, and the story soon ran out of steam. The fact that he was gay was widely known at Westminster, where the existence of homosexual politicians was an open secret among political journalists – some of whom are also gay.

However, the story did serve to initiate a long-drawn-out process to bring Mandelson out of the closet, which has had a deep impact on him personally and politically. At the time, it was a devastating blow. Realisation of what was about to hit him had broken earlier in the day. John Chapman, the reporter who wrote the story, put it all together on the Saturday morning. His newsdesk told him to follow up a throwaway paragraph about Mandelson's complex love life that had appeared in *Private Eye* a couple of days previously. He contacted Ms Carbery, and found her surprisingly helpful, given the nature of his inquiries. Ashby was also more co-operative than he probably expected at the time.

Chapman wrote his story on the Saturday afternoon, just as the Tory assault on Labour's tax plans was beginning to impact. He telephoned Walworth Road several times to speak to Mandelson, or any Labour Party press officer. He was not put through to the director of communications, who instead took at least one call from Ashby about how he had been 'doorstepped' by the *NoW*. Mandelson calmed his lover down, telling him not to talk to the reporter. It was too late. Chapman rang every ten or fifteen minutes, according to press-office staffers, but Mandelson stayed in his office. Press Officer Andy McSmith took the call, noting that Mandelson's refusal to handle the controversy himself depressed his colleagues in the office, who by now thought of him as a star, with the reputation of being able to deal with anybody. Chapman asked if Mandelson would have the courtesy to answer his call, and McSmith saw red. 'I told him he was a rat, something out of the sewer. I would let him come and interview Peter, but I was going to ring ITN and the BBC and invite cameras to come and film him interviewing Mandelson so the world could see "Fleet Street's finest" at work. It was a bluff. I don't know what I would have done if he had said yes. But the telephone went dead. I was doing this in the middle of the newsroom whilst Mandelson was in his office. He was ashen. He heard me . . . and he started nodding, "That was OK".'[1]

Mandelson telephoned the *NoW*'s editor, David Montgomery, later in the afternoon, asking for the story to be 'pulled'. Montgomery, a right-wing Ulsterman with scant respect for Labour politicians, entertained several of his executives in his office, playing Mandelson's plea over a loudspeaker phone. 'Obviously there was a bit of wry amusement,' said one of those present. 'Obviously, Montgomery was playing to the gallery a bit.' Mandelson could be heard pleading, 'I would really appreciate it, David,' as the newspaper's staffmen listened. Montgomery turned him down flat. The story ran. There were no writs, and no complaints.

That was to be the pattern in ensuing years; no denial, simply a refusal to comment. For public consumption, it has been a substantially effective policy. In the gay world, it is regarded as inexplicable. But it is important to remember the background. When Peter Mandelson was growing up, homosexuality was illegal. It was not until July 1967, when the Sexual Offences Bill became law, that homosexual acts in private between consenting adults over the age of 21 were made legal. It was not until late 1974, half-way through his university career, that he could engage in legal gay sex.

Homosexuals maturing in that era inherited the atmosphere and practice of secrecy that had become second nature to previous generations of gay men. The idea of gay pride, expressed in street marches and festivals, was still a long way off. Public demonstrations of affection were simply out of the question. It seems clear that Mandelson began his relationship with Peter Ashby in the late seventies, and the relationship continued for a decade, surviving Ashby's fathering of his son. Neil Kinnock and his wife, Glenys, were quite aware of the relationship, and, according to gay writer Steve Wakelam, also a friend of the Kinnock family, they were always 'very fatherly' to Mandelson. 'When the relationship broke up, which would be in the late eighties, I got a call from Glenys, saying: "Peter's relationship has broken up." It was bad news for them, "because we know how efficient he is".' Would it affect his work? They wondered. 'They [the Kinnocks] were certainly afraid it would. He had nowhere to go. No London base.'[2]

It is pertinent here to consider later developments on this issue. Mandelson's entry into Parliament in 1992 put his homosexuality into a different perspective. He was now a public figure, and his political and social life came under the fierce scrutiny of Outrage!, the campaigning homosexual group dedicated to 'outing' known homosexuals who – in their view – voted, spoke or behaved in a hypocritical or demeaning way about gay men and lesbian women.

By this stage in British politics, only one parliamentarian, Chris Smith, the Labour MP for Islington South, had 'come out' voluntarily. His action had no adverse impact whatsoever: quite the reverse. He was praised for his honesty, his majority increased and he progressed swiftly through the ranks to the parliamentary party to join the shadow Cabinet. It could not be said that coming out did him any harm, though it may be plausibly argued that cosmopolitan Islington bears little resemblance to working-class Hartlepool.

There is certainly anecdotal evidence that Mandelson believed coming out could damage him in the North-east. At a Christmas party thrown by Neil Kinnock in the Commons around the time of his capture of the Hartlepool nomination, Steve Wakelam asked Mandelson if he had been asked by Labour people in the town if he was gay. 'They were much too polite, Steve,' he replied. But what if they had asked him? pressed Wakelam. 'I would have denied it,' Mandelson said. Wakelam, an openly gay man, was devastated. 'I can remember at the time not knowing whether to admire the sheer ruthlessness of it, or to dislike it,' he said later. 'I have come to dislike it.'[3]

But Mandelson stayed shtum. He was never seen in a gay bar or club. He refused to give interviews to the gay press, and he never publicly endorsed any campaign for gay rights, such as Stonewall's

Club 2000 Campaign. Nor did he sign parliamentary motions on the repeal of laws discriminating against homosexuals.

Outrage! examined his voting record on the age of consent, and decided he had done 'the bare minimum' but nothing more. The group's spokesman, Peter Tatchell, argued, 'You would think someone in his position might want to support worthy causes like Lesbian and Gay Switchboard, London Lighthouse and the Kennedy Trust. Outrage! discussed outing him. Our policy is that we only support outing where a public figure is being hypocritical and homophobic, and if they actively endorse discrimination by voting for anti-gay laws. We have recently thought of him as a borderline case.'[4]

In fact, Outrage! went so far as to write to Mandelson, urging him to come out. In January 1995, a group of around thirty gay activists belonging to the group met at the Central Club in the old YMCA building off Tottenham Court Road and drew up what they regarded as a 'polite and sympathetic' letter to Mandelson. The two-page 'strictly private and confidential' letter said that Outrage! had received information 'from sources which we believe to be reliable and credible' that he might be gay or bisexual. They urged him to make 'the morally responsible choice' and come out voluntarily. The letter continued, 'Hiding one's homosexuality reinforces the idea that to be gay is shameful. This adds to prejudice which promotes intolerance, encourages discriminatory laws and gives legitimacy to homophobes and queer bashers. With so few public figures being truthful about their sexuality, many homosexuals find the pain of isolation is intensified and can develop feelings of low self-esteem.'

Fear of coming out, Outrage! argued, was far worse than the consequences. It need not damage an MP's political career: indeed, being honest could contribute to a reputation for courage and integrity. Chris Smith had increased his majority tenfold, the gay activists pointed out, and John Major had said that being gay was no bar to a Tory MP holding a ministerial position in his government. Michael Brown, at that time Conservative MP for Brigg and Cleethorpes, had been outed against his will, yet the adverse consequences he feared had not materialised. 'He now wishes he had come out a long time ago!' In fact, Brown went on to lose his seat in the 1997 general election, but does not believe that the 'outing' contributed materially to his defeat in the Labour landslide. Stephen Twigg made no secret of his gayness, yet he took the greatest political prize of the election – Michael Portillo's seat at Enfield Southgate in north London. And Ben Bradshaw, a BBC journalist, captured Exeter for Labour in the teeth of a 'family values' campaign by the Conservative incumbent. Since then, several other Labour backbenchers have come out, chiefly in the run-up to the vote for equal rights at 16 for homosexuals, which won a massive majority in the Commons but was defeated in the Lords.

The Outrage! letter, which was sent to nineteen other MPs on all sides of the House, urged a collective coming-out by several parliamentarians, to remove the possibility of any one of them being singled out as a target by the tabloids. It concluded that Mandelson, if he was gay or bisexual, had a duty to himself for his peace of mind, as well as a moral obligation to other gay men and to lesbians, to be open about his sexuality.

'Our view was that he would help himself and the wider gay community,' Tatchell insisted. 'We didn't get a reply from Mandelson. We were half expecting not to. But we had no other agenda than trying to persuade him, and we decided to take no further action.'[5]

However, six months later, Mandelson was outed for a second time by none other than Bryan Gould, his former boss as campaign co-ordinator at Walworth Road during the 1987 election. In his autobiography, the former contender for the Labour leadership recalled that on May Day bank holiday that year, 'Peter Mandelson and family' came to tea at Brook House, the Goulds' country cottage in the valley of the River Dorn, Oxfordshire. 'Peter was at that time living with Peter Ashby, who was the father of a small boy called Joe. The two Peters saw a good deal of Joe and both were very fond of him. We were delighted to see them all, and very much enjoyed their visit.'[6] This was two months before Mandelson was outed by the *News of the World*.

Further disclosure was in store. Gould recalled the 'scurrilous attack' by the *News of the World* during the election campaign. 'Peter was terribly upset, not so much on his own account, since he had long ago decided to "come out", but on behalf of Peter Ashby and little Joe,' he wrote. Gould recollected being asked at a press conference, launching a range of publicity material, whether, in the light of the story, he had lost confidence in Mandelson. 'I rejected the suggestion with contempt, and pointed to the material as evidence of Peter's value to the campaign.'[7]

To Gould's dismay, these two passages were given the same 'shock, horror' treatment by the *Sun*, sister paper to the *NoW*, as if the original outing had never taken place more than eight years previously. Trevor Kavanagh, the paper's political editor, wrote that in his book Gould had 'sensationally exposed' one of Blair's closest allies as a homosexual. He claimed that at Westminster, the 'charge' of Mandelson being gay would be seen as Gould's revenge on the man he blamed for wrecking his leadership bid in 1992, when John Smith was elected Labour leader. Only in the *Sun* could the disclosure of Mandelson's sexuality be turned into a 'charge', but, as before, he refused to rise to the fly hovering over the water. A spokesman in Hartlepool was wheeled out to say, 'He is on holiday in deepest Devon. This is just a rehash of an old smear story. No one is served by raking over a *News of the World* story of ten years ago.'[8]

Gay-rights activists would have disputed whether no-one's interests would be served by the second outing of Peter Mandelson. Though he declined to comment, privately Mandelson was furious, and consulted solicitors. Gould later disclosed: 'I told that story in the book in perfect good faith. It simply never occurred to me that the telling of the story would do any harm. As far as I knew, it had been all over the Sunday papers and Peter hadn't ever denied the truth of the matter. I told the story to show, in a sense, what a good relationship we had at the time, and all of that. But when the book was published, some of the Tory press ran stories, the thrust of which were that "Gould

Outs Mandelson". More than the thrust. The *Sun* headline was "Top Blair Whip is 'Outed' By Gould", with a sub-headline Mandelson "is gay".'

'I was pretty aggrieved about that,' said Gould. 'I contacted my libel lawyer. The implication was that I had deliberately tried to damage him by outing him.' Coincidentally, Mandelson and Gould shared the same law firm. 'Peter used the same solicitor, and had consulted him about his remedies in the situation. I received a message via my solicitor from Peter. "Peter believes that if you were to sue for libel, this would simply do further damage and give further currency [to the story] that he is not keen to promote." So at that point I said, "OK, I will drop it." It still surprises me that Peter does not publicly acknowledge his homosexuality. As far as I know, it is common knowledge.'[9]

He did not, but the story still refused to go away. In January 1998, the relaunched, raunchy *Punch* magazine published a ten-page special. 'Mandy in the Spotlight'. Half a page was given over to an article, by Peter Tatchell, about Mandelson's sexuality. In it, he recalled that when the *Independent on Sunday* contacted a former boyfriend, Mandelson rang the paper to close down the line of inquiry, arguing, 'The time may come when I want to talk about these things, but not yet – and not at this stage in my political career.' Tatchell said he knew the truth, or some of it. He claimed that Mandelson had had a 'rendezvous' with a friend of his (thought to be known as Billy) and a member of Outrage! on a trip to Moscow a few years previously. 'This was not a "honey-trap" outing plot,' insisted Tatchell. 'My friend fell quite genuinely for Mandelson's charms and good looks. He is regarded as highly fanciable by many gay professionals, once being voted into the top ten "Hunks of the Year" by readers of the gay magazine HIM.'[10]

The issue of Mandelson's sexual orientation will not go away, certainly not until he makes a clear, unambiguous statement that satisfies his gay critics. He is already under renewed pressure from members of Outrage!, who see further signs of hostility to the gay community, even if these appear to be minor matters to the wider world. His book, *The Blair Revolution*, proposed a £5,000 state dowry for newly-weds, but Mandelson has rejected the idea that this benefit might extend to same-sex couples.

It is further argued that Mandelson is responsible for 'de-gaying' Labour Party policy, particularly the 1992 election manifesto promise – on which he first stood for Parliament – of a swift review of changes in the law required to give lesbians and gay men 'genuine equality'. This was taken to mean that Labour would end the ban on practising homosexuals serving in the armed forces. Mainstream Labour opinion now finds little electoral advantage in lifting the ban, though public opinion (as expressed in a *Panorama* poll of 1997) would probably support gay enlistment. Mandelson did not vote on the issue when it was debated on 9 May 1996.

Tatchell says the topic is kept under constant review. 'Recently, there have been discussions in Outrage! about reports that Mandelson has played a leading role in de-gaying Labour Party policy, and dumping some of the party's previous gay-rights commitments,' he revealed. 'That is causing disquiet, both within Outrage! and the wider gay and lesbian community. In the past, it was widely felt that he was doing less than he could to help advance the cause of gay equality.

'Now, the concern is that he is possibly actively undermining the party's long-standing commitments. The issue of outing him may come back on the agenda if these allegations can be substantiated. There is a lot of disillusion over Labour's record. The end result has been virtually nothing of substance.'[11]

The question arises: why does Peter Mandelson deny his sexual orientation? Indeed, not only deny it but go to great lengths to avoid any public discussion? His hints are of the most oblique variety. Six months after the 1997 general election he was happy to discuss the subject of relationships in the abstract. He believes that marriage is 'so obviously the ideal way of living'. But it is not for him. 'I don't condemn people who don't get married,' he said. 'I am not married myself, and will never get married.' Nor will there be any descendants, though he shows a genuine affection for children and is godfather to four. 'I don't want to have any children because I am not going to get married. But I love everyone else's.'[12]

His gay acquaintance Steve Wakelam concedes that Mandelson manages to 'get back in the closet' when he is outed. 'And yet he is as camp as hell. That's one of his great charms.' But he criticises Mandy's lifestyle. 'He is living as if it is still the 1950s. He is certainly not helping [the gay cause]. For a man who is so supremely self-confident, he is only looking after his self-interest. I think he has no emotional life, and I think it will trip him up, finally. He gets invitations to the best parties. But he goes home to a fairly lonely house.'[13]

Others argue that Mandelson uses his gayness as a political and social weapon. One gay journalist at Westminster, who asked not to be identified, said, 'His gayness drives his personality. He tries to exploit his sexuality where he can, where he hopes it can curry favours.' But he is exceptionally prudent. 'He has very discreet drinks parties, but he would be far too clever. He would not only have gays, but luvvy types, pretty people who can go both ways.' Nor does he confide easily. 'He never confirms he is gay, unless he absolutely knows who it is. He is fiercely discreet about who he sleeps with. He is paranoid about the press turning him over. He is paranoid about it, how it will play in Hartlepool. He will not make a "Paul on the Road to Damascus" statement unless your book outs him, and then he is talking to his closest advisers about what he will do.'[14]

It is not a question of 'outing' him, however. Peter Mandelson's private life is not only a fit subject for a biographer, it is critical to his public persona, if, in the gay political correspondent's phrase, 'his gayness drives his personality'. Even more so, if, in the words of the same source, 'it is a fundamental flaw in his character' that he has difficulty coming to terms with it. It means that a vital part of his life has to be permanently hidden from view, for fear that it might impair his political advancement. Is it really worth it? A life lived in that kind of denial almost makes the case for Outrage!

8

HARTLEPOOL COUP

The general election of 1987 was a setback for the Labour Party, but not for Peter Mandelson. He had secured much of the credit for the positive side of the campaign, while shuffling off the responsibility for losing. Essentially, his argument was that style and presentation could do much, but he could not sell a dud product. Labour's policies – rather than the leader, and the packaging of Kinnock – were wrong, and the voters had sussed them out.

With his reputation as an organiser and a leader-loyalist firmly fixed in the minds of the media and the Whitehall village, Mandelson began his real search for power. From his playground days in Hendon, when he began the chant of 'PM for PM', his ambition had been only thinly disguised. Within months of the general election, he began to look around for the vital vehicle for the next stage of his reach for the top: a seat in Parliament. He knew more than anyone that the newspaper hype of him being 'the real deputy leader' or 'the most important man in the party' was precisely that, and no more. In order to be taken seriously as a political figure in a mature democracy, he had to stand for election to Westminster, the last camp before the final assault on the summit. And a very agreeable one, too.

But, like most mountains, it was not as easy as it looked. To begin with, he had to move discreetly. There was a convention, if not a rule, in the party hierarchy that full-time officials should not use their privileged position as a springboard into Parliament. It was a reasonable principle. Officials at Walworth Road or in the regional offices often knew well ahead of aspiring Labour politicians which MPs might be thinking of retiring, or so close to death that a by-election was imminent. This was sensitive information that could be abused, but should not.

Furthermore, for a full-time official as highly placed and well-thought-of as Mandelson, quitting ahead of an election that Labour had substantial, if misplaced, hopes of winning, was little short of treachery. It would be seen as the action of an ambitious man willing to put his own interests before those of the party and of the leader. In fact, it was tantamount to a vote of no confidence in the leader, because it clearly signalled a lack of faith in his ability to win.

There were other, practical, difficulties. In 1987, the Opposition parties slashed the Tory majority from 144 to 101, bringing twenty new Labour MPs into the Commons. Accordingly, there were fewer safe seats ripe for plucking. Mandelson was not particularly interested in going through the tedious proving-ground of contesting an unwinnable or barely marginal constituency before landing himself a prime slot. He wanted a ticket for the game.

In the early autumn of 1987 he confided his plans to his mentor Bryan Gould, with whom he had worked closely during the election campaign. Gould and his wife, Gill, drove down to Foy one weekend, as he recollects, in September that year. After tea, Mandelson suggested a walk across the fields. As they walked, Mandelson disclosed that he would like to become an MP. 'I said, probably unwisely, "Why would you want to be a backbencher with no influence when you are such a powerful figure as director of communications?" I saw him, I confess, at that point as a functionary,' Gould recalled. 'He never struck me as a politician, or having any political views. He looked to me as somebody who operated on a day-by-day technical, not strategic, basis. He said, oh well, he would not necessarily always stay on the backbenches. I said that was a long and arduous road. I think he hoped I would say, "Peter, you are a person we want, you must get in, I will find you a seat." Possibly, I missed a trick there.'[1]

As far as Gould (at that stage shadow trade and industry secretary) understood, Kinnock had extracted an undertaking from party staff, particularly senior figures, that they would not seek a seat during the current Parliament, so that they could concentrate on winning the general election four or five years hence. If so, Mandelson clearly did not regard the bar as applying to him. An oblique, but shameless, application for the job which should have rung alarm bells in Walworth Road appeared in September 1988, in the *Daily Mirror* colour magazine. Alastair Campbell tracked Mandelson down to his 'farmworker's cottage' in Herefordshire for an interview. Campbell wrote that it was no secret that he might fight the next election as a candidate rather than a campaign strategist. Mandelson was suitably modest. 'The job I do can be very frustrating,' he confessed. 'I have strong views about what's going on in Britain, and what can be done about it. There are times when I think that rather than fixing press notices and election broadcasts for others, I could be presenting Labour's case directly.'[2]

His interest alighted first on Stoke-on-Trent, capital of the Staffordshire pottery industry and regarded by psephologists as the most favourable city in England to the Labour Party. Here, Jack Ashley, the deaf MP and champion of the disabled, was hinting at retirement at the next election. He had been MP for the constituency since 1966, and had a majority of more than five thousand in 1987. Mandelson's antennae quivered. In 1988, he began calling friends and contacts in the area, surprising one with the warmth of his interest in the affairs of Stoke-on-Trent Labour Party. Sadly, he was unable to help, and Mandelson's interest swiftly dimmed. He discovered that the seat was already spoken for. He also made inquiries in the west Midlands, where the safe seat of Warley West was also coming up for grabs. Its Labour member, Peter Archer, a former Labour attorney-general was the first MP to announce he would not stand again. Once again, Mandelson was warned off, this time by the Black Country Labour 'mafia'. The seat was being kept warm for John Spellar, a right-wing electricians' union official who subsequently became a junior defence minister.

His attention then shifted to Hartlepool, a tough seaport and once a strong steel-making, shipbuilding and engineering centre on the north-east coast of England. This was unlikely territory for a 'soft southerner', particularly one with a disdain – dislike, even – for trade unions. It had massive housing, health and jobs problems. Unemployment in the 1981 census was 20 per cent, and it only came down to 17 per cent at the time of the 1987 election.

But it had much going for Mandelson. Hartlepool was the only parliamentary constituency to record no swing at all from Labour to the Conservatives in the 1979 election when James Callaghan lost power – one of Labour's ten best results in England. The constituency was next door to that of his new hero, Tony Blair, at Sedgefield. It was essentially in the gift of the General, Municipal and Boilermakers' union, the GMB, a politically moderate slice of the Labour movement known for its loyalty to the party. And Hartlepool's long-standing MP, Ted Leadbitter, was retiring at the next election, bequeathing an impregnable majority of 7,289. No doubt about it: Hartlepool would suit Mandelson's purposes admirably.

He was spotted on the terraces of fourth-division Hartlepool football club in December 1988, a sure sign of his determination to impress upon the people of the town his credentials as one of them. Technically, he was an invitee of the GMB, which was sponsoring the match. His appearance was a charade – Mandy had shown no previous interest in soccer – but a necessary one. 'I felt as if I was entering a family for the first time,' he gushed later.

There was immediate suspicion about the Londoner eyeing

votes. A trade-union-sponsored candidate was already in the race
for the nomination: Steven Jones, backed by the Transport and
General Workers, which had a high profile in the area. Jones
worked as a political adviser to the Labour leader of Cleveland
County Council. He was the son of a Labour MP, Barry Jones, a
member of Kinnock's shadow Cabinet as shadow Welsh secretary.
There was also considerable interest in the nomination among
local Labour councillors, and from others outside the constituency.
It looked sewn up. Not if Mandelson had anything to do with it.

His first port of call was in Claygate, Surrey, a far cry from the
crumbling shipyards, but close to the real seat of influence – the
headquarters of the GMB union. Some time in the summer of
1988, only a year after the election, Mandelson went down to
Claygate for a personal interview with John Edmonds, the union's
general secretary and chief power-broker. He had already been
spotted hobnobbing with the union's top brass at the GMB
conference in Bournemouth a few weeks earlier. At that time, the
unions still sponsored around two dozen MPs with substantial
annual grants of money to their constituency, topped up at
election times by much larger donations running into several
thousand pounds. The unions also affiliated large branches *en bloc*
to the local Labour Party, giving them a powerful say in the choice
of would-be MPs – 40 per cent of the votes, in the case of
Hartlepool. Internal reforms such as 'one member, one vote' have
subsequently swept away their political clout, but in the late
eighties, if you wanted to secure a safe working-class seat, it was
more important to know how to play the system than to want to
change it. And Mandelson was a maestro. He secured the personal
support of Edmonds, known as 'treble chins' for his magnificent
jowls. 'Edmonds saw that this guy was very talented, and was
probably flattered that he wanted GMB backing,' said a union
insider. 'Edmonds' motive was to say to Kinnock, "I can control
this party; not control, I am a player. I can take your star centre-
forward and place him in a new team."'

Coincidentally, the GMB sponsored Hartlepool United Football Club. The lay president of the GMB that year was Mrs Olga

Mean. Conveniently, she lived in Hartlepool and her husband was a leading figure in the Hartlepool constituency party. The union was strong in what was left of the shipping industry, and in the local authority and the NHS. Edmonds could not dictate what the local branches did, but his influence through the union's north-east regional secretary, Tom (now Lord) Burlison, was far-reaching. Mandelson was soon on board as a sponsored candidate for the nomination and began making regular visits to the town. Few, even today, when tourist attractions beckon, travel from the metropolis to Hartlepool out of casual interest.

While Mandelson was looking for a way out of the top-level loop, Kinnock had other ideas. He wanted Mandy to switch from Walworth Road to his office as press secretary to the leader. Patricia Hewitt, a first-rate thinker and strategist but never really at home with the press, quit the job in late 1988 to run the left-leaning Institute for Public Policy Research. Finding a replacement of the right calibre would be difficult. Alastair Campbell, a friend of Kinnock then working for the Mirror Group, was mooted, but Kinnock was adamant that he would not take any favours from Robert Maxwell.

Charles Clarke, the leader's chief of staff, cast around for a suitable alternative, and came up with Mandelson's name. He first put the idea formally to Kinnock on a plane back from Belfast in early January 1989. Clarke had his own doubts, particularly about Mandelson's ability as a team player, but respected his talent for handling the media. Kinnock offered Mandelson the job, on condition that he gave up his parliamentary ambitions. This was a tricky one. Mandelson had set a new course, and was not to be deflected from it. Yet a refusal would look like – and indeed, would be, and was – a political betrayal. Kinnock offered him the job three times. His wife Glenys added to the pressure on Mandelson. 'This was the leader of the Labour Party, the leader of the Opposition,' said a top Kinnock aide. 'And Mandelson turned him down. That was quite a moment. Mandelson saw his loyalty to his own career as more important than his service to the party, and particularly his service to Neil Kinnock. His ambition was greater.' Thrice rejected, Kinnock was left without a media handler, and the operation never quite recovered from that blow.

News of Mandelson's impending coup in Hartlepool broke in the press on 11 October 1989, less than a month after Ted Leadbitter told his local party of his intentions. Thereafter it was a media war. The *Guardian* opened the shelling with a story suggesting that a row was brewing over 'importing candidates from the South' for a safe seat in the north. Its coverage, complete with a 'downbeat' picture of the run-down town centre, incensed the local *Hartlepool Mail*, which ran a leading article attacking 'upper-crust, arty Liberal types' who begrudged the town its progress and regeneration. Mandelson was as arty as the next liberal, if not more so, but he could recognise a rich seam when he saw one. 'They must have scoured Hartlepool for the picture, which is untypical of the town,' he raged to the *Mail*. 'It makes my blood boil.'

The rage may have been synthetic, but it was first blood to Mandy. More than he could have realised at the time, the people of Hartlepool, stuck out on a North Sea promontory, have long felt different. They are known locally as 'the Monkeyhangers', after an unfortunate incident during the Napoleonic wars when a shipwrecked monkey was mistaken for a French spy, and hanged by the locals on the foreshore. The port had once been England's third most important, handling coal, iron, timber and all manner of industrial goods, but, like the shipbuilding industry, it was in decline. Interestingly, Hartlepool was not a dyed-in-the-wool Labour seat. In the nineteenth century, it sent Liberal manufacturing barons to Westminster, but it was Tory for most of the twentieth century until 1945. The constituency was captured briefly by the Tories in 1959, but returned to the Labour fold in 1964 and has remained there ever since.

Nominations opened on 23 October, and Mandelson faced a strong field of contenders. Apart from Steven Jones, local politics yielded Ray Waller, 50, a former mayor and native of the town, who felt that Hartlepool was 'separate and unique'. Russell Hart, a 42-year-old local accountant threw his hat in the ring, arguing that the town needed an MP who lived there 'not someone who's using Hartlepool as a stepping stone to a parliamentary career'. Mandelson, whose main home was still in the Wye valley two hundred miles away, did his best to establish local credentials. He described Hartlepool as 'a real place', adding, 'It's a town I strongly identify with, I like the people and I want to make my home there.' But he admitted that unless he was its MP, he would not move there.

Within a week, the Mandelson machine was clearly at work. The *Hartlepool Mail* reported prominently that a local branch of the TGWU had gone against the wishes of the union's national leaders and decided to throw its weight behind Mandy, earning a rebuke from the district organiser for doing so. Mandelson was not quoted in the story. He was well aware of the party's strict rules against media canvassing by candidates for selection. However, there was no doubt where the inspiration came from. Labour's north-east organiser, Andrew Sharp, wrote to all members of the 500-strong Hartlepool constituency Labour Party telling them to 'refrain from contact with the media' because it could only be prejudicial to the choice. 'It is absolutely essential that this selection is not conducted by the media, but in accord with the rules and guidelines of the party.'

With Mandelson in town, fat chance there was of keeping this contest a media-free zone. On 16 November, the *Hartlepool Mail*, fast becoming Mandelson's favourite paper, 'exclusively revealed' another victory for him. Brus Ward had voted to back him, and in a secret ballot. Steven Jones fared badly in the poll, which the paper described as 'another blow for the TGWU'. Waller didn't get a single vote. Instead of condemning the leakers, Andrew Sharp observed that the members were simply making their minds up.

The media coverage was all one way. On 19 November, the *Sunday Telegraph* – probably not the staple diet of Hartlepudlians – devoted almost half a page to Mandy's parliamentary campaign. It was, of course, a good story: sharp operator from the south takes on local talent. Political correspondent David Wastell calculated that Mandelson had pulled ahead of his rivals, 'albeit by no more than his neatly trimmed moustache'. By now, he had the support of all Hartlepool's nine GMB branches, plus the National Union of Public Employees. In vain did Steven Jones hit back at the steady drip-drip of the Mandelson machine. He pointed out that officials of the rebel TGWU branch had invited Mandy to address its members, and the union had sixteen branches in the town, of which only one supported the interloper. His complaint appeared on the letters page of the *Mail*. Mandelson could command the front page, though not always for the right reasons.

On 27 November, only days before a short-list of contenders was drawn up by the constituency executive, it emerged that Kay Jones, wife of aspirant Steven Jones, had formally complained to party chiefs of 'rule-bending' by Peter Mandelson. In a letter to the regional organiser six days earlier, she accused him of giving press interviews and canvassing support while the selection process was under way. She further accused him of holding receptions for local party members in the town's Grand Hotel, and of telling potential voters, 'Neil wants me to stand. I can help him even more as an MP.' He was also alleged to have said that Kinnock had promised he would be 'a minister from day one' of the next Labour government. He had clearly been up to something. Olga Mean, the GMB president, disclosed, 'He said he hoped he would be able to persuade some big government departments and some big industry to come up here and give people lots of jobs. We thought he would be able to pull strings.'[3] He was: the strings of influence to win his own nomination.

But both Walworth Road HQ and regional officials were quick to exonerate Mandy. Sharp said he had investigated the complaint, and found there was no case to answer. He saw no reason to stop the procedure and go back to the beginning. Joyce Gould, the director of organisation at HQ, faxed a strongly worded letter to Northern Region office, which hand-delivered it to Mrs Jones at 10 p.m. on the night of 27 November. The letter warned her to 'desist from false claims' and threatened expulsion. Mandelson further wrote to Jones accusing her of making her complaint available to 'Murdoch papers'. Mrs Jones was evidently a strong-willed lady, who took a dislike to Mandelson at their first meeting. 'I met him only once really at a social gathering,' she said. 'He struck me as rather a shark in a pool, quite cold-blooded if not downright bloodless. I just got the feeling he was assessing the electoral worth of everyone.'

She had made several complaints to Sharp at regional HQ. 'He said the national office was very anxious that Mandelson should not be embarrassed at this selection and that there was no way he was going to rock the boat,' she said.[4] Mandy himself kept up the line that he was not talking to the press, and if there was any misconduct it was coming from the other side. 'When you've been there ten minutes you'll realise that there are two campaigns going on,' he told a reporter – notwithstanding his refusal to speak to the press. 'One, the majority 90 per cent campaign which is orthodox, well-mannered and sticks to the code of conduct, and two, a minority 10 per cent which is loud, by and large outside the code and not typical of the Hartlepool Labour Party. I'm being damaged by it.'[5] The row rumbled on, and even surfaced at Westminster, where 24 Tory MPs signed a mischief-making Early Day Motion describing the selection as 'an utter shambles and travesty of fair play'. They called on Neil Kinnock to dissociate himself from 'a very sophisticated campaign full of dirty tricks'.

It was an unequal struggle. As well as local GMB sponsorship, effectively, Mandelson had the support of the Walworth Road machine, the regional party officials and the outgoing MP, Ted Leadbitter. The local paper found him interesting. Even the TGWU began to disown its official candidate. Joe Mills, the right-wing regional secretary of the union, dismissed Mrs Jones's dossier, saying he had no complaint against Mandelson and her complaint did not have the authority of the TGWU. She lost her post as secretary of a TGWU branch. Steven Jones was reduced to lamenting, 'There can be no cause for saying Peter Mandelson is suffering from any disadvantage in this competition.' By 1 December, a fortnight before the selection conference, Mills was advising Jones to drop out, citing the 'controversy' stirred by his wife. Jones fought on, but he was fatally weakened by the adverse publicity. The controversy refused to die down, and the *Hartlepool Mail*, feeling under siege from *The World at One* and the *Independent*, felt strangely moved to defend its coverage of the selection. The paper rejected charges of favouring one candidate over another, or of creating an 'unseemly squabble'. It added, 'No *regular* [author's italics] informal briefings have taken place with anybody, although occasionally reporters do receive information in confidence.'[6] This admission covers a lot of ground. It is a moot point as to how regular briefings need to be if they are to be effective. It would be naive to assume that Peter Mandelson did not choreograph his own media campaign. It was, after all, what the Labour Party paid him to do and what he was best at. His denials have all the credibility of Labour's initial denials that Bernie Ecclestone, the Formula 1 racing boss, had given £1 million to the party.

At a meeting in Hartlepool Civic Centre on 17 December, Mandelson was duly chosen to be the Labour candidate at the general election. He swamped the five other candidates, taking 63 per cent of the votes. Ray Waller, the former mayor, took second place with 21.5 per cent. Barbara Hawkins, an executive with the Fabian Society, took 3.8 per cent, Russell Hart, the accountant, picked up 3.3 per cent and Steven Jones trailed in last with only 2.9 per cent. It was a crushing victory for the Mandelson machine. It was 'the proudest day' of Mandy's life. 'This is the first and only constituency in which I have put myself forward because this is the town where I want to make my home, live and work, as well as representing it at Westminster,' he said. Neil Kinnock welcomed the result, through gritted teeth, insisting that Peter would be a fine representative for the people of Hartlepool. The selection was not universally popular. Mandelson was labelled a carpetbagger, a charge he loftily dismissed. 'The kindest response I can make is to ignore those comments,' he said.

A briefing note drawn up by defeated contender Steven Jones after the selection procedure analyses Mandelson's detailed strategy. The chief complaint was that he used a complete membership list to conduct systematic canvassing of wards prior to their nomination meetings. It also said that he used his position to influence local press comment, dining editors and reporters and offering them deals for favourable coverage. 'His leaks and briefings have dominated press coverage,' the note argued. 'These factors imply an unfair advantage, particularly where the full membership list is concerned.'[7] However much the party denied it, the list could have come from Walworth Road. No other candidate had one. Furthermore, a senior officer of the party also enjoyed access to members of the national executive and trade union bosses, and many people felt that the party could not afford to have one of its senior officers defeated in a constituency selection. Labour officials could also promise significant favours in return for support. These factors militated against a fair and open selection contest, the briefing note reasoned. It recommended that Labour should think about a ban on senior officers standing for Parliament while in the party's employment. It called further for the replacement of the cumbersome electoral college with one member, one vote selections, and a new regime of open, positive campaigning, with all candidates having access to the membership list. Finally, the note poured scorn on Walworth Road's denials. 'Colin Byrne, Peter Mandelson's deputy, has claimed to the press that Mandelson adhered strictly to the code of conduct – to the extent that he has placed himself at a disadvantage. This is a nonsense. The code has been used to bully and silence critics. It has been circumvented by a consummate manipulator of the press.' There was no question of Mandelson being at a disadvantage, 'only the privilege of being at the heart of the party machine with powerful friends. He has "banked" his advantage.'[8] These charges resurfaced in *Tribune*, in an article by Steven Jones, in which he suggested that all aspiring candidates should be able to do what Mandelson had done and run well-planned campaigns in the media, among the membership and the unions. Mandelson did not sue.

He did not need to. He had won. The furore would die down. The election was still more than two years off, and everyone would forget how he had won. He was not slow to exploit his new-found status, appearing on BBC TV's *On the Record* on 15 January 1990, to comment on an imaginary 'look back' at Britain in the nineties viewed from the vantage point of the year 2000. This rather stagey device was used to paint a bleak picture of declining competitiveness, horrendous environmental problems and political uncertainty. Mandelson confined himself to platitudes about mobilising the efforts and resources of both North and South to tackle the nation's ills. Public and private resources would be needed to overcome the social divisions and disparities that had disfigured it during the 1980s. Reality lay outside the studio. At the national executive monthly meeting ten days later, Mandelson was ordered out of the room while party bosses decided what to do with their ambitious high priest of spin. Some wanted to keep him on as director of communications and campaigns, while others were angered by his defection from Labour's high command before a critical general election. He was not the only offender. Peter Kilfoyle, the party's Merseyside organiser, had landed a safe seat in Liverpool, and two head office researchers had also won nomination in winnable constituencies. Eventually, the executive agreed that Mandelson should go before the general election. The precise timing would be negotiated.

Neil Kinnock was in a quandary. He didn't want to lose Mandelson, but could not ignore the weight of NEC opinion building up for his removal. Furthermore, he didn't approve of his 'core people' going for parliamentary seats. Nor did his chief of staff, Charles Clarke. 'We could all have done it,' said Clarke. John Reid, who became defence minister in the Blair administration, was ousted from his post in Kinnock's private office when he went for a seat in his native Scotland before the 1987 election.

Kinnock had watched Mandelson's increasingly high-profile role in Hartlepool during 1989 with mounting irritation. Not only was Mandy putting personal ambition before the party, but he was telling key people in the party that he had the leader's blessing to go for the seat. Charles Clarke is clear on this point. 'I remember Tom Burlison calling me, and saying, "Is Neil supporting his candidature. Is that the case?" I didn't say "no".[9] Burlison, ever the GMB loyalist, said that, if Kinnock wanted him, the union would have him. 'That was not the case. It was also not the case that he [Kinnock] wanted to behave like a complete shit. Peter Mandelson has never acknowledged the fact that Neil's restraint and my restraint actually enabled him to be selected. We didn't say we didn't want him to be selected. I believe if we had, he would not have been. He has advanced through the self-restraint of others.' Now, however, Mandy was on a high. He did not believe he would have to resign as director of communications.

It was true that losing Mandelson from the inner circle would be damaging for Labour. But Kinnock decided he had to go. At the NEC Organisation Committee meeting in Walworth Road in February 1990, the party leader angrily denounced those who used their party position to get into Westminster. After the meeting, there was an altercation between Kinnock and Mandelson in the car park behind Labour HQ. Mandy approached the leader as he got into his car, and Kinnock began shouting at him, to the intense delight of party staff watching from the press office three floors up. Mandelson resigned rather than suffer the indignity of the NEC sacking him, which in the view of those close to Kinnock is what would have happened had he not done so. But his departure was neither swift nor discreet.

Initially, Mandelson wanted to go as soon as possible. He was dissuaded by Kinnock, who wanted a longer hand-over period. It was agreed that he would stay until the party conference in Blackpool the following October. The issue then arose: how was he going to earn a living? Labour might not have paid very well, but his salary at Walworth Road funded a comfortable lifestyle. He had a home in the country, and a pied-à-terre in London. On top of that, he would now have to spend much more time in the North-east, nurturing his constituency. As soon as practicable, he would have to buy a home there. Money became an imperative.

One option would have been to keep Mandelson on as an adviser to Neil Kinnock, paying his salary from the £1 million a year the Opposition received from public funds, but this was not pursued. By the early summer of 1990, it was clear that Mandy was heading for the world of corporate affairs. He landed a job with SRU, a blue-chip management consultancy, working in the boardrooms of some of Britain's biggest companies – including some who were large donors to the Conservative Party. The salary was £28,000 a year, about the same as he had been receiving at the Labour Party. Mandelson insisted that there was nothing incompatible in working for firms like Marks & Spencer and BAT, which gave money directly or indirectly to the Tories. 'I am not going to do anything which is incompatible with my beliefs,' he said. 'Labour now has a very good dialogue with a whole range of companies where executives do not agree with all our policies.'

The newspapers reported that Mandelson had been headhunted for the post, though it did not go unnoticed at Westminster that Dennis Stevenson, chairman of SRU, had known him at the British Youth Council. He had also been chairman of Newton Aycliffe Development Corporation, in County Durham, a few miles from Mandelson's new constituency. Stevenson was one of a trio of high-flyers who founded SRU in 1972. He was also chairman of the Tate Gallery and a director of the media group Pearson, which had given £25,000 to the Conservative Party in 1988. The other two were Colin Fisher, a member of Labour's unpaid panel of industry advisers, and Peter Wallis, better known as Peter York, joint author of *The Sloane Ranger's Handbook* and a former style editor of *Harpers & Queen*. SRU had more than forty people on its payroll and was regarded as one of the most financially secure consultancies in Britain. Among its clients were ICI, Unilever, BAT, Clarks Shoes, Allied Dunbar, Thorn EMI, WH Smith and Ladbroke.

Stevenson had no qualms about hiring his old friend. 'Peter's political colours are quite irrelevant,' he declared. 'I am not the slightest bit worried about the effect of employing him. Our clients will back us.' He described Mandelson as one of the most able people of his generation, 'a superb strategist and marketing person'. In which case, they were getting him quite cheap. 'We are employing him for his brain power, not his political preferences,' said Stevenson. Mandelson was rather more modest about his contribution to the firm: 'I am going to SRU to contribute to its day-to-day work, not with elevated status as a public relations adviser or image-maker. I will be starting at the bottom all over again.'[10]

Stevenson suggested that the relationship with SRU could flourish even after Mandelson's entry into Parliament. In those discreet days, before the exposure of 'cash for questions' and dubious lobbying by MPs, it was perfectly above-board to take on well-paid consultancy work in addition to a parliamentary salary. Stevenson said that if Mandelson worked only a three-day week at Westminster 'he will pack in what most people do in five'. Mandy quickly rejected the idea, insisting that he would be a full-time MP. 'I have long wanted to gain knowledge of industry and business and the period before the general election gives me my chance,' he argued. 'It will make me a better MP.' Indeed, in Hartlepool, it was billed in the local paper as a north-east consultancy job, taking up only three or four days a week – leaving him more time to spend in the town.

However, he was reluctant to relinquish his hold on the levers of political influence. Kinnock had agreed that he should continue to give advice on an informal basis, even if he had rejected his overtures to work for the leader full-time. Mandelson still felt he was invaluable to the party's election effort. Indeed, shortly after being selected at Hartlepool, he told Charles Clarke: 'Don't you understand how important I am? You can't win the general election without me.' That is his view today. He thinks if he had stayed on as director of communications, we would have won the 1992 election because of his tremendous talents . . . by 1989, his vanity was becoming overwhelming – I would say overweening.'

Mandelson's relationship with Kinnock came under fresh strain when he moved into a flat in Bloomsbury in August 1990, to share with Julie Hall, a former ITN reporter recently appointed the leader's press secretary, and Colin Byrne, his protégé and Labour's deputy director of communications. The joke at Westminster was that the trio were 'living in spin', and journalists ringing the telephone number they shared had a choice of three sources from whom to get a top-level briefing on the issue of the day. 'This caused us massive problems,' confessed a Kinnock aide. 'Mandelson became very disruptive. He picked up the telephone all the time.' Naturally, journalists wanted to believe that he was still speaking with the authority of the leader, and Mandelson's critics say he did nothing to disabuse them of this notion.

In Hartlepool, Mandelson immersed himself in the minutiae of local politics. One month, it was a campaign for a lay-by outside a school. Another, it was a campaign, ultimately fruitless, to save the town's Rolls-Royce plant. In April 1990, he became president of the town's toy library, and had his picture taken for the *Hartlepool Mail* with a group of children. He was in an inclusive mood. 'Play is important not only for children, but for adults and the whole community,' he told the paper. In August that year, he persuaded Tony Blair, Labour's employment spokesman, to pose in front of the local Cameron's Brewery in a sweatshirt supporting a management buy-out of the plant to avert closure. Mandy also posed in a hard hat on the site of Hartlepool's marina development. Blair was back in the town a month later, visiting a scheme for retraining ex-offenders.

Mandelson's party finale was the Blackpool conference, which was generally agreed to have been a consummate success in presenting Labour as a government in waiting. Not only were the delegates well dressed – and well drilled – but the brilliant platform appearances of future Cabinet figures – Gordon Brown, Tony Blair and Jack Straw – were a portent of what was to come. Political commentator Anthony Howard noted, 'It was not merely the Left that was permitted no place in Mandelson's script: just as firmly banished was the entire tradition of "Old Labourism".' This was the first hint of the subtle redirection of the party towards New Labour, a social democratic party shorn of ideology.

Mandelson bought a substantial terrace house at 30 Hutton Avenue, Hartlepool, in the autumn of 1990. He said at the time, 'I've spent all my savings on buying this house and I needed a job.

Obviously, I'll have to cut the frills and the few luxuries I enjoyed.'
He did however make a handsome profit on his country cottage in
Foy, Herefordshire. Mandelson bought the property for £31,000
in 1984, and sold it for £71,500 to a Mrs Meeks. Originally, he
had been asking for as much as £95,000, but the market was weak
and surveyors said a great deal of work was needed on the house.

In late October, he was noisy in his defence of the family,
condemning the Tories' £1-a-week uprating of child benefit as 'a
mere sop' offered by a prime minister panicked by her government's deepening unpopularity. Mandelson showed his demotic
skills, relating the child-benefit squeeze to the problems of
Hartlepool's families. The town's children had been deprived of
£1.5 million since 1986, he calculated. By contrast, in its first year
a Labour government would increase the benefit 'by at least
enough to make up the loss in value since the last election.'[11]

He also showed he could bring the big shots to his constituency,
getting Gordon Brown, shadow trade and industry secretary, to
the town in late October to address the local Labour Party.
Mandelson embedded himself in local life, joining the
Community Health Council in January 1991, arguing that it
would help him keep in touch with the real issues facing
townspeople, particularly the NHS. It was a neat move, as was his
support for a campaign to prevent the siting of toxic-waste
incinerators in Cleveland – despite the presence locally of the
highest concentration of chemical factories in the country. He
kept his name at the forefront of local politics, chiefly in the
Hartlepool Mail, intensifying his efforts after Labour's share of the
vote in Hartlepool fell by 15 per cent in the May 1991 council
elections, while the Conservative share rose by 11 per cent. A
swing of those proportions at the general election would sweep
away Labour's majority, and the pundits began speculating that
Mandelson might have a real battle on his hands.

First, however, he was drafted into a preliminary skirmish with
the Tories in Monmouth, where a by-election took place on 16
May 1991 owing to the death of the Tory MP, John Stradling-
Thomas. This was an opportunity for Labour to prove its

superiority as a fighting force, and Neil Kinnock asked Mandelson to drop everything and go down to the constituency to beef up the campaign. The story of Monmouth is a cameo of Mandelson's life: a good piece of work converted into a myth of virtual omniscience and omnipotence. To begin with, the seat was more winnable than the 9,000 Tory majority in 1987 suggested: it had been held by Labour from 1966 to 1970. And though the opinion polls were unpredictable in the wake of John Major's succession to Margaret Thatcher the previous autumn, the government was still unpopular. It had not won a single by-election since William Hague retained Richmond in 1989, and had just lost ultra-safe Ribble Valley to the Liberal Democrats on a swing of almost 25 per cent. Labour had a reliable candidate, Huw Edwards, while the Tory contender, barrister Roger Evans, was something of a right-wing maverick. Spring in the southern Welsh marches was a welcome diversion for Mandelson. He could use his home in Foy as a base, and win back some much-needed political capital within Labour's high command.

The campaign was brief, sharply fought and victorious. Edwards won with a majority of more than two thousand on a swing exceeding 12 per cent. His victory was subsumed by Mandelson's. The newspapers were ecstatic about how he had masterminded the by-election. In one version, he 'nailed down Monmouth and its 100 villages so that nothing moved without his knowledge'. A profile in the *Sunday Times* on 19 May, three days after the poll, waxed lyrical: Mandelson was 'an operator of genius', who would put Kinnock into Downing Street. The truth is that Labour would have won even if Mandelson had not set foot in the constituency. The party put into the campaign around 70 professional paid workers, some of whom had fought twenty or more by-elections. He was fighting only his second, and his contribution had not prevented a Liberal win in the first, seven years previously. Andy McSmith, who covered the by-election for the *Daily Mirror*, dismisses the hyperbole around his role as 'nonsense', but points out that the myth-making was helpful to the Tories. Chris Patten, chairman of the Conservative Party, mentioned Mandelson three times in his post-poll briefing to journalists, and the Tories blamed him for masterminding a 'big lie' during the campaign that Trust hospitals would be able to opt out of the NHS. It was useful for the government to identify a Machiavellian figure in Labour's ranks.

While the by-election was in full swing, a vicious little power struggle began back at Walworth Road between Mandelson's successor as communications director, John Underwood, and his deputy, Colin Byrne, responsible for press and broadcasting. Underwood wanted to sack Byrne, who was Mandy's acolyte. Senior party figures shared Underwood's concern that the briefings emanating from the Bloomsbury flat owed more to Mandelson's political destination and strategy than to Labour policy. He was pursuing his own agenda. In particular, Mandelson's enthusiasm for Britain's role in the Gulf war was blamed for the bad press received by Robin Cook and John Prescott over their more lukewarm attitude.

Underwood decided to lance the boil by ousting Byrne. But the latter had powerful friends. Kinnock wanted the two of them to continue working together. Underwood backed down from outright dismissal, but insisted that he would not have Byrne as his deputy. The dispute dragged on into June, despite the intervention of Kinnock and Larry Whitty. In the media, Byrne got the better write-up. It was said that Whitty regarded his performance as 'faultless', though he had suggested that Byrne leave Walworth Road. The respected commentator Donald MacIntyre described him as 'the consummate professional . . . tirelessly available, blunt speaking, intelligent and pro-active.' His style ('an active, if sometimes tempestuous relationship with print journalists', as MacIntyre described it) and continuing links with his ex-boss prompted speculation that Mandy was still calling the shots. Mandelson himself tried to shake off the criticism by denying a charge that had not been made – that post-Monmouth he was looking for a more influential role in directing party strategy. 'No proposal has ever been made and nor would one ever be considered by me that I should play a national election role. Why it suits some people to keep speculating about this beats me.'[12] That was not the issue. The issue was his constant meddling in the current conduct of communications policy. The hideous expression 'pro-active' might have been invented for Peter Mandelson.

Underwood, according to the ubiquitous friends, wanted Mandelson to concentrate on winning Hartlepool and keep his nose out of party communications. He felt that Mandy represented the advertising culture in film-making, and sought a return to more content-based party broadcasts, rather than the image-based films of his predecessor. He also saw himself as a servant of the party at Walworth Road, the national executive and the shadow Cabinet as a whole, rather than of the 'beautiful people' – most notably Tony Blair and Gordon Brown – whom Mandelson was promoting so assiduously in terms of TV and radio slots. Some rather elderly ITN research was trotted out to prove that this theory did not hold water, but the hand of Mandelson was detected everywhere.

His handiwork was certainly spotted by Bryan Gould, still his friend but becoming increasingly sceptical. Gould later identified Mandelson's game plan. 'It was becoming clear to me over this period that Peter Mandelson was working to his own agenda – on what I and others began to call the "Mandelson Project". The "project" was to ensure that Peter's protégés – Gordon Brown as the Prime Contender but with Tony Blair as a fall-back – should succeed to the leadership,' he wrote.[13] Kinnock was now 'merely a player' in the Mandelson strategy. It was important to the strategy that Kinnock remained as leader long enough to allow this younger generation to mature in shadow Cabinet office, ready to succeed when the time came. 'In my opinion,' said Gould, 'a good deal of the Mandelson strategy therefore concentrated on clearing the way for the eventual succession by undermining as much as possible the credibility of other possible contenders.' If his choreography was ever questioned, Mandelson could simply say he was being loyal to the leader. Gould was incensed. He believed that Mandy's game of 'playing favourites' caused a great deal of unhappiness, particularly among those who felt they were his victims. 'It probably did more to undermine Shadow Cabinet unity and to distract major players from the job in hand than any other factor.'[14]

The war for supremacy at Walworth Road ended, superficially at least, in Mandelson's favour. Instead of taking his case to the NEC, where he would almost certainly have won because of Mandelson's mounting unpopularity, Underwood approached Kinnock for his personal support in the battle with Colin Byrne. It was a fatal move. The leader, who had not wanted him in the first place, did not give it. On 5 June, Underwood quit. The newspapers treated the episode as another feather in Mandy's cap, but the reality was rather different. Buried in the archives of the Kinnock Collection in Churchill College, Cambridge, is a letter dated at that time from Mandelson to Charles Clarke, the leader's chief of staff. In it, Mandelson is contrite, thanking Clarke for his help in 'what I had not realized before was such a difficult situation', and adding: 'I am trying to put my bruised feelings aside'. He was practically apologetic about stealing the credit for Monmouth, but said, 'I think I can contribute more in the same way . . . [although] I know you don't share this view.'[15]

The Tories seized on Underwood's downfall with glee. John MacGregor, leader of the House, cheerfully allied himself with the Labour Left in a speech on 7 June 1991, saying, 'I find myself most unusually in agreement with Mr Ken Livingstone, who said in a newspaper article recently, referring to the Labour Party's former Director of Communications, "The result of 'the Mandelson-isation' of Labour is that we seem to stand for nothing positive and clear whatsoever. Labour has projected no clear positive positions of its own, but simple opposition to the Tories."[16] And the removal of Mr Underwood shows that they are determined to keep it that way. All glitzy image, nothing underneath.' Mandelson pretended that the Underwood affair was none of his business, insisting, 'The circumstances of Mr Underwood's resignation have nothing to do with me. Journalists are using my name to spice up a story and turn a drama into a crisis. I have got my own life and home in Hartlepool and my own campaign to prepare in the town. I will always respond to request for help as a good foot-soldier, but there is no question of my going back to headquarters.'[17] This is classic Mandy-speak, combining the false modesty of 'the good foot-soldier' with the pretence that he was not involved.

To his regular weekly column in the *People*, Mandelson now added a similar contribution to the *Hartlepool Mail*, though it was not always an unqualified success. In August 1991, he apologised for giving his address in the town as Hutton Arcade, not Avenue. A slip of his handwriting, he insisted. In the main, he championed the obvious causes: the NHS, jobs for young people, and law and order. He attacked the 'criminal sorts' who stirred up communal violence on nearby Tyneside in September 1991, claiming, 'I would not hesitate to round them up at the first sign of trouble.' He also took a hard line on young offenders, suggesting that they should lose their liberty and be 'taught a lesson' away from other criminal elements.[18]

Mandelson sometimes seemed to be suffering from culpable garrulity. On ITV's *This Week* on the eve of the Labour conference, he disclosed that Neil Kinnock felt his policy U-turns on nuclear weapons and state ownership were a 'betrayal' in the minds of his party's Left. The leader had told him, 'I'd rather get my betrayal in before the election than after.'[19] Mandy's indiscretion prompted a rather manufactured political furore from the Conservatives, whose chairman Chris Patten seized on these comments and said once again that no one had the remotest idea what Labour stood for. Mandelson argued that his interview had been 'mangled' by the Tories to give it a false meaning. All that he had said was that Kinnock was honest enough not to make election promises he could not keep in government. It was an unconvincing retreat. He attended the 1991 Brighton conference as a delegate – in fact, as a prospective parliamentary candidate – 'cheering loudly, rather than acting as a cheerleader'. Less obtrusively, he also went to the Conservative Party conference in Blackpool the following week to see what the opposition was up to.

Mandelson was back into the campaign fray that year, just

across the Tees in Langbaugh, where the last by-election of the parliamentary session was fixed for 7 November. It was caused by the death of the incumbent Tory MP, Richard Holt, and presented Labour with another opportunity to humiliate the government. The party's candidate, Ashok Kumar, a research scientist with British Steel, was bidding to overturn a Conservative majority of just over two thousand votes. Mandelson was his usual energetic self in the autumn campaign. But his presence raised eyebrows, because he was now an adviser to the BBC, courtesy of his old friend John Birt, the director-general. There was clearly a potential for conflict of interests, as the Conservatives swiftly appreciated. In late October, thirty-five Tory MPs signed an Early Day Motion at Westminster, 'noting' that Mandelson had been appointed to his BBC post after he resigned as Labour's head of communications and campaigns, that he had been staying at the Cross Keys Inn, Guisborough, throughout the by-election, and that he had been photographed in the *Independent on Sunday* as campaign co-ordinator and named in an internal party document as a member of the campaign management team. The Motion further noted 'the obvious conflict of interest in what is supposed to be an impartial public service' and called on the BBC to terminate his contract, in the same way as it had ended the part-time contract for Graham Robb when he became Tory candidate for Hartlepool.

For once, Mandelson sought to hide his light under a bushel, insisting that he was only 'helping out' in the campaign, leaf-letting and canvassing. However, his name appeared on an internal party agenda for an organiser's meeting, dated 31 October, just a week before polling day. He shared the number-six slot with regional organiser Andrew Sharp, introducing a report on 'strategy for the last week'. It was plainly not the case that he was 'just helping out'. The Tories had a point. The BBC dived for cover. A spokesman said, 'We don't want to be drawn on this. We have no comment whatsoever.' Despite an embarrassing disclosure over dealing in British Telecom shares, Kumar won the by-election, only to lose the seat in the 1992 general election.

To Mandelson's relief the BBC 'conflict of interest' affair died away, and he concentrated on bread-and-butter constituency issues as the election neared. But the mini-scandal resurfaced in February 1992, when the *Daily Express* reported that the BBC had severed its links with Mandelson. The Tories were delighted, offering the over-the-top comment that the corporation's 'generally socialist bias' was hopefully now curtailed. Mandelson denied that he had been sacked, saying he had quit voluntarily to work on his bid to enter Parliament. 'I told the BBC some time ago that when the likely date of the election became known I would want to concentrate all my time and efforts on the campaign in Hartlepool,' he declared. 'I am now doing that. My move has not come about as a result of complaints from Tory MPs.' Polling-day, 9 April 1992, was not actually set until a month later, but the three-month delay in his departure from the BBC had served its purpose. The story was lost in the pre-election hysteria.

Hartlepool was a three-cornered fight. Mandelson was the clear front-runner, benefiting from a rising tide of support for Labour. His Tory opponent, Graham Robb, aged 28, a former BBC Radio Cleveland disc jockey, was almost a local boy, hailing from Middlesborough. He was now making his way in the public relations world, acting as PR man for the Conservatives on Cleveland County Council. The Liberal Democrats fielded Ian Cameron, 45, a taxi and garage proprietor in the town who had fought the seat as an independent in 1987.

Mandelson entered the fray in a lyrical frame of mind. He told visiting journalists that he had chosen Hartlepool very carefully. 'I wasn't just going in search of a constituency,' he effused. 'I was going in search of a home. A place where I could feel emotionally secure and supported, as well as where my political base would be. A place I would be able to put my arms around.'[22] Presumably, he would have said the same about Stoke-on-Trent, or Warley.

The election was a pushover, but Mandelson kept up the theatricals. He confessed that 'nothing prepared me for the anxiety and elation of my own election night in Hartlepool. I'd seen other candidates put through the mill, but this time MY future was on the line.' As the votes were counted, his supporters said it looked good from the spectator benches. 'But from where I was sitting, the piles [of ballot papers] looked the same and I became tense.'[21] Of course, he had no need to worry. Labour increased its majority, taking over half the votes cast. On a turnout of 76 per cent, Mandelson received 26,816 votes (51.9 per cent of the total), while Robb won 18,034 (34.9 per cent). Both benefited from a slight fall in votes cast for the Liberal Democrat, who polled 6,860 (13.3 per cent), as well as from the improved turn-out, up 3 percent on 1987. Overall, the swing from Conservative to Labour was, at 1.2 per cent, on the low side. But it was enough. Mandelson could look forward to twenty, or even thirty, years of job security.

9

BACKBENCH NOVICE

In his column for the *People* on 12 April 1992, Peter Mandelson struck a note of mourning. 'The Labour Party this weekend,' he said, 'is like a grieving family.' He argued that the voters had not returned the Conservatives because they felt that John Major deserved another turn. The Tories got back in because people believed the lies they told about Labour, in particular the claim that voters would have to pay £1,250 a year more in taxes if they put Neil Kinnock into Downing Street. A coalition of voters already hit badly by the recession plus the well-off wanting to keep all they had was enough to give the Tories their majority.

But he appeared unrepentant. 'Labour cannot shrink from making the rich pay their fair share in taxes for good health, schools and other public services,' he wrote. 'This may leave the party vulnerable to the Tory's atrocious smears but if truth matters in politics – and it does – if Labour is to remain true to its ideal of social justice – and it must – the party has to be confident about its fair taxation policies. Labour has won with that appeal in the past. It will certainly do so again.'

The little bit of truth about politics that Mandelson did not divulge was that, as these words were being written, he was holding secret talks with Tony Blair and Gordon Brown to ditch John Smith's shadow budget and reinvent Labour's economic policy so that the rich could indeed hang on to their riches. Two days after the disastrous results became clear – Major was back in with a Commons majority of 21 – Brown travelled down for a series of private talks with Blair. They were joined for the third session, held at County Hall, Durham, by the new MP for Hartlepool.

Top of their agenda was the succession to Neil Kinnock. Bitterly disappointed at being a second-time loser, and blaming himself for the rout, the party leader swiftly signalled his desire to stand down at the earliest opportunity. John Smith, the shadow chancellor, was clearly in line to take over. But who should be his deputy? Brown was excluded by virtue of his origins – there could not be two Scots on the ticket – and by his personal loyalty to Smith. Blair was strongly tempted to go for the deputy leadership. Mandelson privately urged him to stand, but the future leader stalled and his vacillation cost him the opportunity. Margaret Beckett decided to run, and the Smith-Beckett 'dream ticket' was born.

Its dreamlike qualities did not extend to Peter Mandelson. Neil Kinnock had valued him, but John Smith did not, or not to anything like the same degree. Smith was part of Labour's old Right, a constituency that was suspicious of the outgoing leader's house-trained Machiavelli. Moreover, Smith had a personal distaste for Mandelson, linked in part to his flatmate Julie Hall. In October 1988, when he had his first heart attack, Smith had been approached in his intensive-care ward by Hall, then an ITN reporter, for an interview. Recovering from a close brush with death, he was appalled by this sickbed journalism, and never forgave her. But Smith's chief reservations stemmed from the hugely ambitious policy-making role that Mandelson felt was his by virtue of simply being right. In a *Fabian Review* article published soon after Labour's defeat, Mandelson praised Smith's 'neat and clear-cut Shadow Budget', but implicitly criticised him for failing to connect with the electorate. 'The Tories were able to exploit the lack of specific spending figures relating to the manifesto commitments,' he wrote.[1] Labour, he argued, had a deep-seated credibility problem. The only way to resolve this was to drive forward the process of renewal and change, developing 'new and distinctive' policies. Mandelson singled out Labour's internal democracy, its institutional links with the trade unions, its behaviour in Parliament and local councils and the calibre of the leadership team.

Mandelson lost no time in flattering the dream team. He described Smith as having the strength of character to unite the party around its policies and put them across to the voters, even if he was 'clear to the point of bluntness'. Despite his covert campaign to persuade Blair to go for the deputy leadership, publicly he called for a woman in the number-two slot, arguing that Margaret Beckett was 'as good as any male . . . pleasant, diligent and open to reason, but she's tough – and once she has made up her mind, wild horses won't sway her'.[2]

As a new MP, he had the usual complaints about not being given an office and a desk immediately on arrival at Westminster. His first week in Parliament was 'among the most bizarre, as well as the most exciting, of my life'. He whinged about not being able to find his private locker, and made his first mistake by sitting at the Tory end of the MPs' smoking-room. All in all, it was an unremarkable debut. He delivered his maiden speech during a Ways and Means debate shortly before 7 p.m. on 14 May, after two other new Labour entrants, Tessa Jowell (Dulwich) and left-winger John Austin-Walker (Woolwich), had made theirs. As is the custom, he began by praising his predecessor, Ted Leadbitter, and retelling an old story about his telephone pole rebellion. He also recalled Hartlepool's first Labour MP, David Jones, whose memory was particularly special 'because he was a friend of my grandfather when he was a Member of this House', a suitably oblique reference to Herbert Morrison. He commended the civic pride and sporting prowess of Hartlepudlians, before proclaiming his vision for the future. 'The task of the coming decade, as we approach the 21st century, is to transform a new industrially-poorer and less confident Hartlepool into the thriving industrial community of the future that it can become.' There followed much more in the same vein, optimistic but generalised and vague. He appealed for 'a new partnership, the business community and the government, based not on dogma but on co-operation to secure objectives in the interests of the economy as a whole'. The people of Hartlepool were not looking for handouts or subsidies, he insisted, but what the town and the North-east desperately needed was 'not another cyclical invitation to share in the nation's fortune, only to find that no place is set for it at the table'.[3] This was a laborious reference to a comment by R. H. Tawney that willing the ends without willing the means was akin to inviting unwelcome guests to dinner in the certain knowledge that circumstances would make it difficult for them to attend. He concluded with a tribute to the values of the Labour Party and sat down after sixteen minutes. It was a workmanlike, rather than impressive, first appearance. Mandy observed in his *People* column, 'In line with convention, I wasn't barracked or interrupted, but reading was difficult because I had nowhere to put my notes. Perhaps autocue should be the next parliamentary innovation.' Hardly the sentiments of a Michael Foot. However, Nick Brown, a fellow North-east MP, welcomed his speech as 'absolutely first-rate', but cautioned Mandelson against rivalling Ted Leadbitter's drinking skills. 'Without casting any aspersions on his willingness to get in his round, I hope that it is one area in which my hon. Friend will not emulate his predecessor.'[4] He need not have worried. Mandelson has always avoided Westminster's many bars, and the MPs and lobby correspondents who frequent them, though he was spotted in the plotters' pub, the Red Lion in Whitehall, closeted with Robin Cook, during the leadership campaign.

John Smith was duly elected party leader on 18 July at a special party conference in London's Royal Horticultural Hall. Mandelson was not present. He was in New York, observing the US Democratic Party convention with Gordon Brown and Roy

Hattersley. He found it 'fun, but with a serious message'. He wasn't sure about the American razzmatazz, though he amazed everyone with his stamina: listening to the tedious conference debates all day, and networking his way round the city by night. Back home, reporters found no sign of Mandelsonian red-rose glitz at the ritual enthronement of John Smith. His influence was already on the wane.

There was no question of the new leader finding a place, not even a lowly private parliamentary secretaryship, for Peter Mandelson in his shadow administration. None of the 1992 intake was given a job, and had they been he would not have been among them. So he busied himself with his *People* column and various political causes, including Europe and the National Lottery (of which he was passionately in favour) and the campaign to sustain Cleveland County Council (to which he was equally passionately hostile). He was put on the Commons Committee responsible for scrutinising the Finance Bill implementing Norman Lamont's budget, and regaled his readers with tales of parliamentary derring-do. In late June, the committee sat up until five in the morning discussing bingo duty. Some MPs thought these hours were ludicrous, he commented, and the public might worry if they knew taxes were being debated at that hour. 'But I'm not sure it's wrong for MPs to earn their pay researching by day and talking at night. And there's certainly something special about eating eggs and bacon as day breaks over Big Ben.'[5] His assiduity earned him election to the secretaryship of Labour's backbench Treasury Committee, where he lined up squarely behind the new shadow chancellor, Gordon Brown. He continued to fawn publicly on John Smith, however, remarking on his Commons performance in late September, 'Sitting two benches behind him as he destroyed John Major, I could see the effect he was having on MPs of all parties. On the Labour side, morale went sky-high.'[6] He was also unctuous about 'Labour's First Lady', Elizabeth Smith. The leader's wife, he said, had in abundance the qualities required: tact, discretion, the ability to be nice to people at all times, a sense of humour, a belief in her partner's work and an understanding that politics is a crazy world. By now, and not surprisingly, his editorial masters at the *People* were beginning to have doubts about Mandelson's weekly column. It was too flattering to the Labour hierarchy, and lacked edge.

But his ideas were gaining ground in the party. At the annual conference in Blackpool, party bosses decided to try out Mandelson's proposals for increasing membership. In a pilot project, selected constituencies would be able to cut subscriptions in a bid to build up membership, which nationally had fallen to a post-war low of 261,000 despite an official campaign launched three years previously to drive the figure up to 1 million. As a result, Labour had a £2.5 million overdraft and would have to cut spending by 30 per cent, involving job losses. Mandelson argued that the party should 'throw open its windows locally' and make itself more attractive. Only by being a better party would it become a bigger party. In a description that was only too recognisable, he complained that many new members felt ignored, frozen out of decision-making and put off by boring meetings. 'They might as well have stayed in front of the telly with a six-pack, watching the latest video for all the difference joining the party makes,' he observed acidly.

Within weeks of the conference, Mandelson learned that he was to be sacked by the *People*. His departure was partly connected to big editorial management changes at Mirror Group Newspapers, but there was also disquiet about his copy. On 21 November, his column for the next day's paper was held out on the instructions of the new editor, Bridget Rowe. Mandelson agreed to replace the lead item, which attacked Buckingham Palace press aides for failing properly to represent the royal family, but later heard on the grapevine that he had been fired. With endearing naivety about the ways of the tabloid press, he told the *Independent on Sunday*, 'I have received no direct communication whatever from the editor, but I understand from other sources on the paper that it may be discontinued. I hope this is not the case.' Mandelson's case was linked to general concern in Labour's high command that the Mirror Group might renege on its traditional support for the party. John Smith was said to feel 'let down' because the millionaire businessman and Labour peer Lord Hollick, who was part of MGN's new top management, had not kept him fully informed of developments.

Senior Labour sources worried that 'Peter's dismissal will add to the atmosphere of crisis between the paper and the party'.[7] There was undoubtedly a sense of unease that David Montgomery, the ex-Murdoch new chief executive of MGN, might take the group's titles in a different political direction. The fears proved generally unfounded. And the notion that the War of Mandelson's Column might have played a major role in this delicate political balancing act is absurd. New editors dispose of existing columnists faster than paper handkerchiefs, and Mandy was no exception. It was left to Londoner's Diary in the *Evening Standard* to dispose of the notion that dropping the column was a deliberate blow to Labour. 'Perhaps so,' commented the diarist. 'But others might take the view that Mandelson's weekly whinge should have gone a long time ago – or, better still, never started. I cannot remember it raising any question more important than whether or not the author should shave off his moustache.'[8] With brilliantly insulting style, Rowe offered Mandy's column to the unreconstructed hard-Left MP Dennis Skinner, 'the Beast of Bolsover'. He turned it down on the impeccable Old Labour grounds that MPs, on £30,000 a year, should not 'moonlight' in the media, particularly on newspapers where members of the NUJ were being sacked to make economies.

Mandelson had no such scruples. By mid-December, he had found a new media outlet: *The Times*, no less. He appeared on 'The Thunderer's' facing leader page with a long feature about the royal family, sympathising with the very spin-doctors he had been only too happy to criticise in the tabloid press a few weeks earlier. He advised the Prince of Wales to get himself a new image, urging, 'He should take a long, cool look at what he is trying to achieve, how he is going about it and how that is being communicated to those he aspires to lead,' wrote Mandelson.[9] He might just as well have written, 'Hire Me'. Despite his constant new theme that he

Labour Party 'Republican Away-Day trip' to Boulogne on the day Charles and Di married. (left to right) Sue Nye, Alan Haworth, Conor McCauley, Jack Dromey, Alan Griffiths, Mike Gapes, Peter Mandelson, Averil Donohoe, Stuart Hercode, Chris McLaughlin.

Peter Mandelson launches his report on 'Youth Unemployment: Causes and Cures' in April 1977. The report received wide coverage in the press.

Mandelson (far left) seeking the support of Edward Heath for legislation on youth issues, July 1980.

On the terraces of his local team's ground, Hartlepool FC.

The Mandelson Roadshow.

Rite of the North East: Mandelson carrying a tribute to his constituency.

'Shall I compare thee . . . ?'. Peter Mandelson, the Red Rose man.

Work hard, play hard: Mandelson is a fitness fanatic.

The constituency MP: working at home in Hartlepool.

With Neil and Glenys Kinnock at Hartlepool Marina.

Mandelson with
Councillor Bernard Carr.

Cheers! Shadow Chancellor Gordon Brown visits
Mandelson's constituency.

Peter Mandelson MP speaking at the 'Hard Labour' conference organised by Tribune in October 1988 at Kings College, London.

Demonstrator and Mandelson clash at the Islington launch of his book in March 1996.

THE DOME'S CENTREPIECE IS REVEALED....

INSIDE YOU CAN SEE WHAT SPIN DOCTORING DOES TO THE BODY

Chris Smith, Michael Heseltine, Tony Blair, John Prescott and Peter Mandelson (left to right) witness the 'topping-out' ceremony to mark the completion of the highest point of the Millennium Dome's roof.

Getting his nose dirty: Mandelson during his visit to Kellingley Colliery in West Yorkshire.

Newly appointed as Secretary of State for Trade and Industry, Mandelson arrives with George Robertson and Alistair Darling for the first meeting of Tony Blair's reshuffled cabinet, July 1998.

Mandelson blows a kiss to supporters following his party's landslide general election victory, May 1997.

Waiting in the wings: Peter Mandelson and Tony Blair at the Farnborough Airshow.

Mandelson on the steps of his ultimate ambition: 10 Downing Street.

An artist's impression of Peter Mandelson.

wanted to be seen as a proper politician, not just a spin-doctor, the old instincts could not be suppressed. Prince Charles had an immense public relations problem, he declared. He could either continue going downhill, or use his 'changed circumstances' (his divorce from Princess Diana) to re-present himself to the public. But the opportunity would not last long. 'If the prince fails to grasp it and does not carry out the overhaul many would like to see, it will be a great shame for the people he wants to help and a personal tragedy for him.'[10] It was to be five more years before the royal family took his advice.

At the year's end Mandelson sought to speed up the passage of the Tory government's Bill to ratify the Maastricht Treaty. He sponsored a Commons Motion, signed by 85 Labour MPs – one in three of the parliamentary party – to support rapid completion of the Bill's remaining stages. It was his first foray into serious Commons politicking, and he secured the backing of Neil Kinnock, Roy Hattersley and former shadow foreign secretary Gerald Kaufman. Mandelson was careful to stay on side, however: 'John Smith will be very reassured by this backing for his pro-Maastricht stance.' Whether he was or not, the Motion marked a minor watershed for Mandelson, from *People* columnist to aspiring player.

He raised his profile in the new year, arguing that Labour's modernisation project should be accelerated, not ditched. *Tribune*, the left-wing weekly, disclosed that the argument about why the party had lost in 1987 was still raging fiercely among Labour leaders. The modernisers insisted that the party must adapt to social change and shifts in voter attitudes, while the traditionalists suspected a wholesale abandonment of socialist values. Their fears were sharpened by the constant offering of Bill Clinton's successful campaign for the US presidency as a model for Labour. 'Clintonisation' became a code word, and in some quarters a dirty word, for this process. Mandelson was unmoved. 'The argument that, having changed many of its policies between 1987–92 and still lost, the party should now reject further change is akin to blaming the electorate rather than ourselves for defeat – the show was great but the audience poor.' He was encouraged by grass-roots experience in Hartlepool. Encountering a jobless constituent, he rehearsed the party line about work-for-benefits being wrong, and what the unemployed needed were 'real' jobs – only to be met with an anguished scream that nothing was worse than being on the dole with nothing to do. 'Everyone must abandon slogans and start some real thinking instead,' he wrote to *The Times*, though he could not resist a sideswipe at old Labour. 'In other times, in another generation, Labour would have supported nationalising unemployment.'

Mandelson was busy on the backbenches in early 1993. He supported the Bill setting up the National Lottery, earning the gratitude of the Tories. He raised the murky issue of British Airways' ethics towards Virgin Atlantic – the flag-carrier had been up to dirty tricks – and pondered why no one resigned at the top in BA. He also kept up his interest in the media, intervening in a debate on a private member's Freedom and Responsibility of the Press Bill in late January. Surprisingly, in view of his 'outing' by the Murdoch press six years previously, he sided – without mentioning it by name – with the *Sun*, which had exposed the dire state of the royal family. Apart from facts and lies, he argued, there was a third category of journalism: interpretation. 'In the case of the marriage of the Prince and Princess of Wales, journalists were interpreting the information they had, and the heavens opened and they were damned for doing so. It then turned out that they were accurate,' he reminded MPs. He intervened twice more in the morning debate, to support the Press Complaints Commission and its voluntary code of practice for journalists, and to mock the prime minister for letting it be known through his press secretary that he was now against statutory regulation of the press. 'Was that,' Mandelson mused aloud, 'because he sensed Kelvin MacKenzie's tanks rolling down Whitehall and approaching No 10 Downing Street?'[11] He was also hyper-active during the debate on the European Communities (Amendment) Bill giving effect to the Maastricht Treaty. He was so vitriolic that Peter Hain, a Eurosceptic Labour backbencher, asked him to 'restrain the sharpness of his tongue'. Mandelson shot back, 'Talking about sharpness, I do not need to take any lectures from hon Friends about the effectiveness with which I represent my constituents.' He interrupted several more times, accusing Hain of 'ducking and weaving', until the deputy speaker called a halt and told him to keep quiet.

The party moved decisively in Mandelson's direction after a special meeting of the shadow Cabinet on 15 February 1993. He had no direct role in the summit, but he appeared on BBC radio to articulate Labour's changing view of the world: aims and policies that would offer the greatest opportunity and fulfilment. In other words, a return to the policy review begun by Neil Kinnock, and that was the route that John Smith now took.

But first, one final opportunity for Mandelson to weave his by-election magic. With the tragic death of Judith Chaplin, John Major's former political secretary, the government lost one of its Commons majority and the rural Berkshire constituency of Newbury had to find a new MP. Smith agreed to send Mandelson down to Newbury as the 'minder' for Labour's candidate, Steve Billcliffe, a 42-year-old Unity Trust Bank executive. Billcliffe had worked alongside Mandelson at Walworth Road for four years in the late eighties. Contemporaries at party HQ said they couldn't stand the sight of each other. Billcliffe was unashamedly pro-trade union.

The 6 May by-election was held amid continuing speculation that Labour might come into if not a formal pact with the Liberal Democrats, then at least some kind of working arrangement. At Newbury, the Liberal Democrat contender, David Rendel, an old Etonian management consultant and Oxford rowing blue, was best placed to overturn the Tories' 12,000-plus majority. Labour's candidate at the general election, Richard Hall, went so far as to suggest that the party stand down in favour of the Lib-Dems. The parliamentary party rejected this idea, insisting on a fight. Sending Mandelson down to Berkshire was a sign of political earnest, even if Labour's performance in 1992, winning fewer than 4,000 votes, made Billcliffe a rank outsider. Pausing only to sign a statement drafted by Baroness Thatcher that demanded Western troops be send to war-torn Bosnia, Mandelson engaged the enemy in Newbury. But not to any great effect. His best sally was to tease Rendel about his Eton background, addressing him in public as 'Dave'. Seasoned reporters noted that Mandy's interest level was low. 'He passes the time annoying the media with clever sarcasm and personal goads,' said James Dalrymple.[12] He had already sold the pass on poor Billcliffe by admitting that Labour would help mobilise the protest vote against the Tories, without benefiting from it.

On polling-day, the party did worse than even the most unfavourable opinion polls had suggested, taking only 1,151 votes – 2 per cent of the total, where it had once scored 30 per cent. It was Labour's worst performance in a parliamentary election in living memory. Unlike at Monmouth, Mandelson did not claim the credit. But the result was still spun in his favour by the faithful *Sunday Times*, which recorded that Labour's token campaign, directing its fire against the Tories and giving the Lib Dems a clear run, showed a possible way forward for power sharing between the two parties of the centre Left. 'For Peter Mandelson, Labour's minder at Newbury, honour was thus satisfied while the desired result was achieved,' wrote Michael Jones.[13] That 'desired result' was the humiliation of his own party in pursuit of a chimerical goal of political realignment.

Mandy's bitchy side emerged during a Commons spat on 17 June with Mo Mowlam, Labour spokeswoman on women's affairs and MP for Redcar. In a debate on the future of Cleveland County Council, Hansard recorded that he interrupted her ten times. As they left the chamber, Mowlam told him, 'You win some, you lose some.' He hissed back, 'So will you.' But mostly he bothered himself with mundane issues. Should *News at Ten* be moved from the slot it has occupied for a quarter-century? Should the royal yacht *Britannia* find a final resting-place at Hartlepool marina? Could he find a niche of influence in the row between British Airways and Virgin over 'dirty tricks'? He was in touch with both Colin Marshall of BA and Richard Branson. But the great aviator said, 'He is not representing us.'

It was a tiresome period in Mandelson's life. Essentially, he was marking time, operating on the margins of politics, principally because John Smith did not trust him or his new assistant, Derek 'Dolly' Draper, of whom the leader was heard to say, 'What's that little bastard been up to now?'[14] Mandelson was not critically involved in the long summer campaign to win over the trade unions to Smith's 'one member, one vote' (OMOV) reform, which was to dominate the 1993 Brighton conference. This was a device to dilute union influence in the selection of parliamentary candidates and the party leader. Mandelson was a strong supporter of the reform, even though he had been a substantial beneficiary of the unions' patronage in the fight for Hartlepool. The big trade unions were opposed, but Mandelson's influence there was negligible. At the Transport and General Workers' conference in July, delegates rejected the proposed changes and urged Smith, 'Don't listen to the yuppies and spin doctors.' Mandelson retorted that the TGWU decision was neither a surprise nor a blow. Greater democracy in the party, with a much larger membership 'can and will and must come', he declared.

When he returned from his summer holiday in France in late August, Mandy's famous trademark – his neatly clipped moustache – was gone, after twenty years. Even the security men at Westminster failed to recognise him. Mandelson helpfully offered, 'I was at a dinner party. A friend's daughter told me that the ends were turning grey, so a general vote was held. I nipped upstairs, shaved it off and returned to tumultuous applause.' Of course, as any barber will confirm, there are no such things as grey hairs, only white; and hairs do not turn white (or grey) at the ends. Yet again, the anecdote was turned to advantage. 'When you've had a trademark for so long people begin to know you only by that trademark. Now they are beginning to notice the man behind the moustache.'

If they were, it was not obvious. Mandelson was not asked to weave his magic in the next by-election, at Christchurch, Hampshire, in July 1993. This was probably just as well, as reporters on the ground there discovered that Mandelson was not the one who had invented Labour's red rose symbol. That credit went to Leigh Hatts, twice a Labour candidate in Christchurch, who wore a real red rose in 1974 and 1979, when Mandy was still cutting his teeth in the British Youth Council. Hatts had a less grandiose motive than Mandelson. He simply didn't like rosettes, which he thought made candidates look like prize-winning cattle.

Mandelson sounded a warning note after Christchurch, which was another by-election triumph for the Liberal Democrats. He paid tribute to the energetic campaign team, whose effort was 'well-directed and executed, but futile'. Labour won a mere 1,453 votes, only a handful more than in Newbury, yet had started with a higher share of the 1992 poll. Writing in the *Independent*, Mandelson argued that Labour could be in trouble in a number of important seats 'if, heaven forbid, the Lib-Dem surge increases'. He argued that to win over floating voters, Labour had to persuade them that it would govern sensibly – and not tax or spend more for the sake of it. he was also subtly critical of the leadership. 'What's lacking in Labour's approach is not the policies but success in spelling out the basic themes and messages underlying them.'[15]

Mandelson kept up a profile of sorts in the Commons, intervening in Prime Minister's Questions in October to demand an autumn budget that raised revenue without preventing recovery. He urged Chancellor Kenneth Clarke to target tax-dodgers rather than harm pensioners and families by increasing VAT on fuel, and argued that at least £5 billion of revenue was being lost by individuals, companies and wealthy foreigners – twice the amount expected to be raised by the hike in VAT. Two days later, he 'celebrated' his fortieth birthday by appearing on BBC TV's *Question Time*. After the show, the programme team presented him a cake decorated with the red rose symbol. Fellow-panellist Robert Key, the roads minister and a tenor, sang 'Happy Birthday' for him. He was gradually getting a little less disliked at Westminster.

That same month, Mandelson hired a new part-time researcher, Emily Barr. She had previously worked for (and had an unhappy love affair with) the Tory MP Hartley Booth, who had succeeded Margaret Thatcher in the north London constituency of Finchley. Ms Barr (who later became a journalist on the *Guardian*) did not stay with him long. Four months later, Mandelson remarked, less than gallantly, 'Emily Barr worked for me temporarily, two days a week, typing letters. She has not worked for me since January. I have absolutely no knowledge of the circumstances of her previous employment or her alleged relationship with Mr Booth.'[16] This is surprising since the story of Ms Barr and her middle-aged MP lover had been splashed all over pages 2 and 3 of the *Sunday Mirror* the day before, causing the hapless Mr Booth to resign his post as parliamentary private secretary in the Foreign Office. Prior to that, he had rung her on the internal Commons telephone in Mandelson's Westminster office, and once even called there to say he had delivered to Ms Barr's flat a parcel containing a valuable oriental rug.

Mandelson's steady application to work had brought him to the notice of Labour's power-brokers in November 1993, when a vacancy occurred on the Treasury Commons Select Committee. His name was mentioned as a contender, but the very idea raised growls of protest on the backbenches. Giles Radice, a senior Labour member of the committee, said it was 'a very complicated process', made by the whips, the frontbench, the chairman of the parliamentary party and the chairman of the backbench Treasury committee. Mandelson proved unable to line up all these cherries on the parliamentary one-armed bandit.

Mandelson had rather more success in elections for the executive Tribune Group of MPs later that month, when Peter Hain the former cricket-match saboteur of the early 1970s was despatched into the wilderness for advocating economic policies more radical than the party line. MPs openly blamed Hain's defenestration on a campaign involving Mandelson to court votes for Janet Anderson, MP for Rossendale and Darwin.

The beginning of 1994 found Mandelson in something of a trough. He could still mount a good campaign behind the scenes as, Hain had found to his cost, but he was still not very popular among his own kind at Westminster. Even his lowly post as secretary of the Labour backbench Finance Committee was coming under threat, after only a year. Still, *The Times* was always ready to indulge his foreign-policy flights of fancy. On 7 January, the paper printed a letter from Mandelson contradicting his own leader on NATO, which the MP for Hartlepool found lacking in credibility. He argued that the question of extending NATO membership to Poland, Hungary, the Czech Republic and Slovakia was 'one of timing rather than principle'. If these former communist states were not allowed into NATO, they might form their own rival body, promoting 'undesirable fragmentation' in the region. The resultant uncertainty would be more, not less, provocative to Russian security. Mandelson complained that the ex-communist countries should be offered partnerships with NATO clearly identified as 'staging posts to membership'.[17] It was a well-argued letter, which showed the man who would dearly like to be foreign secretary was well abreast of his subject.

The threat to his Finance Committee position came out into the open in mid-January, when Tribune MPs began talking up the 'definite' prospect of a contest for the committee secretaryship. To a degree, he was being used as a stalking-horse against his mentor Gordon Brown, whose position on tax-and-spend was under attack from some of Labour's traditionalists, but the fire was also directed at him personally. He sought to lift his game in a debate on the Finance Bill on 25 January 1994, when he rounded on a remark by Treasury Chief Secretary Michael Portillo that Harriet Harman's comments on unemployment were fatuous. 'Cutting unemployment is fatuous?' he yelled at Portillo, repeated the phrase a dozen times more.

The higher profile may have done him some good when the Finance Committee contest ensued a few days later. Roger Berry, MP for Kingswood, a university lecturer in economics before entering the Commons and co-author with Peter Hain of Tribune pamphlets critical of the new direction of Labour economic policy, stood against Mandelson. Berry was, and remains, a respected figure on the backbenches. He was supported by the left-wing

Campaign Group of MPs. However, it was a poor turnout, and Mandelson was re-elected by a margin of 39 votes to 30. The result was probably more due to efficient vote-whipping than anything he said on the floor of the House. His victory was topped off by being appointed parliamentary adviser to the First Division Association (FDA), the so-called 'mandarins' union' that represents Whitehall high-flyers, soon after. Mandelson could not disguise his immodesty. 'It's something of a coup. It shows that Britain's top civil servants look to the Labour Party for their champion.'

In fact, it was a little more complicated than that. The FDA's general secretary was Liz Symons, a devoutly pro-Labour figure closely allied with the party's modernisers. Her loyalty was subsequently rewarded with a life peerage, and Baroness Symons of Vernham Dean became a Foreign Office minister in Blair's first administration. Her husband, Philip Bassett, then industrial editor of *The Times*, who was professionally and socially well acquainted with Mandelson, later joined the Downing Street Strategic Communications Unit, under the watchful eye of the minister without portfolio. It is a fair bet that members of the FDA applauded the appointment on grounds of getting a big name on-side. But it was also useful that Mandelson was such an effective networker. He quickly showed his usefulness, taking the FDA's part in a row over the conduct of four ministers, two of whom were alleged to have used 'the F-word' to civil servants. There were further allegations that ministers treated advice from their staff with contempt. The FDA demanded a tribunal of privy councillors to rule on 'ethical dilemmas' raised by civil servants. Mandelson was quick off the mark. 'These complaints raise very serious issues and show the need for a code of ethics,' he declared. 'Civil servants should be heard with courtesy and respect. It is no wonder that the government is forced to make U-turns on half-baked legislation when it is not listening to advice from officials.'29 In fact, a code already existed, and the Cabinet Office insisted that no specific complaints had been made.

Mandelson clashed with *The Times* in March 1994, over an

article in *Tribune* in which he demanded that Labour should offer a convincing diagnosis of Britain's economic problems, and show that it had a worked-out and workable alternative. He warned against specific tax and spending pledges. The *Times* report drew attention to Labour's Economic Policy Commission, which was not due to report for another year, whereas Mandelson was warning that voters in the forthcoming local council elections would inevitably ask: 'What will Labour do instead?' *The Times* speculated about a 'policy vacuum', prompting Mandelson to fire off a letter of complaint, claiming that the story attempted to set him against John Smith and Shadow Chancellor Gordon Brown. He hurried to display his loyalty, insisting that Labour had two years to develop its policies.

Considering that he had never before exhibited a passionate interest in war veterans, Mandelson's sudden explosion over government plans to celebrate the fiftieth anniversary of the D-Day landings on 6 June 1994 was a fascinating case-study of his ability to alight upon and exploit an issue. On 15 April on Radio 4's *Any Questions*, Mandelson lambasted the government's plans to celebrate the occasion as being in poor taste and an act of cynical opportunism. Elections for the European Parliament were due on 9 June, and Labour suspected that the Tories were trying to whip up a 'feel-good factor' among the people to minimise their electoral losses. The live radio audience applauded Mandelson's criticism, and he scented a rich potential source of embarrassment for the government.

He tabled a parliamentary Motion calling on the government to scrap its programme of 'festivities and public relations stunts' and demanding that the landings should be commemorated instead by a single, respectful national service of thanksgiving in grateful memory of those who gave their lives. His Motion accused the government of misjudging the mood of the country and called for the cancellation of proposed street parties, spam-fritter cooking contests and fireworks displays, in favour of 'a commemoration, not a celebration'. Mandelson's hype was swiftly taken up by the *Sunday Times*, the *Daily Mail* and the rest of the right-wing press (with the exception of the faithful *Daily Express*). His protest also found some support among ex-servicemen, but the British Legion was ambivalent and the government was largely unmoved. One Tory backbencher described the affair as 'a largely synthetic row'.

Still, the D-Day affair gave Mandelson a higher profile, casting him in the role of defender of the war veterans. It was a useful boost to his standing. But he was still out in the cold as far as the Labour leadership was concerned. No amount of populist noise on the backbenches could propel him into John Smith's inner circle. However, the cruel hand of fate was preparing to rescue Peter Benjamin Mandelson from political obscurity.

10

THE BLAIR PLOT

Shortly after eight o'clock on the morning of 12 May 1994, John Smith was struck down by a massive heart attack in the bathroom of his home in the Barbican, London. Little more than an hour later, he was pronounced dead at nearby Bart's Hospital. Labour was plunged into collective grief. But his personal and political tragedy was Mandelson's opportunity. He did not miss it.

Within ten or twenty minutes, according to key players in the drama that followed, the Mandelson calculating-machine was working at full revs. He discreetly but vigorously briefed journalists on the phone (his favoured instrument of spinning) that 'It's got to be Blair.' Senior politicians, including members of the shadow Cabinet, were aghast, but could do nothing to stop him. They knew what his agenda was. 'Mandelson was out there doing this, and causing an enormous amount of resentment among his colleagues,' said a ranking shadow minister. 'It was almost a fait accompli. That was important for Mandelson because it began to marginalise Brown. That was why it was so crucial for it to be done early, because it was already becoming accepted that Blair, not Brown, should be the candidate.' Blair knew this too.

He was on a European election campaign visit to Aberdeen when he heard the news of Smith's death. He called his wife Cherie, and then the arch-fixer, Peter Mandelson.

But Mandelson was playing a double game. Later that morning, he went round to Gordon Brown's London flat in Great Smith Street, where the shadow chancellor was grief-stricken. Sitting with a circle of close confidants, Brown was trying to compose an obituary of his old friend and mentor for the *Daily Mirror*. His thoughts were not on the leadership, as Mandelson swiftly divined. He took the temperature of the Brown camp and took off on his sedulous campaign to promote Blair.

Charlie Whelan, Brown's press secretary, said later, 'We didn't have any clue while this was going on that people were plotting for the leadership. It didn't register at that stage.' But Brown himself was aware of the chicanery. Indeed, he had been conscious for some time of concerted moves to downgrade his leadership chances in favour of his erstwhile friend's. While the shadow chancellor got on with the unpopular job of revolutionising Labour's economic policy, he had unwisely relied on Blair and his supporters to defend him from the London media establishment.

Brown spent little or no time in London at weekends, preferring to be in his Fife constituency. And in any event he had a great deal of disdain for the weekend party circuit that took in the Alastair Campbells, the Harriet Harmans, the Peter Mandelson's, the Tony Blairs and the odd journalist from the *Guardian*, the *Independent* and a few other papers. It was not a social error, but a political one. While the shadow chancellor reformed Labour's tax-and-spend image, taking the flak from the media and traditional Labour, Blair's supporters – most notably Mandelson – promoted Blair at Brown's expense.

So, while no-one could have predicted that a second heart attack (Smith had already had one, in October 1988, from which he completely recovered) would kill the leader, the Blairistas were in a position to move quickly and in an organised fashion. That night's London *Evening Standard* set the pace, with Blairite commentator Sarah Baxter writing about 'Why it should be

Tony'. Other papers followed suit.

On Saturday 14 May, only two days after Smith's death, Mandelson broke the official party moratorium on campaigning, during an appearance on Channel Four's *A Week in Politics*, presented by another Blairite, Andrew Rawnsley. He argued that contenders for the leadership had to consider 'who will play best at the box office, not simply appeal to the traditional supporters and customers of the Labour party'. This was a thinly disguised attack on Brown's leadership hopes. He knew that the shadow chancellor had courted unpopularity in the modernisation of Labour's economic policy, but still retained a strong power base among party traditionalists. Mandelson also wondered 'Who would fully maximise support for the party in the country?' This was another unsubtle hint that Blair was the man most likely to broaden support for Labour in middle England. To be fair, his analysis chimed with public opinion. Three opinion polls in the following day's broadsheet press gave Blair a commanding lead over Brown. It is unthinkable that the man who boasted of his polling skills when he applied for Labour's top communications job was not aware of the general lines of those polls when he gave the interview.

But this steer to the media, amplified in private conversations with political journalists, was not enough. Mandelson also felt compelled to intervene directly. On 16 May, he wrote Gordon Brown a brilliantly crafted but subversive letter that ostensibly offered to help him run for the leadership, but actually sought his withdrawal from the campaign. It runs as follows:

Monday

Gordon, I think I should give you my best view of the situation from the media standpoint.

You are attracting sympathy from the Lobby for your position. You are seen as the biggest intellectual force and strategic thinker the party has. Most people say there is no one to rival your political 'capacity.' I have thought a lot about your fear that you are being written down (out) by the press, and I have re-read everything very carefully. I don't believe your fears are justified. Nobody is saying that you are not capable/appropriate as leader, merely that the timing is bad for you or that you have vocal enemies or that you have presentational difficulties.

You have a problem in not appearing to be the front runner. It's not that people question whether you could catch up – people accept that your support is currently being understated – but that it would now be difficult for Tony to withdraw in your favour (how would it be explained in the polls etc?) and that by standing you would trigger Cook and possibly others and this would surely not be in the interests of the party.

If Tony felt he had to stand, and you did too, what would be the consequences? I think you both, and our cause and the party would all be hugely damaged. It would be a gift to our enemies. Because you would be appearing to come in as second runner, you would be blamed by the media for creating the split. I think the media would attack you and that your standing in the party would suffer.

The only way to overcome this media resistance to you is to mount a massive and sustained briefing which concentrated on your political skills, ability to unite and manage all sides of the party, dominance in the House, blend of party tradition and modernising agenda. I have not encountered much trouble in selling this so far but to be effective it would have to be greatly escalated, begun immediately and, I am afraid, only done by explicitly weakening Tony's position.

Even then I could not guarantee success. Ultimately, the card the media are playing for Tony is his 'southern appeal'. He doesn't need to point it out or build it up: it is there firmly in their minds and it is linked to their (and our) overriding question, is Labour serious about conquering the South?

My fear is that drift is harming you (cf BBC lunchtime news). You either have to escalate rapidly (and to be effective I think I would need to become clearly partisan with the press in your favour) or you need to implement a strategy to withdraw with enhanced position, strength and respect.

Will you let me know your wishes?

Peter

The typed letter was faxed from Hartlepool to Brown, with a handwritten note at the top telling the shadow chancellor that Mandelson was in his office 'if you want to chat now'. Gordon Brown did not want to chat. Nor did he answer the letter. It was clearly calculated to undermine his position. The suggestion that 'it would now be very difficult for Tony to withdraw in your favour' was a cruel device to exploit the close relationship between the two. Of course, Blair was not even a candidate at the time – nobody was – so the question of his 'withdrawal' was a red herring. As was the warning that by standing Brown would trigger Cook 'and possibly others' to run, which would not be in the best interests of the party.

Brown has a powerful, instinctive loyalty to Labour. Mandelson's accusation that his leadership ambitions would 'hugely damage' the party and the cause of the modernisers was a dagger to his political heart. Had Brown acted on the proposal that he 'escalate rapidly', it would have been a clear breach of the formal moratorium on campaigning. Furthermore, John Smith had been dead for only four days. Brown was still grief-stricken. He had lost a close friend and ally; Mandelson had merely lost an enemy who stood in his way, a man who had once memorably observed of him that 'he was so devious he would one day disappear up his own something or other'.[1] Equally, the reference to 'the overriding question' – Labour's need to conquer the South – may also be read as an ill-concealed dig at Brown's Scottish origins, though no such criticism had ever been levelled at John Smith. Quite the reverse: he was the archetypal Scots bank manager, trustworthy and respected.

The subversive nature of the letter makes all the more unconvincing Mandelson's offer to become 'clearly partisan with the press in your favour' if Brown did escalate his non-existent campaign. It is true that, on the day after he sent the letter,

Mandelson had been seen in the Commons tea room at Westminster telling Labour MPs that he was backing the shadow chancellor. But even Blair's sympathetic biographer records the suspicion that Mandelson was playing a double game. 'Brown's supporters thought he [Mandelson] was exploiting his unpopularity in the parliamentary party to push wavering MPs towards Blair.'[2]

It was a natural enough suspicion, substantially confirmed by Mandelson's pay-off line, arguing that Brown should implement 'a strategy to exit' with strength and respect. The whole burden of the letter leads to that conclusion, and is designed to do so. The letter angered Brown and dismayed his friends, in particular his two brothers, who were closely engaged in his thinking at the time. It was proof that the Blairites would play every card in the pack to propel their man into the leadership.

In the days after John Smith's emotional funeral in Morningside, Edinburgh, on 20 May, Mandelson stepped up his campaign on behalf of Blair, ceaselessly briefing the media. His role was kept secret, because some MPs – including shadow Cabinet member Mo Mowlam and Merseyside fixer Peter Kilfoyle – had declared that they would not vote for Blair if Mandelson was part of the operation. Derek Draper, Mandelson's aide, later recalled: 'Mandelson's mode was near-subterranean, providing a constant stream of advice to Blair and his fledgling spin-doctors . . . and contacting only the most senior and discreet journalists.'[3]

Mandelson met Blair's campaign team frequently at Blair's home in Islington to plot strategy. His role was central to the Blair coup.

In the face of this concerted campaign to block his leadership ambitions, Gordon Brown finally withdrew from the race on 31 May at his famous dinner with Tony Blair at the Granita restaurant in north London. His self-sacrifice made his old friend a certain winner. When the coronation finally took place on 21 July, Blair romped home, with 57 per cent of the votes cast, against 24 per cent for John Prescott and 19 per cent for Margaret Beckett. Moreover, Mandelson's preferred candidate for deputy leader, John Prescott, also secured a convincing win over Mrs Beckett, taking 56.5 per cent of the votes.

Now that his man was in power, the pretence that Mandelson was not involved could be dropped. At his victory party, Blair ostentatiously paid tribute to 'Bobby' – the campaign code name for Mandelson – thanking for him all he had done in the weeks and months since John Smith's death. A flattering myth has grown up that he was given the *nom de guerre* as a reference to Bobby Kennedy, the kingmaker for President John Kennedy. But Derek Draper says that the choice of 'Bobby' was pure coincidence – the random choice of Blair's diary secretary, Kate Garvey, who wanted a name that would never be associated with Mandelson. 'He narrowly escaped being forever known as Terry,' wrote Draper.[4] For ever? It is difficult to believe that such a proletarian-sounding code name would ever have been spun into the Mandelson myth.

Public praise was not his only reward. After taking over the reins as leader, Blair appointed his little helper to the Whips' Office. It was not a popular appointment, either inside or outside the ranks of Labour's business managers. The chief whip, Derek Foster, made no secret of not wanting the leader's favourite courtier in his office.

Being a whip inevitably diminished Mandelson's parliamentary speaking appearances. However, before taking up the job he did manage to create a scene during defence questions on 19 July. Jeremy Hanley, the defence minister, was asked what plans he had for the royal yacht *Britannia* following her decommissioning in 1997. Mandelson was immediately on his feet. Three weeks previously, he had written to Defence Secretary Malcolm Rifkind, suggesting that *Britannia* should receive a comfortable and dignified retirement 'as befits her age' in the new maritime heritage centre – and outstation of the Imperial War Museum – and marina at Hartlepool. 'Is the minister aware that I have discussed the matter personally with the Queen who has expressed her interest in that? Will the minister confirm—'

At this point, Speaker Betty Boothroyd interrupted, with some feeling. 'Order!' she demanded. 'I am sure that the hon. Gentleman is proud, but he should not be divulging conversations that he has had with Her Majesty.' Seemingly oblivious of this reproof, 'proud' Mandelson ploughed on. 'Is the Minister aware that Her Majesty's private secretary has graciously given me permission to disclose that information? Will the Government, therefore, confirm that they will consider the option most positively?' The minister replied that 'if such are Her Majesty's instructions' he could do no less. This was too much for Madam Speaker. 'It is the Speaker of the House who rules here and not Her Majesty's private secretary,' she thundered.[5] This time, a chastened Mandelson stayed in his seat.

However, selling Tony Blair proved to be a stimulating and rewarding task. The new leader began forging a new style of Labour politics, much closer to Mandelson's vision. He moved the party firmly into the centre ground, winning plaudits from the largely Conservative press and from former SDP grandees like Roy Jenkins, Shirley Williams and Bill Rodgers. It was time for a great leap forward. On holiday in the south of France, Blair, in consultation with Gordon Brown and Peter Mandelson, decided to take the historic step of ditching Clause IV of Labour's constitution. Mandelson had long hankered after the abolition of this catch-all nationalising measure, which since 1959 had been printed on the back of every party membership card. One year, while director of communications, he had printed new cards without the hallowed Clause IV. There was an immediate outcry from party traditionalists. All the cards had to be pulped and new ones issued. Mandelson dismissed the embarrassment as a printing error. It looked more like a Freudian slip.

Mandelson was brought into this radical project, along with Alastair Campbell, newly appointed press secretary to the leader. The work went on in secret until the annual conference in Blackpool, which took place under the new slogan 'New Labour, New Britain' on a green background to the platform. In his first leader's speech on 4 October 1994, Tony Blair did not actually come out and say, 'We will abolish Clause IV.' He merely promised a new statement of the party's objectives to take its place in Labour's constitution for the next century. It was left to Mandelson and the other spin-doctors to explain to journalists covering the conference the nature of his radical intentions. Not that Blair fooled the veteran left-winger Arthur Scargill. The miners' leader got his spin in even before Mandelson, vigorously denouncing the 'betrayal' during the standing ovation for the leader.

Some commentators detected Mandelson's hand in the Blair speech, particularly *Times* staffers with whom he had dinner early in the week. But Campbell, still writing a column for *Today*, was quick to set them right. He acknowledged Mandelson's role in the spin operation, but added, 'Having been a close friend since the days before he started wearing cufflinks, I have none of the traditional hang-ups about Peter, and fully intend on becoming Blair's press secretary to exploit his expertise, which in some areas is second to none. Speech writing, however, is not one of them, but such is his ubiquituous appeal that *The Times* yesterday suggested he had helped write Blair's speech. I know from the days when Peter was a *People* columnist that writing was never his strong point, and that he had to look to his friends to help him out.'[6] Mandelson responded in kind: 'I have known Alastair Campbell since he was in T-shirts and my huge admiration for him is well documented. It is an honour to receive brickbats from the hands of such a great speech writer and trainee spin-doctor.'[7]

The Campbell–Mandelson show had got off to a shaky start. However, Mandelson was perceived to have had a good conference, back in his familiar role as the leader's Svengali. But now he could appear in his own right, and proceeded to do so, appearing on BBC to denounce Scargill and 'Red' Ken Livingstone as the 'enemy' within the Labour Party for undermining the work of the modernisers. Livingstone, who has had an ambiguous political relationship with Mandelson, reacted humorously: 'There must be something really tragic that happened to him in childhood, but I am so used to his views I am prepared to forgive him his bitter little asides and I hope he will get better soon.' Austin Mitchell,

MP for Grimsby and a former television journalist, was more scathing. Mandelson was 'the chosen middle man, speaking half truths to the media, media talk to the leader, and all at inordinate profit to himself. Just like any middle man'.

The general view after Blackpool was that Blair and his team had got away with an audacious move, and with the goodwill according to an incoming leader there would never be a better time to ditch the most significant piece of Labour's ideological baggage. More out of nostalgia than political reality, delegates had actually reaffirmed the party's commitment to Clause IV, two days after Blair's speech, by a 51–49 per cent margin. But few doubted that Blair would get his way, even if the campaign to redesign the constitution got off to a slow start. A new statement of objectives was promised by the end of the year. It eventually emerged in March 1995.

Mandelson had other things to think about. With Labour consistently ahead in the polls, he was determined to stamp his authority on the coming general election campaign. On 31 January 1995, he sent Blair a two-page personal memorandum supporting fears expressed by Jonathan Powell, the party leader's new chief of staff. 'Jonathan is right in his note to you that we are dangerously late in commencing the detailed planning of our general election campaign. At the equivalent stages of the last two parliaments both strategic message development and design of the three-week campaign were more advanced.'

He blamed 'lack of structure' for the mess, and complained that 'We lack a concerted message, we are not making full advantage of media opportunities and we are failing to control the media agenda.' The main gap was in the area of political management and co-ordination of strategy and day-to-day tactics.

Mandelson conceded that the case for a strategy committee set up by the party NEC, composed of NEC and shadow Cabinet members was strong. It would have legitimacy and provide 'an indisputable political and decision-making focus'. But he was opposed to it, ostensibly on the grounds that it would take too long to set up, and would involve too many people, and might also replicate the existing NEC Elections and Campaigns Committee chaired by John Prescott.

Instead, he proposed an alternative Leader's Committee. This body, for which he cited precedent, would oversee all strategic and planning activity. In effect, it would be the real engine of the election. 'You would have a relatively free hand on membership and its authority would be considerable,' Mandelson told his leader. 'If you were to go along this route, the real work would then be undertaken by a smaller election strategy committee.' This would be chaired by Gordon Brown (he could not leave the shadow chancellor out of the frame: Brown had already been appointed general election co-ordinator) and it would report to the Leader's Committee. Through the maze of Mandelson's prose, a clear route is discernible: control over the election campaign should be wrested from Walworth Road, the NEC and party officials, and placed in the hands of a carefully picked group of New Labour trusties.

It got better. Mandelson could not resist a mention of his previous brilliance. 'In 1987, the surprising strength of our three-week election campaign following the awful buffeting of the preceding six months was due to the separation of long-term planning from short-run handling,' he argued. 'I suggest that a separate election planning group is given responsibility for preparing technical papers on the election itself for consideration by the Leader's Committee.'

This group would comprise half a dozen individuals with expertise from Blair's office and Walworth Road, plus outsiders whom otherwise it would be difficult to use. These 'outsiders' were not named, but earlier in the note Mandelson pointed out that Philip Gould had been drawn in further to assist in formulating strategy and 'his role needs to be formalised'. Not surprisingly, the MP for Hartlepool wanted to chair this secretive, six-member election planning group using 'outsiders' and reporting directly to the leader. It would, he argued, 'help to legitimise my role and membership of the strategy committee and presentation to the Leader's Committee.'

Quite so. Gordon Brown spotted the nature of Mandelson's initiative immediately. He fired off a (much shorter) note to Blair, accepting the idea of a strategy committee but firmly rejecting Mandelson's plan for it to be subordinate to the Leader's Committee. With the existing NEC Campaigns and Elections structure still in place, a parallel body would blur lines of authority and hamper the decision-making process. 'Only an NEC-based committee can be open and above board, bind in all members of the NEC, make staff at John Smith House wholly accountable and therefore have clear influence and authority.' It might take longer to set up, but the delay would be worth it. Brown wanted a two-tier structure, with an NEC Election Strategy Committee meeting monthly, and a small Executive Committee, meeting more often and embracing politicians and their party experts. If necessary, the executive could commission 'informal groups' to carry out work on specific issues. In other words, Brown wanted a party-based operation, rather than a leader's clique that also brought in outsiders. The distinction is important, because Mandelson's plan marked a further concentration of power among a small number of people gathered round Tony Blair – some of whom were not even party insiders.

Mandelson laughed off reports that he might have a reselection battle on his hands in Hartlepool. The suggestions, which first surfaced in late 1994, were traced to dissident members of the GMB, the union that had got him the job in the first place. He was also embroiled in a personal row with his next-door parliamentary neighbour, Frank Cook, MP for Stockton North, over the abolition of Cleveland County Council. Mandelson supported abolition, on the politically astute grounds that Hartlepool would get its own borough council. Cook, a native of Hartlepool, wanted to keep the unloved and unwieldy county council. 'I don't know where Mr Mandelson was born, and frankly, I don't care,' he said. Mandelson replied that where he was born was 'beside the point' because 'I know where my duty lies'. He even defied the party line on abolition, abstaining in the Commons vote in January 1995, an act which prompted calls for his dismissal as a whip inside the parliamentary Labour Party. He was not sacked, and Cleveland council duly disappeared. Mandelson toasted its passing at a champagne and smoked salmon victory party.

These were good times for Peter Rabbit. It seemed that he could have his won way over anything, including who should fill his vacant desk at Walworth Road. In February 1995, the party advertised for a new director of communications. Joy Johnson, the 40-year-old political news editor of the BBC, a senior figure in the broadcasting world who had revolutionised live coverage of party conferences in recent years, was asked to apply. The political intention was to re-merge the communications, campaigns and election elements of party work. It was a big job, but Johnson, a long-standing Labour supporter, was a direct and aggressive performer. John Major once famously asked, 'Who is that woman who makes me feel like a criminal?'

At a discreet meeting in the roof bar of 7 Millbank, Mandelson vetted her for the £50,000-a-year post. He approved. Her one regret is that she passed that test, because from day one it didn't work. Johnson was expected to channel everything through Mandelson, though his role and status in the scheme of things were ambiguous. She protested, and Blair slapped her down, saying, 'You *must* talk to Peter.'

Johnson ignored the edict, and with Gordon Brown's office was responsible for the hugely successful 'fat cats' campaign which highlighted the vast personal profits being made by the bosses of the privatised water, gas and electricity industries, and paved the way for the windfall tax that is funding Labour's 'new deal' on jobs and training. Friends warned Johnson that Mandelson was not a man to cross, but she carried blithely on. Mandelson told her to 'spin' Labour's message to the parliamentary press lobby, but Johnson (whose motto came to be 'You can't win by spin') declined, pointing out that her great strength was in the broadcasting field. Mandelson was not pleased, and told her, 'You'll have to do it sooner or later.' Then, she knew the writing was on the wall, though it was chiefly her doing that Labour's campaign and communication team moved from Walworth Road to the gleaming skyscraper on Millbank, down the road from Westminster. After the 1995 party conference, which was a brilliantly successful showpiece for New Labour, stories began appearing in the papers that she was on her way out. The parting of the ways came in January 1996. At the time she told friends, 'Mandelson couldn't let anybody else do the job – or it would have to be someone who would bow to him. My idea was to make the news agenda, to think in terms of a newsroom, to give it the urgency of deadlines.' That radical reform survived her departure, and is now being copied by the Conservatives. An idea that figured in conversation with Mandelson did not come about. An exasperated Johnson one day blurted out, 'We will be Tony Blair's Labour Party next!' To which Mandelson replied, 'If only we could.'

He was never far away from the headlines: calling for the ban on Sinn Fein representatives speaking on television and radio to be lifted, being 'paired' with a smooth snake at London Zoo for charity, or being awarded the title of 'Parliamentarian to Watch' by the right-wing *Spectator* magazine. Previous winners of this prize included Tony Blair and Gordon Brown, he noted.

While he continued to work discreetly as a spin-doctor for Tony Blair, Mandelson was also planning to lift the intellectual profile of New Labour. He decided to write a book, choosing as co-author Roger Liddle, his friend of Lambeth Council days who had defected to the SDP but who was now preparing to rejoin Labour. The book was originally billed as Liddle's idea, putatively titled *Birth of a New Labour*, and Mandelson would be *his* co-author. Mandelson was reported as rejecting the idea, but the gossip columnists alerted a waiting nation for 'some sort of project announcement' in July.

In fact, Mandelson had already written a 22-page synopsis that was sent out 'in confidence' to prospective publishers in the spring of 1995. It was political dynamite, far ahead of anything that even New Labour had yet contemplated. His covering letter, on House of Commons notepaper, to the confidential draft predicted that interest in how Tony Blair 'will govern' would intensify as the election neared. His book would explain 'how New Labour will govern differently both from the Conservatives and "Old" Labour'. It would give an insiders' character study of Labour leaders, their ideas, 'and what makes them tick'.

He pointed out that he had been at the centre of events in the Labour Party since 1985, first as campaign director and now as an MP 'close to Tony Blair'. His co-author, Roger Liddle, a wealth of experience in politics, having been a special adviser (to Bill Rodgers) in the last Labour government. He had since played a leading role in the SDP and Lib Dems 'and is now rejoining Labour'. Mandelson promised that the book would engage the general reader as well as being indispensable to informed and academic readers. 'It will be a mixture of topical analysis, history and anecdote,' he trilled. 'In the year ahead, I do not think there should be doubt about its marketability.'

Given that Blair's own press secretary had only recently disclosed that Mandelson was not much of a writer, publishers might have been forgiven for harbouring some doubts. But the synopsis of the ten-chapter tome looked promising. The authors claimed to have 'special insight' into Tony Blair's thinking and intentions. The draft sharply criticised the previous Labour government for 'a steadily corrupting relationship' with the trade unions, which ducked necessary industrial relations reforms. The price Labour had to pay to the unions ossified industrial structures, damaged economic performance, inhibited the development of modern social policies and public service reform, affronted popular ideas of liberty and, 'worst of all', distorted Labour's sense of right and wrong. Mandelson and Liddle would back up their charges with examples of 'undue influence of trade unions and the timidity of Labour ministers in standing up to bullying behaviour'. They would set out a plan for completely changing the unions' role in the party. This was strong stuff. The unions had, by and large, gone along with Blair's reforms, but, had they known the leader's close friend was proposing to say such things, they would have been up in arms.

Turning to the economy, the synopsis suggested that students repay the cost of their university education through higher taxes, 'workfare' for the hard-core jobless, and child care for single mothers only if they agreed to training. Mandelson and Liddle excoriated John Smith for his obstinacy in sticking to a doomed shadow budget in the 1992 election, and predicted, 'This time, Labour will not reveal its new plans until much nearer the next election, but the authors will spell out what they think Labour's tax policy should be.' It would not be an increase in the tax burden for the mass of voters.

In a chapter describing a Re-United Kingdom, the authors proposed:

- special courts to deal with anti-social behaviour
- abolition of universal child care benefit
- compulsory private pensions to supplement the state pension
- reform of the social security system
- 'no strike' deals for public service employees, tied to an independent pay review system
- entrepreneurial innovation in the public services
- opting-out from local authority control for all schools

If it had been leaked at the time, this wish-list of ideas would have created mayhem in the party. There was more to come. On Europe, Mandelson and Liddle favoured a Labour government joining the single currency, and a referendum on a more integrated Union. But the most radical proposal was left until the penultimate chapter, 'Does Labour Need a Coalition to Succeed?'.

Essentially, the answer was yes. The Labour–Lib Dem writing alliance argued that a programme of renewal for Britain would take more than one five-year Parliament. A Blair-led government 'will' be facing re-election by a possible sceptical or hostile public before the results have been delivered, they declared. 'It is impossible to predict what, if any, overall majority Labour will achieve at the election, and rather than wait and deal with events as they come, there is a strong argument for working out in advance what understanding Labour should forge with the Liberal Democrats.'

Of course, they were not to know that two years later Labour would win with the biggest landslide in modern political history. But their thinking appeared virtually to rule out an overall Blair victory, and certainly did not envisage a second Labour-dominated Parliament. The Lib Dems, they claimed, had support 'that even Blair cannot touch'. Mandelson and Liddle insisted that the left of centre had to stick together. No doubt some in both parties would explode at the prospect of doing a deal, they admitted. 'But the majority would prefer to see a longer-term stable left of centre government than a risky, short-term, go-it-alone attitude prevailing.' The worst scenario would be to dismiss any idea of a pact, only to be forced to confront it later if the election went less well than expected. 'Taking on the issue in advance is the better option.'

Few would have accepted that argument. It smacked of defeatism, and it clearly indicated that Mandelson and Liddle had their own version of The Project: a 'left-of-centre' government that would remain in power for the foreseeable future. But not a Labour government. Had the book really pursued this private agenda, they would have risked political oblivion. So they didn't write it.

Mandelson was cast in his old role that summer as by-election supremo, masterminding Labour's campaign to win the seat of Littleborough and Saddleworth on the west Pennine slopes. The marginal constituency became vacant through the death of the Tory MP Geoffrey Dickens, but it was regarded as a three-way contest with the Liberal Democrats starting as favourites. Labour's candidate was Phil Woolas, a former president of the National Union of Students who had known Mandelson in his British Youth Council days. Woolas, director of information for the GMB, was initially suspicious, but the great fixer's organisational brilliance and sheer hard work won him over. The pair conducted a faultless, and ruthless, campaign, first seeing off the Tory candidate, and then eroding support for Chris Davies, the Liberal

Democrat rival, by portraying his party as soft on drugs and high on taxation. The Mandelson Project might call for a long-term political partnership with Paddy Ashdown's party, but in the by-election, no quarter was given. The joke in the Lib Dem office was that the price of co-operation with Labour was proportional representation and no government job for Mandelson. It was talked of as the dirtiest by-election in years. Once again, Mandy's tactics did not produce a win, though he did take Labour to within a few thousand votes of success. He had a few words of congratulation on the result for himself: 'It will do much to extinguish the self-doubt in the party about the appeal of New Labour.'

Had he succeeded in winning the seat, some of the bitterness that followed might have been avoided. Weeks later, Richard Burden, Labour MP for Birmingham Northfield, loosed off a salvo in the *New Statesman*. He was sharply critical of Mandelson's conduct of the by-election, and accused Tony Blair of a 'Kremlin' leadership style. Burden was an obscure backbencher, but his comments were swiftly taken up by traditionalist MPs keen to exploit the opportunity to attack Mandelson, implicitly, if not by name. The growling got louder in mid-September, with the leak to the *Guardian* of a confidential document prepared by Mandelson's friend and close political ally Philip Gould.

The Gould memorandum was sent to Blair, but Mandelson also had a copy. The self-appointed guru did not mince his words. The party revolution was unfinished. Labour was not ready for government. The reforms must go deeper and wider. The leader and his inner circle should have greater power. Blair himself should be 'the sole ultimate source of campaigning authority'. The trade-union link should be further diluted. Peter Mandelson should have a greater role.

It mattered little that the memorandum had been written seven months previously. The judicious timing of the leak – just before the party conference in Brighton – prompted speculation that Labour's high command was deeply divided. John Prescott, the deputy leader, was not among those who had been brought into the Gould exercise. It was self-evidently a manoeuvre to take the ground that Mandelson had failed to gain in his January bid for greater power through a Leader's Committee. He had lost that argument. A general election strategy committee had been set up, and it met every day. But Gordon Brown was firmly in the chair. Prescott had been given an assurance by Blair that there would be senior political control of the campaign: it would not be delegated to a junior whip and his cronies in the advertising world.

Perhaps to assuage his wounded feelings, Blair promoted Mandelson to a frontbench job after the party conference. He became Labour's spokesman on the civil service, with a brief open to the widest interpretation. He was to become the scourge of Whitehall bureaucrats, who might seek to frustrate the Blair revolution. In that capacity, he would call to account the Cabinet Office, traditionally the preserve of the deputy leader. Despite setbacks, life was going rather well. He shook off an attack from the left-wing MP Brian Sedgemore, who said in a new book that a huge majority of Labour MPs were united in their hatred of 'the Prince of Darkness'. He claimed that 'The level of hatred is consistent throughout every geographical area and cuts across gender, class, social background and occupation.'[8] Mandelson adopted his usual stance: a tiny minority were attacking him because they could not find fault with Tony Blair's leadership. This onslaught was 'laughable'.

But then he received an unexpected early Christmas present. On 23 December, the *Observer* carried a full report on his 'confidential' book synopsis, and the news-hungry tabloids fell upon it like wolves on the fold. The *Daily Mail* called it 'quite simply dynamite'. Left-wing Labour MPs queued up to denounce him and suggested that if he was so much in love with the Liberal Democrats, he should go off and join them. Mandelson was unrepentant. 'This book will contribute to the public's understanding of what new Labour stands for and its thinking on a range of policy issues.' It would expound and 'enlarge upon', rather than contradict, party policy. 'With my record,' he said, 'I would be the last person to want to do that.' His colleagues who had been 'wound up' to react to the book before the publication would be 'pleasantly surprised' by its contents.

Quite so. The manuscript had been toned down to diminish the risk of a political brouhaha. An aide in Blair's office responded dismissively: the synopsis was written before Mandy became a frontbencher, and highlighted areas to be examined in a book that didn't happen. Random House, the original publisher, had decided not to go ahead with the project, so Mandelson and Liddle turned to Faber and Faber, who agreed to bring out *The Blair Revolution* as a paperback in February 1996. The original title – *Can Labour Deliver?* – had been relegated to a subtitle, giving rise to the joke at Westminster, 'Can Mandy deliver?' His protestations that the book would not actually call for a Lib–Lab pact, or the abolition of child benefit, did not cut much ice among Labour backbenchers only too willing to believe the worst of the Prince of Darkness. He must believe in the ideas aired in the synopsis, they reasoned, or he would not have proposed them in the first place.

Serialisation rights for the book were reportedly touted for £500,000, a preposterous sum for a work of beginner's political philosophy. The *Guardian* finally agreed to take it, for very much less. The publishers' 26 February embargo was broken by *Prospect*, a modish new Labour monthly magazine, which published a review by the left-of-centre *Guardian* columnist Will Hutton, whose pop-economics tome *The State We're In* had been a bestseller. It did not seem that *The Blair Revolution* would share the same success. Hutton's disdainful review set the tone. He criticised the centralising ambitions of New Labour, identified in Mandelson's call for a shift away from Cabinet government to rule by a troika composed of Downing Street, the Cabinet Office and the Treasury. Under this dispensation, Blair would run the country at a series of ad hoc meetings. 'No prizes for guessing who plans to attend as many ad hoc meetings as possible,' snorted Hutton.

Media interest in the book centred on Mandelson's proposal for £5,000 state dowries for newly-weds and on his plans for 'superministries' with multi-departmental responsibilities to

tackle the countries economic and social ills. He went on BBC
TV's *On the Record* to outline his ideas, arguing that a prime
minister could not bring about all the necessary change by
himself. He would need colleagues working collectively with him,
'and there are in government what's called wicked issues, the sort
of elusive issues which are difficult for a single minister or department to get hold of '.[9] Peter Riddell, political commentator of *The
Times*, was kind to the authors, exonerating them of the charge of
acting as a proxy for Tony Blair's secret plans. He disclosed that
they felt constrained not to write anything that would embarrass
their leader and give ammunition either to the Labour Left or to
the Tories.

This was not quite how Mandelson saw his magnum opus.
Indeed, on the eve of publication, he sent a handwritten 'In
Confidence' note to John Prescott, saying, 'I know you will not
agree with the way everything is put, but at least no one can
accuse me of not coming clean with what I really believe!' This
was precisely the charge that could be levelled against him.

The book did not give examples of 'the undue influence of trade
unions and the timidity of Labour ministers in standing up to
bullying behaviour'. It merely lamented that relations between
unions and the Labour Party had become 'too close and incestuous'
and unions now had to recognise that putting improper pressure
on ministers 'is the wrong path to take'. There was no mention of
Labour and the Liberal Democrats 'doing a deal', only a re-
affirmation of existing policy about the potential for co-operation
between the two parties. Indeed, such co-operation 'does not
imply or require a pre-election pact or post-election coalition',
whimpered Mandelson and Liddle. This was a far cry from the
injunction in the synopsis that the worst scenario would be to
dismiss any idea of a pact. In the words of Michael Jones of the
Sunday Times, discretion stalked every one of the book's 261 pages.

Nor were his Labour colleagues any more impressed. Roy
Hattersley, his mentor, opined that 'Pretensions mar every page',
and that the book rejected ideology and replaced it with
banalities, such as 'New Labour stands for ordinary families who

work hard and play by the rules.' The only excuse for such triviality, said the former deputy leader, 'is the authors' palpable ignorance of the political philosophy they reject'.[10] The journalist MP Austin Mitchell, gave the book beta minus, adding, 'Peter can't write', even though there was a stubborn desire inside him to be taken seriously. Peter Kilfoyle, MP for Liverpool Walton and a former party fixer on Merseyside, who went on to become a minister in the Cabinet Office, contributed a scathing review to *Tribune*. He recalled that in the heyday of the *Beano* and the *Dandy*, there was a comic character named Roger the Dodger, and a comic called *Mandy*. 'Both came to mind as I began this book, although my humour metamorphosed first into incredulity and then dismay . . . it was a relief to read that the book "bears no one's imprimatur but our own". Its style is condescending, and many of its prescriptions trite. It is also dangerous in its reduction of complex social issues to glib phrases.'

As put-downs go, his review ranks among the cruellest of recent times. But he spoke the truth. Mandelson and Liddle wrote about people as if they were walk-on parts in a party political broadcast directed by Hugh Hudson. They invented imaginary people – Bill Andrews of Milton Keynes, Steve and Jane Stephenson of Basingstoke, and Phil Jones living 'not far away' on a pre-war council estate – to illustrate the impact of life under the Tories and what they would want from a Labour government. These composite figures lacked all credibility. They were created to make a political point, and remained cardboard cut-outs. More than anything, they resembled the authors: packaged, and remote from the rich mess of normal life.

That disagreeable reality caught up with Mandelson when the authors went on tour to publicise their turkey. On 26 March, they appeared at a £5-a-head bash at the Almeida Theatre in Islington to present the case for the Blair revolution, only to be confronted by banner-waving demonstrators protesting about the rights of asylum-seekers. They voiced a series of demands, and Mandelson promised 'as much time as you wish' to debate their complaints after the event. But they continued their vociferous demands, and he yanked their protest banner away. A woman fell to the ground, and one of the men shoved Mandelson. He shoved back, and the two men stumbled. According to a colourful account in the next day's *Evening Standard*, Mandelson, never much of a pugilist, felled a protestor on the stage. It was, said the paper's diarist 'an amusing little scuffle'. His aides played down the embarrassment, insisting that it was 'a little incident, and Peter was not upset in the least'. He had a rather better reception in the City, where blue-chip firms like Sony, Hambros, Texaco and SBC Warburg bought tickets for the Mandelson and Little Show. At a fund-raising dinner for *Tribune*, however, the insults flew. Brian Sedgemore described the book as 'codswallop and trash, from the devil made flesh', while Campaign Group MP Alan Simpson wailed about the environmental cost: 'The trees! Oh, the trees!' A copy of the book was auctioned, and the winner, political cartoonist Martin Rowson, admitted, 'I paid £100 for it. I was drunk.' At least Mandelson was now a celebrity, immortalised in rubber on the television show *Spitting Image*, in which he appeared with his head on the body of a snake.

Mandelson's first Commons outing at the Despatch Box in March failed to impress. The verdict in the MPs' tea room was that 'Two Brains' Tory minister David Willetts won game, set and match against a hesitant Mandelson. In a debate on the privatisation of HMSO, the government printers, he argued against a sell-off. Once transferred to the private sector, HMSO would be subject to market forces and MPs would suffer because the supply of papers they need would be at the mercy of commercial competition. 'We know that, when the chips are down and market forces rule, and when the privatised HMSO inevitably has to face the rigour of competition, it will not be able to put its commitment to Parliament and our needs first.'

Willetts pointed out that the Tories had liberalised the trading regime of HMSO to the absolute limit, but the further liberalisation favoured by Labour would not bring the public-sector body out of long-term decline. Mandelson intervened twice, the second time to demand an undertaking that the Lords would have an opportunity to vote on the measure. Willetts brushed him aside, and then turned devastatingly to Mandelson's book. Not only had the minister read it, but he had reviewed it – 'although, of course, not quite as savagely' as Roy Hattersley – and the book said clearly that 'privatisation has brought about improvements in operating efficiency and facilitated new investment'. Willetts taunted him further, arguing that a future Labour government would not dare to renationalise HMSO because by then it would be thriving in the private sector. The government won the vote with a majority of forty, and HMSO is indeed still a private company.

In the early summer of 1996, the press was full of fresh speculation that moves were afoot to heal the rift between Mandelson and Gordon Brown. Donald Dewar, the chief whip and Brown's friend, was named as the most likely go-between. Since the stories did not emanate from the Brown camp, it is a fair bet that they were inspired by Mandelson, who had more to gain from their currency. Encouraged by Tony Blair, the two men did meet twice in mid-May, and Brown paid public tribute to Mandelson as 'a brilliant strategist who has done a tremendous amount for the party'. They could scarcely avoid meeting: each had a key role in preparations for the election. Brown chaired the strategy meetings, while Mandelson presided over the day-to-day planning. But despite the superficial show of unity, there was no rapprochement between the two men. Mandelson continued to talk up the shadow chancellor in speeches to the business world, while Brown told anyone who would listen his favourite joke about Labour's Machiavelli. 'Mandelson asked me for 10p to call a friend. I said, "Here's 20p. Ring them all." '

Mandelson took his summer holiday that year in Tuscany, at the villa of Geoffrey Robinson, the millionaire Labour ex-minister. He stayed there with friends in August, and when he left Tony Blair took his room. While Mandy was sunning himself in 'Chiantishire', Clare Short, the shadow overseas aid minister, launched a stunning attack on him. She denounced him and his fellow-confidants of Tony Blair as 'the people who live in the dark' and said, 'We go to the Shadow Cabinet. We go to the NEC. Everything we do is in the light. They live in the dark. It is a good place for them.' Everyone knew who she was talking about, and Roy Hattersley confirmed the universal view that she meant Peter Mandelson 'who seems to be in the paper too often, who seems to be on television far too often, and who seems to take himself, and be taken, far more seriously than I think is appropriate'. The Tories were delighted with this friendly fire on Mandelson, particularly as it came on top of an ICM poll in the *Guardian* which cut Labour's lead over the government from 21 points to 12. Left-wing Labour MPs jumped on the bandwagon, too, saying Ms Short was right to fear that the spin-doctors might lose Labour's core vote.

In the build-up to the election campaign, Mandelson was suddenly seen riding around in a chauffeur-driven limousine. The silver Rover, it transpired, was on loan from James Palumbo, son of the Conservative peer Lord (Peter) Palumbo and owner of the Ministry of Sound nightclub, where Mandelson had once been photographed. Of Labour's high command, only Tony Blair had an official limo, but his campaign lieutenant once more dismissed the criticism: 'We are a professional, mobile team and the days of relying on a penny farthing machine are over.'

Much was made of the prospect of a three-way debate between John Major, Tony Blair and Paddy Ashdown (it never happened), but most voters did not hear that Mandelson refused to take part in a three-way debate with his Tory and Liberal Democrat rivals, Michael Horsley and Reg Clark, at Hartlepool Sixth Form College in February. His rivals accused him of being afraid to have a proper discussion, and college vice-principal Duncan Graham said it was a shame that the town's MP would not take part in a debate. Mandelson did not say why he would not argue his case with the other parties. He may have been too busy building up the Millbank political machine, of which he became inordinately proud ('*my* Millbank', he called it). More than three hundred party staffers – media monitors, rapid rebutters, MPs' researchers, trade-union officials and miscellaneous gofers, some of them recruited on short-term contracts, were crammed into the so-called 'war room'. This was Mandy's empire. He was campaign manager, he reminded everyone; Gordon Brown was campaign co-ordinator. Mandelson had his own small office, with a clear view of the open-plan campaign village.

He set a cracking pace for the others to follow. He was in the office before seven in the morning for his first strategy meeting, and did not leave until nine at night. Even then, he waited up for the next day's first editions to be faxed to him before turning in at about midnight. At the start of the campaign, he gave the troops a pep-talk, demanding that they go to bed early (to sleep), avoid alcohol (he stopped drinking on New Year's Eve) and take vitamins. On his own desk rested two bottles of multi-strength vitamin-E pills and three lemons – milk was out, too. And coffee. 'My body seems to have been constructed with this job in mind,' he boasted. But he was also powerfully conscious that this was his last opportunity. 'If we lose, I crawl off into a hole somewhere, never to be heard of again. If we win, then the proper business of my life begins with Labour in government.'

Curiously, however, in the series of interviews he gave during the campaign his own role was more prominent than the way Labour would govern. He 'personally' had been preparing for this campaign since 1985, he told the *Mirror*. He was reliving what his grandfather Herbert Morrison had done in 1945, deliver a landslide Labour victory for a party dedicated to change and reform. To the *Sunday Times*, he was the man in the hard hat who refused to let a Scottish TV film crew making a programme about Gordon Brown into meetings or into the war room. He dismissed suggestions that his rift with Brown ('it has healed') could affect his performance. 'I regard that period as behind me,' he said. 'You don't manage an election campaign without enjoying very close daily constructive relations with your colleagues.'[11] The key word here is 'manage'. The 1997 election was going to be a landslide for Labour, and Mandelson was determined to garner as much credit as he could. 'I am a campaign manager now, not a spin doctor,' he repeated. The theme was taken up by friendly journalists. Brown was merely in charge of election strategy, while Mandelson was 'crowned' campaign manager, Anne McElvoy wrote in the *Spectator*. This made it sound as if Mandelson would merely manage Brown's strategy. 'In reality, things are not like that at all. Mr Mandelson is Mr Blair's true intimate and he often knows of intended changes to policy as soon as – if not before – Mr Brown.'[12] This unsubtle build-up of media attention was clearly aimed at spinning the credit for a Labour victory Mandelson's way, even before the voters had gone to the polls. He also rubbished the 'media bore campaign', claiming that the broadcasters' 'simplistic tit-for-tat coverage is playing into Tory hands'. He argued that the public were crying out for politicians who would concentrate on their concerns, in an article which attacked the Tories by name sixteen times, typically as 'backbiting, desperate and polluting'.[13]

In Hartlepool, Mandelson had three competitors for the seat: Michael Horsley, a public-affairs executive with Dixons plc, carried the Tory banner; Reg Clark, finance director of a steel company, was the Liberal Democrat; and Maureen Henderson was standing for the short-lived Referendum Party. The campaign was uneventful – Mandelson was in London most of the time – but there was a drama on the eve of polling day when his car was hit by the runaway wheel of a lorry that broke down at speed. Mandelson's driver swerved, and the wheel hit the roof, inches from the windscreen. He was shaken but unhurt, and carried on to a speaking engagement at a local Catholic school.

On 1 May, Mandelson was 'absolutely thrilled' when his majority was almost doubled from just under nine thousand to 17,508 over the Tories. In a 65.6 per cent poll – down ten points on 1992 – he took 26,997 votes, 60.7 per cent of the total, though only 181 more than at his first outing. The Tory vote slumped to 9,489, barely 21 per cent, while the Lib Dem poll stayed relatively firm at 6,248. The Referendum Party picked up only 1,718.

During the count, Mandelson gave five radio and television interviews, while an extra table was brought in to hold all his votes. After declaring that 'the sun has certainly shone on Hartlepool today', he repaired to a party in the Sports Bar.

11

THE GREATEST SHOWMAN ON EARTH

Before winning power, New Labour was seriously lukewarm about the Millennium Dome. On taking office, Blair's Cabinet had to decide whether to go ahead with the money-gobbling monster or abandon it. Voters were overwhelmingly against the idea, as measured by public opinion polls, which could have been interpreted as showing no more than their ignorance of the issue. Creative opinion was divided. Playwright David Hare called it 'This insane piece of statist grandiloquence'. It was going to cost £758 million, most of it from the National Lottery, but a large chunk from public spending too. Gordon Brown thought it was a waste of money. John Prescott shared some of these doubts, but struck a characteristically macho pose: if an incoming Labour government could not deliver a big project like the Dome, what kind of signal would that send to the punters? With some reluctance, the Cabinet gave the go-ahead.

The tabloid press was unimpressed. The *Sun* splash headline on 20 June was 'DEAF AND DOME', hyping the decision into Blair's first blunder: ignoring public opinion and lashing out on an extravaganza. Blair admitted that it was his most difficult decision since becoming prime minister. 'I should really cancel it, but my gut instinct tells me otherwise,' he told aides. Most Westminster observers assumed that responsibility for the Dome would go either to Prescott, into whose superministry it naturally fell, or to the culture secretary, Chris Smith, a Londoner with a constituency just across the river from Greenwich where the great tent would be built.

The experts reckoned without Mandelson. The Dome appealed to his sense of history – had not his grandfather, Herbert Morrison, been responsible for the hugely successful Festival of Britain in 1951? – and his vanity. This was precisely the right prestige project for him. Blair invited Mandelson up to the Number 11 flat he occupies to seek his advice. He got more than he asked for. Mandy felt the hand of history on his shoulder. He would build the Dome, and make it a success. It would be a magnificent showcase for his hip view of the world. Think of all those wonderful photo-opportunities to have his picture taken in a hard hat! The sheer delight of talking (as he does) at fashionable London dinner parties of 'my Dome'. The delightful hours to be spent getting his way with trendy designers, creative artists and businessmen bemused by his dynamism! Above all, his name, like his grandfather's, would be associated with success.

The Festival of Britain was not Morrison's idea, just as the Dome long pre-dated Mandelson's entry into top-level politics. The Festival of Britain was first mooted by the Royal Society of Arts in 1943, and Morrison did not assume formal responsibility until 1947. Thereafter, he threw all his undoubted organisational abilities into the project, which he regarded as a great symbol of the regeneration of Britain after the sacrifices of the Second World War. He suggested an area between 'his' County Hall and 'his' Waterloo Bridge, despite the smallness of the site – only thirty acres. Morrison, said his biographers 'had long wanted to see that bedraggled southern riverside turned into something of a credit to London, and a pleasure to Londoners, especially south Londoners'.[1]

Announcing the South Bank site in December 1949, he promised a festival with the theme of a 'new Britain springing from the battered fabric of the old'. The project suffered from the perennial problems of post-war Britain: shortages of materials, including cement and steel, and labour disputes. Morrison kept a light ministerial hand on the tiller, intervening when necessary, on one occasion to give the go-ahead to a statue that the press thought was indecent, and another time to promote Sunday opening of the festival and its associated funfair in Battersea Park. In that endeavour, he failed. But he was determined to cheer Britons up. When the great event opened, he invited the whole country to take part and enjoy it. 'I want to see the people happy. I want to hear the people sing.' The timing might be madness, he conceded, with Britain still gripped by austerity, but it was 'the sort of madness that has put us on the map and is going to keep us there'. Morrison was foreign secretary by this stage of his long career, but he was known colloquially as 'the Lord Festival'.

Mandelson was determined to capitalise on that legacy. Opening an exhibition on the festival, after he joined the Cabinet, he said his grandfather's idea to put a smile on the face of a weary nation had inspired him to make the Dome a success. With almost theatrical emotion, he said, 'If he's up there somewhere, my old grandad, looking down with his one eye, with that great steely look, that firm grip, that iron will for which he was famous, he would be looking down and saying, "It had better be as good as 1951."'

Unfortunately, 1997 was not 1951. Britain was not emerging from a long period of post-war austerity, longing for a cultural celebration that would lift the nation's spirits. It was going through an economic boom, and the public mood was more cynical. There was already more than enough attention-grabbing entertainment around, and individual tastes had changed out of all recognition. Moreover, the chronological imperative was different. The Festival of Britain was staged when it was to mark the centenary anniversary of the Great Exhibition of 1851, a celebration of Victorian scientific know-how and imperial trading success. The year 2000 was the putative two thousandth birthday of Jesus Christ: a time for religious rejoicing for a minority of the population, perhaps, but in terms of an actual event more important for the prospect of computers crashing the world over because of the 'millennium bug'.

In deciding to proceed with the Dome, Labour was picking up a baton dropped by the Conservatives. Peter Brooke, the Tory heritage secretary, had announced in 1992 that Britain would commemorate the millennium in a big way. Michael Heseltine, as deputy prime minister, rejected the claims of the provinces (particularly Birmingham) and ruled that the Millennium Exhibition should be staged in the east Thames corridor, on three hundred acres once occupied by Europe's largest gasworks. The land was polluted with toxic chemicals from many years of coal-gas production. Transport links were poor or non-existent. Greenwich is a notorious black-spot for drivers, and the Jubilee Line tube extension, even when fully operational, would have difficulties coping with Mandelson's predicted millions of visitors in millennium year.

Furthermore, there were monumental organisational problems. Heseltine, a big-picture man who is weak on detail, bequeathed Mandelson a chaotic management structure. He was the minister responsible. Below him was the Millennium Commission, responsible for broad strategy. A separate company, Millennium Central Limited, was set up to take charge of the building and running of the dome. Beneath them came great conflicting waves of designers, thinkers, artists (and not a few chancers), all eager to get a slice of the action. Businessmen were asked to stump up £150 million in private sponsorship money to complement the £400 million of Lottery money being set aside for the project (£208 million is supposed to come from sales of tickets and merchandise). They looked askance at the growing chaos in Greenwich. First, Barry Hartop, the director of Millennium Central quit, to be replaced by Jennie Page, chairman of the Millennium Commission, who all agreed was formidable, and according to a work colleague was 'autocratic'.

The future of the Dome was supposed to have been secured by a cross-party agreement several months before the general election, between President of the Board of Trade Heseltine, and the Labour leadership. Shadow Chancellor Brown flatly refused to spend taxpayers' money on the project. A deal was done in Blair's office at Westminster committing an incoming Labour government to the Dome, but without public spending; Mandelson was privy to the deal. But as the election neared, fresh doubts surfaced. Work on the site continued, but politically the great idea more or less ran out of steam. It was on hold for three weeks after the election, until Blair finally made up his mind at an ad hoc meeting with Prescott. He had previously talked it over with Mandelson, who was keen to take over responsibility. On 20 June 1997 he was given the job and also the sole government 'share' in the scheme. He was jubilant: 'It will provide a window to the future, who we are, how we live and what the future holds for us.' His Dome would be 'the biggest, most thrilling, most thought-provoking experience anywhere on the plant'.

Once the die was cast, Mandelson moved quickly. Into trouble. Uproar greeted the disclosure on 25 June that Mandy had personally sanctioned Labour's first 'fat cat' by confirming a £500,000-plus package for Ms Page. The deal had been worked out in secret between Labour and the Tories just 24 hours before polling-day. She would be paid £150,000 a year for three years – substantially more than Sir Robin Butler, head of the civil service and Cabinet secretary – plus a £67,500 contribution to her pension fund and a £45,000 'success fee' if the Dome opened on time. Heseltine's involvement with the project secured bipartisan backing for the generous pay package, making it impossible for the Tories to attack Labour for getting so swiftly into the fat-cat business.

But new controversy piled on top of old. A week after Ms Page's golden opportunity was disclosed, Mandelson was in trouble again, this time over his award of a £9 million fund-raising contract to the Mark McCormack sponsorship agency (some reports put to the value of the contract three times higher).

Mandelson had to move quickly to defuse the row, insisting that IMG, the sports agent's firm, would receive only 6 per cent commission on its contract to raise £150 million in sponsorship from private firms. The limit to his generosity did not impress MPs, some of whom were 'considerably unhappy' about the deal. Their tempers did not improve when Mandelson hired Maurice and Charles Saatchi, the advertising agency that had handled John Major's re-election bid, to promote the Dome – at a cost of £16 million. Naturally, the Saatchi brothers, who were best known for the 'Labour isn't working' slogan that did so much to get Margaret Thatcher elected in 1979, were absolutely thrilled. They hoped to sell a great many millennium T-shirts and baseball caps, and they would get their hands on a very large advertising campaign on TV and radio and in the newspapers. They were also promised a £2.5 million fee, depending on how many million people visited the greatest show on earth. Assuming they come in their millions.

Mandelson had no public anxieties, but his old boss at LWT, Bruce Anderson, was scathing about his former gofer's prospects of success. 'The Brute', as he is cheerfully known, warned Mandy to beware, lest he overreach himself in attempting to emulate his largely forgotten grandfather. When the public realised that the government was spending hundreds of millions of pounds on temporary buildings 'merely to gratify one politician's vanity' and enable him to rival his grandfather's achievements, the mood might turn angry. 'Grandfather-worship has never been an acceptable motive in British politics,' he admonished. 'The Greenwich Dome may not even be completed on time, and will undoubtedly cost much more than the estimates. If Mr Mandelson is not careful, his political reputation may have been buried before the Millennium celebrations even begin – under a building that will surely be known as Mandelson's Folly.'[2] Fresh embarrassment came from the disclosure that Clare Short, the international development secretary, had described the Dome as 'a silly temporary building' in a pre-election interview, and from a telephone poll for *The Jimmy Young Show* on BBC Radio 2 that showed public opinion running at 20 to 1 against the project.

Hard on the heels of the Saatchi announcement came a writ from the Gwent offices of German company Koch Hightech, which originally been given the £8 million contract to build the skin of the dome. The firm, a leader in its field, had offered to build the entire Dome in glass fibre. This option was rejected by the government on cost grounds, a PVC-covered fabric being the preferred choice. The new version immediately ran into trouble from environmentalists, who claimed that such an enormous expanse of PVC would be harmful. Greenpeace labelled the Dome a 'toxic plastic throwaway monster'. So the government changed its mind yet again. At a cost of £14 million – more than double the original estimate – Mandelson ordered a Teflon-coated glass fibre skin from a Japanese-owned American company, Birdair, a leading rival of the German firm. Koch Hightex immediately claimed £2 million compensation for work already done under the cancelled deal, and rejected a first offer of £600,000. The company accused ministers of being in such a hurry to stave off criticism from Greenpeace that it abandoned plans for a cheaper PVC structure. Mandelson, who held two meetings with Greenpeace to avert possible protests, sought to gloss over the controversy by insisting that the new, eco-friendly version would last longer, and might be dismantled and go on tour. His latest intervention earned him the nickname of 'the Merlin of the Millennium' from the *Guardian* which said it almost defied understanding: 'It's as if Mr Mandelson cannot help himself, rendered helpless by his twin urges to generate controversy and steal the last shreds of Conservative clothing.'

Relative calm settled over the venture during the party conference season, but in November Mandelson was back in the news as the pivotal figure in a £1 million donation to Labour from business tycoon Robert Earl, owner of the London restaurant Planet Hollywood. The Dome appeared in the background. Earl gave Labour the money it needed after the party was obliged to return a £1 million pre-election gift to Formula One motor-racing chief Bernie Ecclestone. It emerged that, after giving the money, Ecclestone had secured an exemption for motor-racing from government plans to ban tobacco sponsorship. When Earl was asked how he came to his decision to give the money, he said his initial contact with Labour had been through advising Mandelson on the Dome. He had concluded that the government was dynamic, honest and absolutely committed to creating a new and better society for Britain. Another first for Mandy's network.

Soon after, he was called before the Commons Culture Committee to lift the veil of secrecy surrounding what was actually going to go in the Dome. Controversy had shifted from construction to contents. At his interrogation on 2 December, Mandelson did not give much away. In a written submission, he claimed that the Dome experience would be a spectacular and emotional performance combining live action, multi-media and special effects . . . an adventure story based on the theme of time. The Dome's outer ring would contain 'vast three-dimensional objects' featuring the latest in 'multi-media environments'. The cutting edge of thinking and research would be brought together to create the most ambitious single exhibition ever conceived, he said. Behind this boastful psychobabble there was little detail. One of the 'zones' in the outer ring would be devoted to 'work, rest and play', with one section called 'Qualify for 20 jobs you never knew existed' and another given over to Surfball, 'the new twenty-first-century sport' that would particularly appeal to young people.

The committee was not impressed. They wanted more and better particulars, especially on where the private sponsorship money was coming from. He refused to go further, preferring to blame the Conservatives: 'When we came in, although there were lots of ideas spinning round, it was very much a blank sheet.' Despite their misgivings, the committee said in a report later that month that the Dome was 'magnificent in conception and likely to be breathtaking in execution'. It would be an indelible creative statement by Britain to the world, and a boost to the British economy. Mandelson passionately agreed with them. 'The last thing I want to be is bashful in presenting to the world the contents of what will be the greatest show on earth in the year

2000,' he wrote in the *Evening Standard*. The small question of the money was simply a matter of time. He did not quote the same report's fears that the Millennium Experience might turn out to be 'not so much a journey through as . . . a journey into the unknown.'[3]

However, there was a danger that he would begin to look like a Minister without Ideas. So Mandelson decided on the bold strategy of a high-profile VIP visit early in the New Year to Disneyworld and the Epcot (Experimental Prototype Community of Tomorrow) Center in the USA. With reporters trailing breathlessly in his wake, Mandy ignored barbs about the Dome becoming a Mickey Mouse enterprise. Ushered past hour-long queues, he braved the aptly named Tower of Terror, in which visitors are dropped at what seems terminal velocity. 'I enjoyed it, really,' he told sceptical journalists. He sailed through an alligator swamp, was sneezed on by a huge shaggy dog, and was drenched in virtual sarcasm by a virtual Jay Leno in a virtual television studio. He carefully avoided being photographed with anything to do with Mickey Mouse, and he dismissed the fake British pub as 'not very cool Britannia'.

Mandelson had come to see how the professionals did it. Walt Disney's masterpiece attracts 23 million people a year, 2 million of them British. But it took a quarter of a century to achieve that, in an American holiday state with myriad other attractions, not in a traffic-snarled corner of south-east London. Even with this expertise, it had taken the company five years to make a success of the Paris Disneyland, yet Mandelson was still claiming that he could get 12 million visitors in the year 2000. There was a risk that the Dome would attract the jokey title given to a printing plant in Glasgow: 'Disnae Land' – because 'this disnae work, and neither dis that'.

At Epcot Mandelson's minders had to prise him away from an interactive computer experience. He also held talks with Judson Green, president of Disneyworld, while an official of the company shook his head in disbelief at the scale of media interest in the visit. 'We had some newspaper stories about this dome faxed over to us,' he said. 'Until this weekend I had never heard of him.'

Mandelson carefully laid on a choice morsel for the press. He revealed that a huge androgynous figure the height of Nelson's column – 150 feet – would dominate the big tent's interior. It would sit with one leg outstretched and the other bent at the knee. The minister had seen something similar in Florida: a high-speed train ride through an 'inside the body show'. He had reckoned without Disney's famous protectiveness over its copyright. An executive of the company warned that Mandy should not steal any ideas from Florida, warning: 'He may be a minister of the British government, but we are the Walt Disney Corporation, and we don't roll over for anyone.'

He had scarcely got off the plane home before another body-blow hit the project. On 9 January 1998, it was announced that Stephen Bayley, the distinguished designer hired to mastermind the interior of the dome, had quit. After six months of arguments, Bayley, a founder of the Design Museum, had had enough. He had clashed repeatedly with Mandelson about what should go in the Dome, and how it should be marketed. Now, Mandy's trip to Disney World evidently proved the final straw. In departure, Bayley was savage. 'If Mandy went down to a voodoo sacrifice in Brixton tonight, he'd come back tomorrow saying "We must have voodoo sacrifices in the Dome",' he said. 'The whole way in which it is being run is pure East Germany. I get memos talking about the "creative task force". It's awful . . . and absolutely scary.' He had no confidence in the management delivering the millennium idea, and feared it might turn out to be 'crap'. Bayley admitted that he had tried to resign three months previously, over a proposal to create fluffy white koala bears wearing Union Jacks. The New Millennium Experience Company had included the flags 'because they didn't want to have Mandy having to answer to truculent pensioners in Cheltenham', he added. The whole job could have been done for £40 million, or at most £100 million, for a world-class event, instead of £758 million, Bayley declared. His resignation was a serious embarrassment to the artistic credibility of the enterprise, but Mandelson played it in his usual dismissive way. The usual 'close sources' said he had met Bayley only once and played down his role as insignificant.

The media had a field day with 'tyrant' and 'dictator Mandelson' headlines, forcing the minister out of his corner. He used the Press Association news agency to put out a characteristic denial. 'I have not been a dictator, but I have been decisive and I have got a grip on a project that was suffering from drift,' he said. Yet he had been in charge for almost nine months, and if there had been 'drift' it had taken place under his direction. The project was 'firmly on track', he insisted. But controversy abounded. Sir Terence Conran, chosen by Mandelson as a creative consultant, said there was no place for Jesus Christ in the Dome, despite the minister's assurances to Church leaders that Christianity would figure prominently. On 15 January, the project took another propaganda hit. Eric Sorensen, the £97,500-a-year chief executive of the Millennium Commission, resigned only ten months into a four-year contract, complaining that he had too little to do since Mandelson took charge. He denied any personality clash with the minister, but insiders said he was fed up at being shut out.

Just as it looked as if the wheels were coming off the project, it was announced that Mandelson would double the time he gave to answering questions about the Dome in the Commons: instead of five minutes, MPs would get ten. The new arrangement was agreed following talks between Labour business managers and the Opposition. It also came after MPs complained that he had spent only eleven minutes at the Despatch Box at Westminster since the election almost nine months before. One issue immediately offered itself for questions. On a top-level visit to Toyko, Tony Blair invited Japanese firms to get involved in the Dome. In return for putting up sponsorship money – sums of up to £12 million were mentioned – big corporations could show off their hi-tech innovations. The names of Toyota, Sony, Nissan and Toshiba were bandied around, and Mandelson beat the Japanese drum vigorously. Firms like Toyota, he said, 'are part of the British way of life'. The Opposition was dumbfounded, claiming that the whole scheme was now open to ridicule. It had been a bad fortnight for Mandy and his great show. The project lurched from resignation to bad publicity and back again. He could still not identify the cash sponsors, nor the contents. The *Sun*, a consistent critic of the Dome remarked, 'A one-man band running a complex of £780 million project has disaster written all over it.'

It was time for something big. On 17 January Mandelson hit back at the sceptics with a sneak preview of the Dome contents. He even invoked the name of the late Princess Diana in an upbeat assessment of the scheme that might help the nation start on an upward course. Promises of £120 million sponsorship money had been collected, he insisted, though no firm had actually signed on the dotted line. Tickets for the show would cost about £15. There would be nine exhibition areas, based on abstract outlines: Who We Are – split into mind, body and spirit; Where We Live – local, national and global; and What We Do – work, rest and play. And, oh, the genitalia-free human body might only be 75 feet high.

MPs were still not impressed. When he answered Dome questions on 19 January, he faced criticisms from all sides, including his own backbenchers, for refusing to publish financial information. He stonewalled demands from Labour left-winger Diane Abbot, who reminded him that it was 'the people's Dome, and the people's money'. And put down Norman Baker, a Lib Dem MP rapidly becoming a thorn in his side, with a lofty dismissal of his claim that the code of ministerial conduct was being broken. The *Daily Telegraph* noted that he left the chamber with a 'supremely satisfied smile'. He was now the smirk of firm government. The following week, he and Michael Heseltine fended off an Opposition onslaught in a special debate on the Dome. The former deputy prime minister hinted strongly that he had suggested Mandelson for the job of sorting out the Millennium. The minister himself came out with a quote of the week: 'If we fail to deliver it, we will never be forgiven, and if it succeeds it will never be forgotten.' Nevertheless, an opinion poll carried out by CAFOD, a Catholic overseas aid agency, found that nine out of ten people believed that the Dome should not be built, and that the money should be spent on the health service, crime prevention, public transport or protecting the environment.

Before his big launch of the Dome exhibition in late February, Mandelson lifted the veil of secrecy on finance ever so slightly. In an article in *Progress*, his friend Derek Draper's magazine, the minister insisted that none of the £758 million cost would be borne by the taxpayer. 'At least £200 million will come from the National Lottery via the Millennium Commission, *twice that if inflation and contingencies demand it*' (author's italics). This was an extraordinary admission, contained in a magazine for the Labour chattering classes. It was an open-sesame for cost overruns, for which the construction industry is notorious. If the funds of the National Lottery could be pillaged in this way, what chance would there be of commercial discipline? Unkind spirits also suggested that business sponsorship was looking shaky. On 16 February, it was reported that British Telecom was on the brink of withdrawing its £12 million investment, on the grounds that the company had insufficient say in how the cash would be used. 'We want something for our bucks,' said a senior BT source.[4] It also emerged that the appeal for Japanese business sponsorship had fallen on deaf ears.

But there was one encouraging sign for Mandelson: his bitterest critic on the Dome – the *Sun* – was about to switch sides. New Labour fiercely lobbied the paper's executives behind the scenes in a bid to get the paper on-side, and the first hint of a U-turn almost as dramatic as its decision to support Tony Blair came on 17 February. In a leader, the paper said the Dome had all the making of 'the biggest white elephant of this or any other country'. But it further noted, 'Sadly, the Dome has passed the point where it could be scrapped without huge loss of face – and money – for the government.' Here was the first evidence of a spectacular public relations coup. He certainly needed it. At a secret meeting with the Opposition Culture Department team on 17 February, he failed to persuade the Tories to stop criticising the Dome. Shadow culture secretary Francis Maude said Mandelson had admitted the project was on 'a knife-edge' and begged for a moratorium on criticism to avoid putting off business sponsors. Maude scorned the appeal, saying, 'Why should I come to the aid of the most controversial minister in the government?'

The minister without portfolio had such a hard ride at his question time on 16 February, when he authoritatively denied that BT was pulling out of the project, that one Labour MP protested to the Speaker about the lack of balance in the questions. The Dome had few friends in the House, but Mandelson hit back with a new line-up of luvvies and experts, including the black actress and children's TV presenter Floella Benjamin, who would advise on the exhibition. This unpaid 'Litmus Group' would ensure both popular appeal and intellectual bite. He was less successful in maintaining his grip over the creative direction. Mandelson wanted Alan Yentob, the BBC's director of television, to succeed Stephen Bayley, but the appointment was blocked by Dome board members led by Michael Grade, former head of Channel Four, who had emerged as the *de facto* 'creative supremo', *The Times* reported. His success was seen as a blow for Mandy and his 'River Café crowd', including film-maker Lord (David) Puttnam and Yentob. Mandelson's troubles were not over. In a *Panorama* interview, Lord Rogers, Labour peer and architect of the Dome, said the project was rudderless and Mandelson was not the right man to be in charge. Francis Maude called on the prime minister to sack him.

In the face of all these pressures, Mandelson remained resolute. He was buoyed up by the final defection of the *Sun* from the ranks of the Dome's critics. On the eve of the unveiling of the exhibition, with consummate timing, the paper repeated that the project had passed the point of no return. 'Griping about it will achieve nothing. Instead, we should all get behind it and ensure its success,' urged the leading article.[5] This was a huge fillip for the project, secured by Mandelson's networking skills. The *Sun* even renamed one of its reporters 'Mandy Millennium corre-spondent', on the lines of its Lenny Lottery stunt.

The unveiling in Morrison's Festival Hall played to mixed reviews. The Dome would now have twelve zones, and the project had so far secured £60 million from private sponsors, including

British Airways, Tesco, BSkyB, Manpower and BAA the airports operator. Tony Blair said it would be an international landmark, the envy of the world and the best day out on earth. The newly converted *Sun* thought it was 'dazzling . . . a great advert for Britain'. The *Sport* said it was 'bollocks', for once in tune with the art critic of the *Daily Telegraph*, who called it a pseudo-experience dreamed up by a marketing man to fill an empty tent and so gratify the vanity of Peter Mandelson; he begged the people to boycott the Dome. The *Guardian* thought the exhibition lacked a connecting idea, and offered Britishness. The paper also tracked down an interesting quote in the *Hartlepool Mail*. Responding to criticism that he was obsessed with making a success of the Dome because his grandfather never got sufficient recognition for the Festival of Britain, Mandy said, 'People have assumed I am trying to do now for the country what my grandfather did then and that's not correct. I don't see it in those personal terms.' What is also not true is that he had a consistent view of the links between 1951 and 2000. Sometimes, as a few months later, he became misty-eyed at will on the relationship with Morrison; at other times, as now, he was dismissive. The tap of affection could be turned on and off at his convenience. It is a strange way to relate to others – not uniquely Mandelsonian, but very much in character.

When the dust had settled, a Gallup poll for the *Daily Telegraph* showed that Mandelson had not moved the people's hearts. Of those polled 98 per cent said that Lottery money should be spent on something other than the dome. Only one in five said they would visit Greenwich – less than half the figure recorded in the year prior to the Festival of Britain. However, when asked if it would work 60 per cent of respondents thought it probably be all right in the end. Six weeks later, a separate poll in the *Independent on Sunday* found that nine out of ten people would not pay £17.50 to visit the Dome. Middle-class people were three times more likely to go than working-class people, and the project was most popular with the 35–44 age group.[6] Mandy kept up his discreet media pressure, lecturing BBC radio and television news editors at Westminster on how to cover his project.

In the meantime, the German firm Koch Hightech launched a second high court action, claiming £2.3 million compensation for materials bought, time spent and loss of profit on its aborted contract. This was on top of the existing lawsuit for £1.3 million.

Nor did it look as thought the British genius of invention was living up to the high hopes of the minister without portfolio. A panel of experts searching for two thousand new British designs to grace the Dome found only 202 by June 1998 – a mere eighteen months before it was due to open. Among the products were a lavatory, a pedal-powered taxi and a new type of duvet that made it easier to change the bed – hardly the cutting edge of intellectual bite promised earlier. Most of the ideas were rejected out of hand. Stephen Bayley, the former creative director, predicted that the Design Council would fail to meet its target.

Then it emerged that Camelot, the National Lottery operators, had offered to sell tickets for the Dome without charge. Since there are hundreds of thousands of convenient Lottery outlets, used by millions of people, this was obviously a very useful development. But hadn't Camelot fallen out of favour with the government for its fat-cat profiteering at the expense of the punters and good causes? Might not their readiness to do the government a favour have something to do with getting back in its good books in time for the renewal of their licence to run a highly profitable business? Camelot's ticket offer, plus a proposal to give business sponsorship, raised the broader issue of relations between big-money Dome sponsors and the government. Were they looking for favours? BAA and British Aerospace both wanted a fifth terminal at Heathrow airport. The plane-makers had a deep commercial involvement in the European Fighter Aircraft, which depended on state investment. BT had lobbied hard to minimise the impact of the windfall tax. Tesco had an interest in government policy on the siting of supermarkets. In the modern economy, business and public policy go hand in hand, and here were some of the country's biggest companies joining hands with New Labour to fund Mandelson's dream. Commentators were quick to point out the dangers of 'sleaze', though Matthew Parris of *The Times* was ahead of the times with his accusation of 'cronyism'. The cash conjunction of the government's friends and the Dome looked, at the very least, embarrassingly friendly, and likely to arouse scepticism about Tony Blair's insistence that New Labour had to be squeaky-clean.

The Dome roof was virtually complete by 22 June, and the prime minister was there to top the project off with a thick layer of superlatives. With Mandelson and John Prescott alongside him, Blair promised a startling and exhilarating success for 'the most famous building in the world in the year 2000'. Mandy went one stage further, comparing it to the Eiffel Tower. That was only a temporary structure, but it was still there, and the Dome would be there for 'many, many years to come'. Among the uses suggested were an Olympic stadium (though this could only be once in a hundred years), a conference centre (though few conferences take up a site twice the size of Wembley stadium, which seats 100,000) and a nebulous 'world university for children'.

Mandelson was unputdownable. At Dome question time on 29 June, he rhapsodised about the commercial benefits of the project. Financially conservative estimates suggested that overseas visitors would spend between £300 million and £500 million on the Millennium Experience. 'The true amount could be double that – £1 billion could be the economic halo effect for Britain,' he said, and he was 'very confident' of reaching the private sponsorship target by the end of the year.[7]

He seemed to have everything in hand. A month later, after the Dollygate 'cash for access' scandal which exposed lobbyists' links with New Labour, the minister without portfolio was asked by a critical Labour backbencher, Gordon Prentice, whether he used lobbying organisations to promote and secure funding for the Dome and its contents. Mandelson replied that the New Millennium Experience Company was responsible for sponsorship, and had not employed lobbying organisations for that or any other purpose.

Prentice was not satisfied: 'I expect a more illuminating reply from a minister who casts such a long shadow.' He observed that

Mandelson had said in a written answer that he never addressed meetings organised by lobbyists. Yet the *Independent* had reported on 9 July that the minister would be briefing clients of GPC Market Access, a fact confirmed by the *Observer* on 12 July. 'Why are those meetings held off the record under Chatham House rules,' asked Prentice. 'What does the minister say privately that he will not say publicly? Will he invite me along to one of those meetings and, if not, why not?' A tetchy Mandelson told the Commons, 'In so far as that question relates to the millennium dome, I can confirm that I neither procure nor negotiate sponsorship for it, and that I certainly do not use the services of any lobbying organisation for that purpose'. Prentice's purpose was clear: he was anxious to establish the degree to which Mandelson could be linked to the cash-for-access affair. Derek Draper, the extrovert lobbyist employed by GPC Market Access whose claims about political influence triggered the scandal, was Mandelson's assistant for several years leading up to the general election. They were still firm friends. The Dome was an oblique point of entry to the controversy, but a useful one even though it turned out to be a dead end.

Amid fresh fears that the Jubilee Line extension would not be up to the mammoth task of ferrying tens of thousands of visitors to Greenwich every day, the minister without portfolio took responsibility for the Dome with him to his new post as secretary of state for trade and industry in late July 1998. Perhaps he had in mind Disraeli's wry observation a century and a half earlier that the 1851 Great Exhibition would be 'a boon for the government, for it will make the public forget its misdeeds'. This was long before the days of universal suffrage, when the public can punish their political masters. What a difference a century makes. In 1951, the year of the Festival of Britain, the Labour government of Herbert Morrison lost power, and it remained in the wilderness for thirteen years.

Perhaps the most accurate assessment to date came from awkward-squad Labour MP Austin Mitchell: 'I am sure that nobody has a better chance of making a success of it than you, and nobody of telling us it has been a success if it isn't.'

There was some competition for that prize. Whatever else failed to happen on time, there was no shortage of critics to tell Mandelson what a miserable hash he was making of the Dome. In a well-timed squib, Stephen Bayley wrote that New Labour had hijacked the millennium as 'a political advertisement' for itself, and though a big advertising sell will probably pull in the required millions of visitors to make it a 'success', the real tragedy of the Dome is the lost opportunity. 'The man responsible for hijacking a project that could have been one of the great international world exhibitions but is instead going to be a crabby and demoralising theme park, is Peter Mandelson.' The difference between 2000 and 1851, he argued, is that then 'the philistines were on the outside, today it's the other way around. The Millennium Tent is a political advertisement full of what Auberon Waugh calls "patronising rubbish".'[8]

12

INTERESTING FRIENDS, FUNNY FRIENDS

I t was a gala social occasion, of sorts. The good and the would-be-great gathered in the Cupola Room of Kensington Palace for an evening reception in late 1989, hosted by the Prince of Wales. Peter Mandelson, shortly to become the Labour prospective parliamentary candidate for Hartlepool, was among the guests. So was Frances Morrell, one-time political adviser to Tony Benn and ex-leader of the Inner London Education Authority. They were both introduced to Prince Charles by Tom Shebbeare, director of the Prince's Trust and Mandelson's contemporary at the British Youth Council.

The ostensible purpose of their presence was to advance the work of the Speaker's Commission on Citizenship, in which the Prince's Trust was involved. That well-meaning initiative is long forgotten. Mandelson and the Prince are not. 'There was a real rapport,' recollects Shebbeare. 'By this time, Peter had very much been heard of, and Prince Charles is always interested in meeting people. He wants to meet everybody. There was a good rapport.'[1]

Yet Labour's ace spin-doctor and former Young Communist was not averse to criticising the royal family – including the Prince of Wales – when it suited him. In his column for the *People*, and in the leader pages of *The Times*, Mandelson could be seriously bitchy. He once described Prince Charles as 'suspended in a half-committed, half-thought-out, half-professional limbo.'[2] Yet the Prince of Wales seemed to have discovered a soft spot for Mandy. Not long after the successful Monmouth by-election in the late spring of 1991, he was introduced to a Labour Party press officer, Lesley Smith, and jested about 'the red rose man' making a comeback.

Mandelson's natural instinct was to get closer to the royal family, as the ultimate extension of his network. If it could work with everyone else, why not the Windsors? In time, his self-appointed role as royal courtier would bring allegations of dragging the royal family into politics, and using them for Labour's purposes. For the time being, he simply talked himself into the royal orbit, using his *People* column. Immediately after the 1992 general election, he told readers that 'it must be great for the Queen to have all those honours to dish out – it means never having to say Sorry.'[3] It wasn't much of a joke. He got more serious a month later, arguing for a slimmed-down monarchy. Mandelson was upset about Andrew Morton's forthcoming book that took the lid off the loveless marriage of the Prince and Princess of Wales. The royal family, he argued, should not discuss their marital affairs with authors. They no longer played as a team, and the solution lay in dropping most of them. 'A slimmed down royal firm should be retained consisting of just two people – the Queen and her heir, accompanied by their partners on certain occasions.'[4] And he condemned suggestions that the Queen was considering paying income tax. 'Respect can't be bought – not even with a fortune as large as the Queen's,' he blustered.[5]

All good knockabout stuff for a tabloid columnist. Mandelson soon changed his tune, however. He was outraged by the publication of intimate telephone conversations between Princess Diana and a male friend, and between Prince Andrew and the

Duchess of York. Anyone who bought a 20-foot radio aerial and spent over £1,000 on a radio scanner was 'going with intent to eavesdrop', he argued. 'The public is going to demand that these people are treated in a similar way to those who go equipped to burgle.'[6] As noted earlier, he was even more gushing about the fate of the royal yacht, about which he claimed to have had his own intimate conversation with the Queen on her visit to Hartlepool.

But it was not until Labour swept into power on 1 May 1997 that Mandelson could really begin to exploit his contacts with the royal family. Once again, the intermediary was their mutual friend, Tom Shebbeare. 'We decided they should meet following the Labour victory,' Shebbeare remembers. 'I reminded him [Prince Charles] about Peter Mandelson. My words would have been something like "Don't believe everything you read in the Press. He is a very supportive person", and very well placed to give advice'.[7] He recollects them meeting again in May or June, very soon after Labour took office.

Then it was the tragedy of Princess Diana's death that confirmed Mandelson's role as royal confidant. He was a key player in the contacts between Downing Street and Buckingham Palace, out of which emerged the indestructible myth of 'the People's Princess'. More to the point, New Labour gained powerful leverage over a royal family torn by conflicting loyalties and prey to the argument that they had to 'modernise' or face extinction. The parallels with the Labour Party and Mandelson's role do not need further emphasis. The Queen ended up with her own spin-doctor, Simon Lewis, appointed in the summer of 1998 at a salary of £230,000 a year (mostly paid by his old firm Centrica, the holding firm for British Gas, on whose payroll he remains). Respect, it seems, might be bought after all. Mandelson played a backstage role in the appointment. He is friendly with Mark Boland, the Prince of Wales's media adviser, and has other friends at court.

Royalty ranks as his most high-profile act of networking, but his links with the business and social worlds are more rewarding. On one level, of course, it's just fun. Mandy is *such* a relentless partygoer. When the row over political lobbying by his old Labour cronies was at its height on 9 July 1998, where was the minister without portfolio? He was escorting his 'good friend' Princess Margaret to a majestic lunch party in Mayfair, thrown by Drue Heinz, widow of 'Jack' Heinz, the baked-bean billionaire.[8] His tastes are as inclusive as his politics. When the Demos think-tank was launched at the National Theatre, he just had to be there, rubbing shoulders with Labour and Tory luminaries, and guests like Anita Roddick from the Body Shop. Naturally, he has also been noticed at Jamie Palumbo's fashionable disco, the Ministry of Sound, a converted warehouse near the Elephant and Castle where the young things dance the night away. For young Palumbo, son of the architect Lord (Peter) Palumbo, it is a £15 million business.

Sometimes the friends are a real help. Remember it was Palumbo Jr who loaned Mandelson a chauffeur-driven car in the run-up to the 1997 general election. 'You know how you just meet someone and you just click,' Palumbo offered later. 'I thought it was just absurd that someone like him should have to drive himself. It seems a bit mad: dangerous.'[9]

Mandelson's network extends deep into the New Establishment, the shifting, glamorous world of business, television, newspapers, advertising and politics, that is so much at home under New Labour. He was an early favourite of Lady Carla Powell, the Italian socialite wife of Baroness Thatcher's top adviser in Downing Street, Sir Charles Powell. Mandy was a house-guest of Lady Carla while his new £500,000 pad in Notting Hill was being done up in his favourite 'meticulous and soulless style'. He met her on a plane to Prague in May 1996 as he travelled to a conference organised by the *National Review*, an American right-wing weekly. They hit it off immediately, and the gossips say that rarely have a pair of such enormous egos graced the same dinner table. Mandy is a constant guest for Sunday lunch.

Consorting with the Powells is not as politically shocking as first sight would suggest. Sir Charles's brother Jonathan, a former diplomat in the British embassy in Washington, is Blair's chief of staff, while his other brother, Chris, is head of the advertising agency BMP DDB Needham, which handled Labour's account. More dismaying for Labour supporters is the fact that on Mandelson's trip to Prague, he applauded Baroness Thatcher's speech and then had lunch with her at the British embassy. Even *The Times* noticed his 'rank opportunism and ideological flexibility'.

Mandy's inclusiveness also takes in Howell James, political secretary to Prime Minister John Major until 1 May 1997. The two evidently talk often on the telephone about the important things of life – art, music, food and politics – and enjoy a close friendship. James, a former corporate affairs director of Cable & Wireless, shuns the limelight, even though he, too, emerged from the television stable. He was head of press and publicity at TVam in the early eighties, when it was at an all-time ratings low. The station's fortunes were magically restored by a cartoon character, prompting James to say he was press officer to Roland Rat. James then moved on to the BBC as corporate affairs director, before joining Major's political office.

When it comes to friends in high places, Mandelson is carefree about political affiliations. He is equally happy spending quality leisure time with Shaun Woodward, former editor of the TV programme *That's Life* and now a rising Tory MP. Another journalist, the columnist Anne McElvoy, was rather ungallantly described as Mandy's leading dance-floor dolly. Certainly, he astounded those who saw his snake-hipped jiving at a Labour Party conference dance in 1997.

Rather more controversial is Mandy's close friendship with Elisabeth Murdoch, boss of BSkyB and daughter of the newspaper mogul Rupert Murdoch. As trade secretary, Mandelson is obliged to rule on company mergers and takeovers, a role with substantial potential for conflict of interest. Mandy was not always Rupie's pal. In January 1994, he wrote scathingly of the Australian-born magnate, 'If Murdoch cannot be beaten – and there are many who believe that his media holdings need to be cut down to size – we should encourage more British media companies to grow, compete and give Mr Murdoch a harder run for his mega-bucks.'[10] These days, however, Mandelson is talked of as a 'semi-permanent fixture' at Ms Murdoch's luxury home in Kingston. Dinner guests say he behaves like the master of the house, though this may just be his natural sense of authority. It was cruelly pointed out in *Punch* that there could be no question of a sexual relationship with his society and business belles, 'but his fondness for powerful women is such that he has been described as the original "hag fag".' With American pungency, Rupert Murdoch put it more succinctly to *Observer* editor Will Hutton in the autumn of 1997. 'Peter's easy,' said the great man. 'He's a star-fucker.'

Naturally, he also enjoys the company of powerful men. Sir Dennis Stevenson, boss of the Pearson Group, which owns among other baubles the *Financial Times*, has been one of Mandy's best friends ever since their days in youth politics. He gave Mandelson a job at his consultancy firm, SRU, when he needed gainful employment after leaving his Labour Party job. Stevenson (ranked 12 in the *Observer* POWER 300 list) was later invited into the New Labour establishment, and headed a study on new technology in schools. Reputedly, he was offered parliamentary seats by both Labour and the Tories, which makes him Mandy-inclusive. Stevenson once observed of Mandelson, 'He is a close friend, but it has nothing to do with politics.'

Mandy's network is as enduring as it is comprehensive. Contacts he made almost twenty years ago at LWT are still bearing fruit. Top of the 'television luvvies' list is Sir John Birt, who was a producer on *Weekend World* when Mandelson was graduating from pouring the drinks for guests. The two formed a close friendship, going on walking holidays in Tuscany together. The alliance proved controversial in November 1998, when BBC chiefs banned their staff and guests from mentioning Mandelson's sexuality on radio and television. Suggestions that there had been string-pulling were emphatically denied – and widely disbelieved.

It would only have been a pay-back. Birt has always been able to rely on Mandelson. In July 1992, he tabled amendments to a

Commons Motion on alleged business links between Birt and David Frost, who was transferring his top-ratings *Frost on Sunday* show from TVam to the BBC. Mandelson denounced the allegations as 'old, untrue and defamatory stories', echoing his old boss's words. The Frost show transferred as planned.

Then, in March 1993, it was revealed that Birt, the new £149,000-a-year director-general of the BBC, was paid not as a corporation employee but through his private company, John Birt Productions – and had been for six years. This was a device to minimise his tax liability. Powerful figures in the media world condemned the arrangement, and Sir Paul Fox, former managing director of BBC Television, called on the governors to 'do their duty' – that is, sack him. Sixty-four MPs signed a Commons Motion demanding his dismissal. But some of the BBC's top presenters lined up behind their chief. Mandelson lined up with them. He defended Birt and signed a letter to *The Times*, admitting that Birt had made 'an error of judgement' but warning that his resignation would be 'a tragedy' at a time when the BBC was going through a period of change. Fellow-signatories included Lady Howe, wife of Foreign Secretary Sir Geoffrey Howe, Margaret Jay (now Baroness Jay, Leader of the Lords) and Graham Mather, a Tory Europhile. Birt stayed.

The LWT network – some call it Labour Weekend Television – brings together a galaxy of New Labour stars. Greg Dyke, former chief executive of the station, is a long-standing party donor and took part in the secretive luvvies' campaign to secure the election of Tony Blair as Labour leader. So did Barry Cox, former director of corporate affairs at LWT. He hired Trevor Phillips, head of current affairs at the station. Mandelson met Phillips on his trip to Cuba in 1978, and they are still close. Mandy was best man at his wedding, and supported the campaign to draft Phillips as Labour's candidate for London's first directly elected mayor. Other leading figures in the New Establishment to emerge from LWT include Lord (Melvyn) Bragg, the former head of arts ennobled by Blair, and Sir Christopher Bland, an ex-chairman of the company, who is now on the Arts Council. Then there is Michael Wills, another former producer at *Weekend World*, an adviser to Gordon Brown when Mandelson was still in his circuit.

It is not surprising that a metropolitan television station with a strong interest in current affairs and the arts should have spawned so many brilliant operators. Independent television offered exciting, intelligent opportunities in the late seventies and early eighties. The significance lay in their long-term political agenda (and, for some, the desire to get seriously rich). Greg Dyke once identified 'a sort of LWT Legionnaires' disease' in the air-conditioning at South Bank. 'Nice, ordinary people come in here and go out crazed and power-hungry.'

Mandelson prides himself on having the most sophisticated, metropolitan and influential circle of friends. It is small wonder that he feels little need to add to them in provincial Hartlepool. But on his way to the top he also made some funny friends, in the sense of funny peculiar rather than funny-ha-ha.

In august 1997, when Mandelson had been a minister for less than four months, it was authoritatively disclosed that he had been targeted by MI5 during his politically militant youth. What is more, the interest of the internal security service had continued right up to 1992, the year he was elected an MP.

These astonishing revelations came from David Shayler, an intelligence officer with MI5 for six years until he quit, disillusioned, in the late spring of 1997. Writing in the *Mail on Sunday*, Shayler disclosed that MI5 had opened a file on Peter Mandelson in the late 1970s, while he was working at the TUC.

Shayler, a 31-year-old former journalist on the *Sunday Times*, said that Mandelson's telephone had been tapped for three years, 'to determine whether he was a threat to national security'. The investigation into his activities took place at the end of the seventies, when the last Labour government under James Callaghan became convinced the industrial unrest was being fomented by the extreme left. 'I saw his main file in the months leading up to the 1992 General Election,' wrote Shayler, 'and was appalled that the Service still had two thick volumes detailing Mandelson's telephone conversations from more than a decade earlier.' Had Labour won the 1992 election, he added, a security assessment of Mandelson would have ended up on the desk of the incoming Labour prime minister.

On the face of it, Mandelson was a prime suspect in the late seventies. He had been a member of the Young Communist League before going up to Oxford University in 1973, and here he was working in the nerve centre of the labour movement. He had also become heavily involved in the activities of the British Youth Council, a strongly political forum for young people, whose overseas work was funded by the Foreign Office. His involvement with the BYC was frowned upon by the TUC hierarchy for bureaucratic as well as political reasons. It was to prove the undoing of his job at Congress House.

In May 1977, Mandelson was elected chairman of the British Youth Council. The year before, the BYC had made 'a conspicuous effort' to establish relations with the – communist-dominated – youth organisations of Eastern Europe. A new committee, chaired by his former Oxford pal Dick (now Lord) Newby, was set up to forge links with Iron Curtain countries. The Youth Council had sent representatives to preparatory talks in Oslo and the Bulgarian capital, Sofia, for a European Youth and Students' Meeting, and had fielded a 'strong and broad delegation' of twenty young people to the conference itself in Warsaw in June 1976.

The Young Conservatives and the Scouts boycotted the event, but Youth Council leaders ploughed on regardless, sending representatives to a 'consultative meeting' of the World Federation of Democratic Youth, an international communist front, called in Balatonalamdi, Hungary, in March 1977. Their task was to discuss a proposed all-European Disarmament conference to be held later in Mandelson's chairmanship year.

The annual report of the BYC for the year in question also records exchange visits with the Committee of Youth Organisations of the Soviet Union. In October 1976, Sir Harold Wilson made the welcoming address to a BYC reception for 400 young visitors from the USSR in the foyer of the new National Theatre. There were further exchange visits with the Union of

Socialist Youth of Yugoslavia and the Union of Communist Youth of Romania. The Council also gave a dinner 'in honour' of Nicu Ceauşescu, son of the dictator Nicolae Ceauşescu, during his visit to Britain in September 1976. And shortly before he took over the chair of the BYC, Mandelson visited Havana, Cuba, in April 1977 as the Council's representative to the Third International Preparatory Meeting of the eleventh World Festival of Youth and Students. The conference itself was scheduled for the summer of 1978, in Havana. It was the first time the BYC had engaged in the work of this Soviet-bloc body, after withdrawing from the Western-orientated World Assembly of Youth (WAY). The WAY had been exposed as a CIA- and MI6-financed counter-organisation to Soviet youth fronts.

In the highly charged security atmosphere of the late seventies, Britain's 'secret state' of MI5 and MI6 saw the hidden hand of Soviet influence everywhere behind the growing unrest over Labour's tough incomes policy. So it was hardly surprising that suspicion should fall on the highly-active young officials at Congress House, who presided over a policy of rapprochement with Eastern-bloc youth movements – knowing that they were totally under the influence of their national Communist Parties – and who ducked back and forth across the Iron Curtain.

In his first set of revelations, David Shayler claimed that a telephone tap had been carried out on Mandelson in the late seventies. According to the MI5 file, which Shayler insisted he had seen, Mandelson had been a member of the Young Communist League (YCL) in 1972, 'joining the Communist Party of Great Britain a year later'. He was active in student politics at Oxford, Shayler continued, and his MI5 notes 'were full of titbits about his student days'.[11] Mandelson worked at the TUC in 1977 when he organised the British contingent to the World Democratic Youth Festival, in Chile that year.

'These occasions used to preoccupy the Foreign Office, which was obsessed with the idea that they were used by the Soviet Union to recruit fifth columnists to infiltrate British life,' wrote Shayler. 'A number of British students attended the Chilean meeting and all their names were sent back to MI5.' But it was Mandelson's 'status as an organiser' that marked him out for special attention. 'F2, the counter-subversive section of MI5, monitored his private telephone conversations to find out if he was a "sleeper" – a covert Soviet sympathiser. The telephone tap stayed in place for three years at astronomical cost. The resulting file contained transcripts of intimate telephone conversations. There were also articles he had written as a student *as well as copies of his membership cards from the CPGB and YCL from the early seventies'* (emphasis added).[12]

Shayler's sensational allegations – he disclosed that Home Secretary Jack Straw and Social Security Secretary Harriet Harman had also been the subject of MI5 surveillance at about the same time – made headline news everywhere. But there are some difficulties with his account. The BYC does not record Mandelson attending any event in Chile during 1977, and it beggars belief that he would have done so. The Marxist President Salvador Allende had been deposed and murdered in 1973, and the country was run for the next thirteen years by a right-wing junta headed by the brutal despot General Augusto Pinochet. It is inconceivable that any youth festival looked on kindly by Moscow would have been held there. Shayler's recollection of the file must have been shaky; he meant Cuba, not Chile.

Furthermore, Mandelson has always denied ever being a fully-fledged member of the Communist Party of Great Britain. He dismissed the *Mail on Sunday* allegations as 'a pure smear', though, as discussed below, it was custom and practice for the CP to expect Young Communists to become full party members when they turned 18. And there is other anecdotal evidence that he was issued with a card. Shayler, of course, claims he saw a copy of it.

Mandelson's would-be revolutionary activities are certain to have been under observation long before the MI5 surveillance began. With his school-friend Steve Howell, he quit the Labour Party Young Socialists to help beef up a YCL branch in Hendon, north London in 1972. Stephen Dorril, an expert on security affairs, comments, 'It is highly likely that there would have been a (police) Special Branch officer taking notes at these meetings, or at least an SB informer. Opening up a branch would have been much more significant and would probably have led the local Special Branch to send a note to Box 500 (i.e., MI5).

'MI5 opened files on all members of the CPGB and, as part of its bureaucratic procedures, required evidence that those targeted were members. However, it wasn't always possible and other material might be sufficient, but would probably need to be passed by an officer up the line. These bureaucratic procedures were, of course, there to protect the Service rather than the target.'[13]

The MI5 affair could not have come at a worse time for Mandelson, who was standing for the Labour Party National Executive Committee in elections due only six weeks after the story broke. He was furious with the secret-service rebel, who was stirring up long-forgotten indiscretions. He was on holiday at the time, and in no position to rebut the leaks in detail. It was of little help that Shayler condemned MI5's actions as 'inexcusable', since in the same breath he revealed that the Mandelson file remained 'amber' — i.e., in place — two years after the fall of communism when the security service still used such data as a reference point.

Mandelson was determined to give the lie to the allegation that his phone had been tapped, and demanded a face-to-face meeting with Stephen Lander, the head of MI5. It took place on 17 September, just ten days before polling for the NEC election ended. Lander, according to reports, assured Mandelson that his telephone had not been tapped for three years, as Shayler had claimed. The minister without portfolio made the best he could of this pledge, turning it into an apology. 'The important thing to me is not so much their apology, but their categorical statement that I was not bugged — because it would have been wrong and totally unjustified to have bugged me,' he said. 'I was not a subversive or a threat to national security. I was a teenager holding ordinary left-wing views.'[14] Ordinary? Communist views were not exactly ordinary. At best, there were 3,000 members of the YCL, perhaps one in a thousand of the teenage population.

Nor was MI5's assurance quite what it seemed. Stephen Lander admitted that Mandelson's file *did* include transcripts of calls he had made to other MI5 targets. This is a classic non-denial by the service. Stephen Dorril points out, 'This is standard practice. One person is named on the telephone tapping warrant as the target in the knowledge that others will be caught on tape. There is no reason to directly tap all potential targets. It is after all time consuming and expensive.'[15] Dorril believes that Lander is unduly economical with the truth.

Shayler was more robust, accusing his former employers of lying. He was on the run from the long arm of the secret state. Following the *Mail on Sunday* disclosures, the authorities were not slow to act. MI5 officers, past and present, owe a lifetime duty of confidentiality to the service. Shayler's revelations appeared to be a clear breach of that responsibility. Attorney-general John Morris set in train a criminal investigation, and Shayler disappeared across the English Channel. But he kept up the pressure in a letter to the *Guardian* on 27 September insisting, for the record, that he had seen Mandelson's personal file, 'and included in that summary, a record of the product from the intercept of Mr Mandelson's telephone'.

The following day, in an open letter to the prime minister from 'somewhere in Europe', he was even more emphatic. 'I know Mr Lander is not telling the truth,' he declared. 'I clearly remember that Mr Mandelson was the direct attack of an intercept because I reviewed his MI5 file.' Attached to the file was the original Home Office warrant authorising the phone-tap.[16]

To the paranoid eyes of the security services, Mandelson fitted the profile of a communist who had been instructed by Moscow to distance himself from the party – just like Kim Philby – the better to spy for his Soviet masters. To the suspicious minds of MI5 and the Foreign Office, despite moving into the political mainstream after university, he 'seemed to be taking on the role of a "sleeper".' And the more moderate he became in reality, explained Shayler, the more the suspicions mounted. 'It was within this atmosphere that in MI5 applied to the Home Office, when Merlyn Rees was Home Secretary, for the warrant to tap his phone.'[17]

According to the fugitive Shayler, what the transcripts showed, in fact, was that Mandelson was a devoted politician who spent most of his life as a moderate left-winger who put a considerable effort into trying to bring the extreme Left round to his viewpoint. 'This counted against him among his watchers because they interpreted it as cover for covert Communist activities,' wrote the former MI5 officer. However, there was no indication that he ever met a Soviet handler or any suggestion that he was trying to communicate with the Soviets. 'He did meet Soviet agents at public functions, but there was no evidence at all to show that he knew they were agents.'[18]

So why did MI5 keep up the surveillance for three years, during which time he left the TUC, and moved on from youth politics to the real thing, working for a member of Labour's shadow Cabinet? Shayler puts this down to 'drift', with the tap being renewed at the end of each warrant until the service 'finally came to its senses' in 1980 and cancelled the tap. His file was not closed at this point, however. Mandelson's final categorisation was '1977. Member: Communist'. Shayler argued that Mandelson was the subject of a classic guilt-by-association assessment by the secret state. 'There is no doubt in my mind that Peter Mandelson was totally innocent of MI5's suspicions,' he told the prime minister. 'It was neither morally nor financially justifiable for MI5 to invade his privacy.'[19]

But Shayler did allow one possible chink of light into the whole murky affair. He disclosed that the Foreign Office was aware that Mandelson was already displaying 'considerable political skills even in his early twenties in arranging the delegation to Cuba'. It could hardly be otherwise. The FO was funding the Cuban venture via the British Youth Council. In the FO's book, nothing could be more useful than a former communist like Peter Mandelson, a democratic socialist with the nerve to take on the Soviet bloc's apparatchiks at an international youth conference. The same would be true for MI6, responsible for counter-espionage abroad.

Stephen Dorril suggests that the British Youth Council was 'a useful place for talent-spotting and a vehicle for the Foreign Office which continued to finance it'. This would be true even after the Council's original links with the CIA and MI6 through its membership of the World Assembly of Youth had been blown in the late sixties. And whereas MI5 would be worried by Mandelson's trips to Cuba and Eastern bloc countries, 'the FO/M16 would have been pleased', seeing them as an opportunity to oppose the Soviet line. Was there, asks Dorril, author of an authoritative history of MI6, anything more to Mandelson's connections with the Foreign Office?[20]

It is important to distinguish nomenclature here, because most people and commentators get the terms wrong. In intelligence/ MI6 terms, an 'officer' is someone who is directly employed by the service. An 'agent' is someone in another organisation, or country, who may be run by the service, who can supply them with intelligence and may report direct to an officer. An 'asset' is someone who is of occasional use to the service, but without any formal arrangement – such as a journalist, a businessman or someone active in public service. 'It is possible', says Dorril, 'that Mandelson was recruited as a schoolboy to infiltrate the communists. It has been done before, but there is no evidence to back this up with Mandelson.'[21]

Traditionally, the most fruitful arrangement has been the 'agent of influence' – someone who operates in the interests of the service. The service (or its talent-spotters) identifies early on the likely candidates who may rise to important positions in politics and government. They are helped along the way. To complicate matters, agents and agents of influence may be recruited and run by third parties, who have no direct contact with the service. The classic example of this is the recruitment of leaders of the international student bodies in the fifties and early sixties. To complicate matters further, agents of influence may be unconscious of the service's interest shown in them, and it may never be made known to them. According to Stephen Dorril, 'If Mandelson was some kind of agent of influence, then he would have been spotted at university. *This is entirely possible*, because it seems that there was some kind of change in his first year at Oxford' (emphasis added).[22] Such a development would fit the known facts. Mandelson moved from the Communist Party to an orthodox social-democrat supporter of the United Nations and the European Economic Community (as it then was) in the months after he went up to university.

Naturally, Mandelson would like to see this embarrassing part of his life completely erased. He demanded that all MI5 files on 'subversives' created during the Cold War should be weeded out and destroyed, because they were 'entirely redundant'. His insistence merely fuelled Opposition interest in his secret past. In October 1997, Dr Julian Lewis, the Tories' witchfinder-general, put down a Commons Motion noting his activities in the YCL, dismissing his 'excuse' that these were ordinary left-wing views, deploring his demand for the destruction of Cold War files and urging the director-general of the security service to 'resist partisan and self-serving political pressure'. Home Secretary Jack Straw ignored the attack on his colleague, but promised not to destroy files of 'historical importance'. Shayler called for the Mandelson file to be shown to MPs.

In a Commons debate on 28 October, Dr Lewis compared the proposal to destroy the files to George Orwell's formula for 1984: 'Who controls the past controls the future. Who controls the present controls the past.' The Tory MP, a contemporary of Mandelson's at Oxford – where, as a Labour Moderate, he fought extremism in the party – put down a series of parliamentary questions designed to exploit the minister without portfolio's embarrassment. He received unsatisfactory replies from the home secretary, and concluded, 'If these files are destroyed, it can only fuel suspicion that the Labour government is seeking to rewrite history and cover up the shameful record of fellow-travellers at the height of our Cold War confrontation with Russia.'[23] He later elaborated: 'One day, when these files are opened, we will be able to see what some of these people were really up to, and those who call most loudly for files to be destroyed are obviously prime suspects as characters who know they have something to hide.[24]

Since Mandelson's greatest political interest was foreign affairs, it was certain that MI6 would also have had a file on him. That would make even more interesting reading. Some expert opinion on the security services holds that, far from being a threat to Western interests, he was an asset, albeit perhaps an unwitting one.

Robin Ramsay, publisher of the political journal *Lobster*, reminds us that the British Youth Council began as the British section of the World Assembly of Youth, which was set up and financed by the CIA and SIS (i.e., MI6) in the early 1950s to combat the Soviet Union's youth fronts. 'By Mandelson's time in the mid-1970s – under a Labour government – the British Youth Council was said to be financed by the Foreign Office, though that may have been a euphemism for SIS,' said Ramsay.[25]

Mandelson has certainly embraced the Western alliance in a comprehensive manner. He plays a little-known but important role in a curiously reticent body called the British-American Project for a Successor Generation (BAP). This is the latest, and arguably the most successful, in a series of post-war initiatives funded by the Americans to promote US values and interests among rising politicians in Britain. It organises seminars here and in the USA, and takes politicians it has talent-spotted to America to gain a greater understanding of the virtues of the American (i.e., capitalist) way of life. It has a British advisory board stuffed with former service chiefs, ex-diplomats and political figures of the centre-Right.

Among Labour luminaries who have benefited from the BAP processes are Mo Mowlam, the Northern Ireland secretary, George Robertson, the defence secretary, Chris Smith, the culture secretary and Baroness Symons, the Foreign Office minister. In its *Newsletter* for the summer of 1997, BAP headlined a 'Big Swing to BAP', congratulating itself that no fewer than four of its Fellows and one of its Advisory Board members had been appointed to ministerial posts in the new Labour government – Mowlam, Smith, Mandelson, Symons and Robertson. It listed them, with the dates on which they became Fellows.

Mandelson, described gushingly by writer Martin Vander Weyer, as 'campaign guru' is of the class of '87. That is to say, within two years of becoming director of communications of the Labour Party, he was actively involved in a US-funded organisation whose defence policies could not have been consistent with those of the party. Indeed, he attended the Atlanticist group's annual conference in 1987, when Labour's non-nuclear defence policy was debated. According to the conference report, British delegates, including Mandelson, John Lloyd of the hard-line electricians' union, the EETPU, and a representative of the Ministry of Defence think-tank, led the discussion. Small wonder, say the critics of Project Fellow Mandelson, that he was so powerfully instrumental in ditching Labour's anti-nuclear policy after the 1987 general election.

Nick Butler, at the time a British Petroleum executive and treasurer of both the Fabian Society and BAP UK, claimed that the Project had 'very little influence on the Labour Party . . . I should think that you would find that Peter Mandelson and George Robertson agree on defence policy, but not as a result of having been to that conference.'[26] This is the old trick of denying something that has not been claimed. The conference was only part of a long campaign to destabilise Labour's non-nuclear policy. Butler was joint author of a pamphlet bringing together material advocating a shift in defence policy from a Fabian weekend school in Oxford that also involved the Shadow Communications Agency promoted within the party by Mandelson. Much of the thinking later appeared in Labour's defence policy review. The clear inference to be drawn from all this activity by Mandelson is that at the very least he was a willing accomplice in the Americanisation of Labour's defence policy, or – more likely – a skilful promoter of the process.

There is a further dimension to Mandy's funny friends: the Trade Union Committee for European and Transatlantic Understanding (TUCETU). This is a successor body to the Labour Committee for Transatlantic Understanding, which was set up in

1976 by Joe Godson, labor attaché at the US embassy in the 1950s. Godson was a close political ally of Labour's first modernising leader, Hugh Gaitskell, in his long campaign against the Labour Left. Robin Ramsay believes that 'The Labour attaché posts may have been used as cover by the CIA.'[27] It may not have made much difference whether he was CIA or not, since Godson reported to the US State Department in any event. TUCETU, which receives over £100,000 a year from the Foreign Office, is organised by two officials of the NATO-sponsored Atlantic Council. It incorporates Peace Through NATO, the group used by then Defence Secretary Michael Heseltine to undermine CND in the early eighties. These origins of Godson's godchild, the TUCETU, are not generally known.

TUCETU published a pamphlet written by Mandelson from a speech he gave to the organisation's conference in 1996, the year before New Labour gained office. In it, he called for 'a strong, continuing alliance with the US which builds on our historic ties and the dependence we have for logistical and intelligence support – and bluntly, military capacity – from the world's one remaining superpower'.[28] This clear commitment to, and dependence on, the USA, has been carried into New Labour's foreign and defence policy, as is plain from Tony Blair's actions in the Gulf, in supporting the US strikes against Sudan and Afghanistan and backing US control of UN/NATO policy in former Yugoslavia.

13

CARRY ON BEING PETER

Power is an even greater aphrodisiac than winning. Mandelson left the all-night victory party to take charge of the nation, or, at any rate, to chair a six o'clock meeting of the campaign team. It began half an hour late, but he was impatient to get control systems in place. So many new Labour MPs had been elected – and not all of them New Labour – that the power centre felt dangerously exposed. Who were these people? Mandelson ordered regional press officers to provide Millbank with a list of the awkward squad, and their personal details. A new age of Excalibur was born, only this one was aimed at Labour's own MPs, rather than at the Tories.

Mandelson helped choreograph the theatrical entry of Tony Blair to Downing Street, cheered on by Union-Jack-waving well-wishers (many of them party workers and their families). He basked approvingly in the prime minister's insistence on the doorstep of Number 10 that 'We were elected as New Labour and we will govern as New Labour.' Then he sat back to wait for the call to ministerial office. He could not expect to vault over his senior colleagues into the Cabinet, but he did have great hopes of a high-profile posting. Initially, he fancied becoming minister for Europe, which would give full rein to his obsessive Euro-enthusiasm. After all, on his application form for the job he had cited his sterling work as vice-chairman of the European Movement. However, the appointment of the more Eurosceptic Robin Cook as foreign secretary ruled out that option. Mandelson had also signalled a private preference to work at Social Security, fulfilling the arid vision of *The Blair Revolution*; and if not there, then at John Prescott's superministry of Transport, Environment and the Regions. Anywhere, in fact, where he could wield power publicly and be taken seriously.

Mandelson filtered his preferences for the top jobs – his own, and everybody else's – through to Blair, but his role was very much secondary to the big hitter next door at Number 11. Gordon Brown, the new chancellor, wielded powerful influence in shaping the Cabinet, and Mandelson's place in the great scheme of things was not as critical as his own opinion of it. Yet, surprisingly, it still proved controversial (the 'what to do with Peter' problem has dogged the Blair leadership years). What followed was worthy of a Whitehall farce. Derek Foster, the former chief whip and another North-east MP, was furious at not being appointed chancellor of the Duchy of Lancaster, the minister in charge of the Cabinet Office. The job went instead to uncharismatic David Clark, yet another member of the North-east mafia, and Foster was offered minister of state at the Cabinet Office.

Foster's dismay was compounded when Blair announced the appointment of Mandelson as minister without portfolio in the Cabinet Office, effectively deputy to Clark. The former chief whip, who had had Mandelson foisted on him in 1994 after Blair took over as leader, resigned on the spot. He let it be known that he preferred to return to the backbenches rather than work under the shadow of Mandelson. His political pique was understandable. He might also have realised that being Mandelson's boss was scarcely a more comfortable berth.

Blair's instinct to keep up his political guard meant that Mandelson had to remain as his chief fixer. 'Peter is to carry on being Peter,' he told colleagues.[1] Mandelson's former aid Derek Draper insisted that the minister without portfolio now commanded unprecedented authority and access to the prime minister. In his pocket was a swipe-card to gain access to Number 10 without leaving the complex of government buildings on the corner of Downing Street. Across his desk flowed a constant stream of confidential civil service and departmental policy documents. He was where he wanted to be, at the nerve centre of the machine. In public, he spoke of his role with a curious mixture of mock-humility and petulance. 'In effect, I am the government's spokesman, instead of being behind the scenes. I'm also in charge of co-ordinating the government's policy. What is so strange or remarkable about that?'[2] Nothing, except that the last politician to lay claim to such a role was Michael Heseltine, deputy prime minister to John Major. And by Saturday morning, less than 24 hours after Major had conceded defeat, the press were already writing up Mandelson as 'the real deputy prime minister'. He was also getting his hands on serious money for the first time since entering Parliament. He did not have a ministry to run – he probably felt he was running the government – but he did have a ministerial salary of £74,985 a year, plus allowances and a chauffeur-driven limousine.

His first controversial task was to defend Blair against the Conservatives' charge of 'politicising' the civil service by giving so many influential jobs to the burgeoning ranks of 'Tony's cronies'. John Major took particular exception to the appointment of Jonathan Powell to the sensitive post of principal private secretary to the prime minister, as part of a virtual doubling of political appointees at the heart of government. Mandelson was dismissive. 'I think the public will welcome the cumulative changes for two reasons,' he said. 'First of all, they strengthen the centre of government, to enable the PM and the Cabinet to carry out the manifesto pledges on which we were elected a month ago. Secondly, they make a very clear distinction between government work and political activity.'[3] Quite how the public's approval was gauged was a mystery, but few seasoned observers were taken in by

Mandelson's plausibility. It was clear that centralisation of power into fewer hands at the very top was the name of the game, and the insistence on Chinese walls between government and party politics carried little credibility. Since he could not explain himself in the Commons, Mandelson answered his critics in a letter to *The Times* of characteristic hauteur. He denied that the strategy meetings he chaired every day in the Cabinet Office infringed the neutrality of civil servants. They were, he wrote, similar in format to those chaired by his predecessor, Michael Heseltine, 'though they are thankfully more effective and decisive'.[4] Heseltine was, of course, given the job of deputy prime minister and chief co-ordinator of policy with the precise purpose of rescuing the political fortunes of the failing Major administration. Only the most naive could have believed that Mandelson's role was not in substantial measure party-political. He lives and breathes party politics, and his – not unworthy – aim is to ensure a second, and if possible third and fourth, Labour government.

Being without a portfolio meant that he did not have to answer for his actions to Parliament. He was rarely seen at Westminster, and never spoke in debates. A persistent new Liberal Democrat MP, Norman Baker, began to put down questions in the House about the minister's engagements. His questions were mostly either rejected out of hand or fobbed off with non-answers such as 'I do not propose to disclose details of conversations, meetings or other engagements undertaken in pursuance of my duties as Minister without Portfolio.' MPs began to speak derisively of an entire 'Ministry without Portfolio' devoted to Mandelson. His office costs were disclosed at £373,000 a year, including two private secretaries, two personal secretaries and a diary secretary. He also had his own adviser, Benjamin Wegg-Prosser (known to intimates as 'Oofy').

But what did he actually do? That summer, the *Sunday Times* put its sleuths on to the trail of 'Pimpernel Mandy', and found he was everywhere except Westminster. In the eleven days leading up to 20 July 1997, he led a peripatetic life. He attended a Treehouse

Party in north London with other celebrities to raise money for autistic children. He passed up the miners' gala in Durham in favour of a lunch with Sir Charles Powell and his Italian wife, Carla. On Bastille Day, he was at the French embassy party, but he rejected champagne in favour of Evian water. Then, it was over to Paris. First, on 17 July, to speak about the spin-doctoring business at a British Council seminar, where he told young journalists, 'If people started to like me too much I would lose all my power.' A hectic round of meetings with French government ministers followed, culminating in dinner with the British ambassador on the rue du Faubourg Saint Honoré, the most elegant street in the capital. More briefing of selected journalists the next day, before a traditional Saturday of speeches to Labour supporters.[5] This was a fairly typical period of activity. Mandy gets everywhere. The following week, he was in Belfast, as a guest of Northern Ireland Secretary Mo Mowlam. When Gordon Brown visited Rome around this time, the minister without portfolio was discovered in the British embassy.

Now, Mandelson turned his attention to the last party bastion still to fall to his charms: the National Executive Committee, once known as Labour's ruling body, but shorn of much of its powers in the Blair era. He was conscious that no Labour politician had become leader of his party without a stint on the NEC, which remained the emotional heart of the party. In July, Mandy surprised his fellow-MPs by letting it be known that he was a candidate in the forthcoming elections for the executive. He might already be sitting on no fewer than eleven Cabinet sub-committees, but he could cope with another one. The spin put on his fresh power bid was that Blair was anxious not to allow the NEC to become an alternative power base to the government, as had happened in the 1970s. Mandelson's role would be to ensure that the executive and the government 'marched in tandem'. That is to say, the government would dictate to the politburo, not the other way round. Mandelson said, 'After modernising Labour, we need to bring about lasting change in Britain. The party and the government working closely together is crucial to achieving this.'

A senior Labour source admitted that while Mandelson had once been unpopular with party activists, 'those days are behind us'. It was nonetheless a calculated risk, for Mandelson himself and for Tony Blair, who supported his candidature. Mandy was running for the seat vacated by Gordon Brown. His closest rival was Ken Livingstone MP, one-time leader of the GLC and now a maverick left-winger on the backbenches, but still a darling of the party faithful.

To raise his profile in the run-up to the 29 September poll, Mandelson agreed to stay in London while Blair was on holiday during the August 'silly season' for news. He shared the task with Deputy Prime Minister Prescott, who had learned to respect Mandelson's professionalism, without feeling the need to demonstrate his admiration publicly. The season was not so much silly as saturated with bad news. Mandelson appeared alongside Lord Simon, when the trade minister announced the sale of his controversial £2 million shareholding in BP. Controversy continued over Labour's by-election defeat in Uxbridge, the scandal over Foreign Secretary Robin Cook's affair with his secretary, Gaynor Regan, and the suicide of Labour MP Gordon McMaster amid claims that parliamentary colleagues were responsible for spreading rumours that he was gay.

Then, contrary to the most basic rule of media manipulation – that the spin-doctor must never become the story – Mandelson hit the news in his own right. He was accused of planting a sensational story that Chris Patten, the former governor of Hong Kong, was being investigated by MI6 for leaking classified documents before the handover of the colony. It was front-page news in the *Sunday Times*, a favourite conduit of the minister without portfolio. The Tories accused him of deliberately leaking the story to shift media attention away from Lord Simon and 'Cock' Robin Cook. Naturally, this was denied. But Jon Sopel, political correspondent for the BBC and a biographer of Tony Blair, disclosed that he had been persuaded to run the story by a Labour press officer who promised that Mandelson would confirm the MI6 angle – if asked to do so in a live interview. His footprints were all over the story. Yet worse was to follow a few days later during a press conference to celebrate the government's first hundred days in office. An irritated Mandelson turned on a BBC reporter and hissed, 'I'm sorry if you're not doing your job properly so that you have to have me write your scripts and fix your headlines.' Shortly afterwards, he became involved in a shouting-match with Radio 4 presenter Martha Kearney on *The World at One*, insisting that the media were preoccupied with news management and 'talking about themselves' was of no interest to the public. He won his point – he rarely fails to do so – but his harsh, splenetic manner prompted dozens of complaints from listeners. For once, they got a public hearing of his private behaviour, and they did not like it. Small wonder that the 'petulant' minister without portfolio emerged in Conservative private opinion surveys as the most disliked member of the government. John Redwood, the shadow trade secretary, said, 'New Labour's first 100 days have identified the weak link in the Labour government. Peter Mandelson is perceived by much of the public as running the government, and our focus group evidence shows the public dislike his tactics and his refusal to answer legitimate questions.' Redwood went on mischievously to demand who was really in charge while the prime minister sunned himself in Tuscany: Mandelson or Prescott? This was now 'the central political issue for the government'.

It was not, of course, but Mandy's vain putdown only got him more unwise publicity. He argued that 'the Tories are trying to destroy me because I'm a threat to the Tory party'. In fact, the furore over Mandy was a godsend to the Conservative Party, desperate to rescue its new leader, William Hague, from his summer doldrums in the opinion polls. Mandelson also said that if he was accused of 'trying to create the truth' he would plead guilty, a harking back to the inventive powers betrayed to the press officer, John Booth, he had fired a decade earlier.

Mandelson sought to re-establish his credentials as a progressive Labour thinker and minister worthy of a place on the NEC in a Fabian Society lecture on 14 August. He announced that the prime minister had decided to set up a special unit in Whitehall to co-ordinate government efforts to tackle the problems of Britain's underclass. This was to be the Social Exclusion Unit, and naturally, he, Mandelson, would be closely associated with it. He also gave a first-hand definition of New Labour. 'Good presentation and effective campaigning were a condition for our success, but were never enough to give us victory. There had to be an intellectual sea change, a revamp of policies. We do represent a genuinely third way, neither old left nor new right.' He expatiated on the government's virtues and its policies, arguing that 'if we are serious about transforming Britain, we cannot be a one-term government. To anyone with a passing knowledge of post-war Labour history, this truth must be self-evident.' This is classic Mandelson-speak. He manages to talk down to his audience, while simultaneously demanding acceptance of his authority. Labour, he went on, should be judged by the people of Britain after 'ten years of success in office'. What? Not at the next general election, or at any intervening point in that decade of rule?

One of the fruits of that success would be a more equal society. 'However,' he emphasised, 'we will have achieved that result by many different routes, not just the redistribution of cash from rich to poor which others artificially choose as their own limited definition of egalitarianism.' The words 'artificially' and 'limited' stand out: only Mandy really knows; the rest simply do not understand. Labour, he concluded, has a vision. 'We know what we are about. We hit the ground running. We are motoring ahead . . . we will deliver it.'

Unfortunately, Mandelson's manifesto failed to have the desired impact. He, not Labour's historic mission, continued to be the story. He hit the headlines again over an attack on the Tories' constitutional affairs spokesman, Michael Ancram, as 'an antiquated Scottish hereditary peer'. In fact, Ancram is an MP, a former Northern Ireland minister respected for his handling of the peace process, who will become the thirteenth Marquis of Ancram when his father dies. It was a cheap shot, and critics suggested that he was trying to prove himself as a class warrior to party electors.

When ballot papers for the NEC poll went out on 18 August, Mandelson claimed he was 'a strong supporter and ally of Gordon Brown' (which came as news to the chancellor's aides). He also promised to make the executive into a 'professional administrative body', which, historically, was the opposite of what it was. Small wonder that John Prescott, a veteran of the NEC, derided Mandelson that day. On a visit to the Millennium Dome site, he christened a Chinese mitten crab 'Peter', and in front of the TV cameras asked it, 'Do you think you'll get on the executive, Peter?' His jibe was taken as clear evidence of tension between the two men. Prescott later put out a statement laced with insincerity: 'I wish Peter Mandelson all the best in his attempt to claw his way on to the NEC. I hope that his pincer move goes well because under his hard shell he has a soft heart.'[6] In fact, Mandelson's power bid was unravelling. Mark Seddon, editor of the traditional-Labour weekly *Tribune*, made a formal complaint to the Labour Party's general secretary Tom Sawyer, claiming that the minister without portfolio was 'in clear breach of the rules' by issuing a press briefing on top of the short personal statement permitted by election rules. The complaint stood no chance of success, but it highlighted the sense of unease among the party faithful. Mandelson had written an article in the *Guardian* to coincide with his manifesto. He portrayed himself as a doughty fighter for the Left. 'There will always be individuals who are more interested in internal argument and fighting their own side than working collectively and taking on the Tories,' he wrote. 'I have no time for infighting or introspection.'[7] Coming from the arch-moderniser who had taken on all comers, this was more than a bit rich. Although privately furious at Prescott's 'crab' jibes, Mandelson put on a good front. 'Politicians have to develop a hard shell, and I have,' he said. 'As John also mentioned, politicians need a soft heart, and I have that as well.'

Not surprisingly, the minister without portfolio dismissed his awful August as nothing more than 'appalling, lazy, journalism'. He was keeping his eye on the big picture – the budget, the

European Council in Amsterdam, and the G8 Summit in Denver. The press, short of news, magnified everything, but the Tory attack was 'frankly grist to our mill'. With magnificent cheek, he blamed the media. 'We don't present many targets to the media, therefore they clutch at any straw. That is the sort of easy, simple journalism that passes as a substitute for good, old fashioned investigative reporting.'[8] Two days later, Tony Blair was back, and the general view at Westminster was that in his absence, 'normal politics' – that is, government-bashing by the media – had been resumed. Labour's honeymoon was over.

In truth, Mandelson had intensified his politicking while the boss was away, but Blair showed no irritation. Indeed, on his return, he went out of his way to endorse publicly his minister's attempt to win a seat on the NEC. It was not going to be easy. Despite his silly-season high profile, half the people had never heard of him, a Gallup poll showed. Only 16 per cent thought he was doing a good job, while three out of four didn't know what his job was.[9]

Mandelson ploughed on. In mid-September, he travelled to Germany to give senior politicians and businessmen the benefit of his views about the future of Europe. He also gave what commentators described as a thoughtful speech, calling for greater co-ordination of government policy. He proposed a 'strong centre' at the hub of government, giving the prime minister a comprehensive grip on the director of his administration. There were no prizes for guessing who should be intimately involved in this centralisation of power. He had already drafted the outline of the new cross-departmental structure in his book *The Blair Revolution*. He was also raising the stakes in Labour's relations with the Opposition parties, accusing Liberal Democrat leader, Paddy Ashdown, of 'deliberate betrayal' and loftily dismissing William Hague. It looked as if his time was coming: could he enter the Cabinet in an autumn reshuffle?

First, however, there was the little matter of the NEC election. On the Saturday before the Brighton party conference, his ubiquitous 'friends' briefed trusty contacts in the Sunday broadsheets that Mandy might not, after all, have secured a seat on the executive. It is a measure of the seeming inevitability of his rise that they could not bring themselves to believe the bad news. The *Sunday Telegraph* reported senior Labour officials saying it was 'highly probable' that Blair's preferred candidate would prevail over the left-wing campaign of Ken Livingstone. Red Ken himself complained that Mandelson's 'five weeks as deputy prime minister' during the summer had garnered him publicity worth £10 million in terms of television and newspaper advertisements. If so, events were to prove that not all publicity is good publicity.

On the Monday morning of conference in the soulless concrete conference centre on Brighton seafront, protected by the tightest security in living memory, rumours began to circulate that humiliation was at hand. Rumour turned into fact at the close of the afternoon session, when the results were declared. Mandelson's power bid had failed. Livingstone won the vacant seat, by a wide margin. He took 83,669 individual votes from constituency party members, to Mandelson's 68,023. The minister came second to bottom in the poll, narrowly missing the ultimate shame of being beaten by Peter Hain, the junior Welsh minister and one-time direct-action protester against apartheid. The humbling of Mandy was the sensation of the day. Livingstone greeted the result as 'amazing', adding, 'Mr Blair will recognise it is a little bit of a prod from the rank and file to say, "You haven't got a blank cheque".' He promptly applied for a job. 'I'd love to be in government,' he said. 'I love running things.' Gloating was not confined to the Left, though NEC hard-liner Diane Abbott MP revelled in his defeat, which she said proved that ordinary Labour members 'did not buy Mandelson's politics . . . This is a tre-mendous blow to Peter Mandelson. A great operator, a great fixer, yet he couldn't get himself operated and fixed on to the national executive.'

Her analysis carried some weight. It may be argued that the NEC elections were an annual beauty contest (they no longer exist in the same form), and that members vote for the candidates they know. But Peter Mandelson could hardly have had a higher public profile in the months prior to the poll, when he was never off the front pages and the television screens. His lamentable inability to energise the votes of thousands of New Labour members who had joined in the Blair years could be counted a personal failure, or seen as a sign of their skin-deep commitment to politics. Either way, it was not a good portent for his future. The media trumpeted his setback as an embarrassing snub to Tony Blair, whose aides hurried to limit the damage. Only Gordon Brown and Blair himself had ever succeeded at the first attempt to win a seat on the executive, they pointed out, missing the point that Mandelson's popularity ought to be at its zenith. Roy Hattersley, Labour's former deputy leader and a long-standing admirer of Mandelson, was withering in his analysis. 'Contesting the election in the belief that gratitude for his part in Labour's victory would see him through was clearly a major misjudgement. Judgement is what Mandelson is supposed to possess in abundance, so the Cabinet seat which he so covets may not be his for years.' His mistake – 'which perhaps, at last, he realises' – was to pursue his destiny in a way that was bound to alienate and antagonise those who should have been his natural allies – including Hattersley himself. 'His problem in life as well as in politics,' wrote the Labour veteran, 'is that he is an obsessive who irritates and offends by working away with a single-minded passion in all that he does.' Hattersley identified 'genuine sensitivity' as a possible reason for Mandelson's manic self-justification. 'His life has been as much dominated by the fear of failure as the hope of success.'[10] This sympathetic assessment, which closed with the hope that Mandelson would get over his posturing and win a seat in the Cabinet, was not as widely shared as the Labour high command might have wished. There were cheers in sections of the hall when the result was announced. The glee was everywhere evident on the conference fringe that evening, even spilling over into a reception for new Labour MPs hosted by the World Cup 2006 Campaign. Mandelson was generously applauded when he introduced the prime minister, but Sports Minister Tony Banks made a sign of the cross with his fingers – a derisive reference to Mandy's reputation as the 'Prince of Darkness'. Mandelson sympathised with the other defeated Labour candidates present and said, 'You will understand why I feel a sudden burst of empathy. I now know what it's like.'

But did he? His initial, staged reaction was, 'Nobody likes to lose and it is humbling when you do. . . . I am obviously disappointed that I didn't secure a place at my first attempt, but a taste of humility is good for everyone, particularly a politician.' His humility was exhibited in all its glory in the next day's *Mirror*, where he was given a column to justify his candidature and turn defeat into seeming victory. He had no regrets. 'I chose to stand this year because I wanted to make a point. Many in the media claim that, as Labour's arch moderniser, I have no popularity in the party. 68,023 votes proved that wrong. I didn't win a place but I was runner-up. And as I was standing for the first time, runner-up is not a bad result.' In fact, he was second to bottom. The spinning continued. He knew he was a controversial figure – 'sometimes too controversial for my own good' – and during the summer he had drawn a lot of flak for his efforts to defend the government. 'Every government needs its lightning conductors, people who are strongly partisan in defence of their colleagues. That may have been off-putting to some people. So I'll readily admit I still have something to learn in treading the media tightrope. But so long as it is the Tories and their supporters who complain loudest about me, I must be doing something right.'[11] So that's all right then. It was all the fault of the beastly Tories, and the media. He had done nothing wrong. His sole fault was defending the government, perhaps too well. As a *mea culpa*, it is remarkably blame-free.

Within 48 hours, Mandelson was back in the headlines over a further excursion into humility. On 1 October, he told a fringe meeting that Labour's long-promised national minimum wage would be lower, or perhaps non-existent, for young workers – the largest group who stood to gain by the reform. The minister without portfolio said that a different statutory minimum 'will' apply to the young. On the platform with him was John Monks, general secretary of the TUC and fully paid-up Blairite, who described the intervention as 'dynamite'. He warned that it would alienate new voters at the next election. It seemed that Mandelson had jumped the gun. Margaret Beckett, president of the Board of Trade, had merely asked the Low Pay Commission set up to advise the Cabinet on the minimum wage to 'consider' a lower rate for those aged 25 and under. Mandelson had taken that line a critical stage further. Was this policy-making on the hoof, was he simply talking out of turn, or had he let the cat out of the bag? Reporters pursued Mandelson off the platform, and he tried to draw the sting from his remark. Whatever 'interpretation' was put on his words, it was up to the Commission to make recommendations on lower rates or exemptions for young people. Quite so, but not an answer to the question. As he knew, the Commission proposes, but the government disposes. And as a uniquely well informed member of that government, he was either in the know, or deliberately flying a kite.

It had not been Mandy's week. It started badly, and fell away. His 'modernising' reforms to strip the annual conference of much of its power and influence had been carried, but his own position was diminished. Winning a seat on the NEC would have proved that he had indeed 'stepped out of the shadows' to become an esteemed politician in his own right, his dearest personal wish. Yet he ended the conference as he had started out in government. The script was still 'Carry On Being Peter'.

14

CABINET

The humility of Brighton, whether real or mock, did not last long. Mandelson bounced back within days, his *amour propre* restored by private messages of support and the extraordinary public endorsement of his Cabinet prospects from no less than John Prescott, the deputy prime minister, the mitten-crab taunter. As delegates to the conference streamed home, Prescott pointed out that under a rule change agreed that week, it was impossible for the minister without portfolio to be elected to the national executive. But hew could yet be appointed to one of the NEC places now being reserved for members of the Cabinet. Speaking on Radio 4's *Today* programme on 3 October, Prescott went out of his way to salve Mandelson's wounds. 'Sometimes we've found ourselves on different sides of the argument and we've both got the kind of temperament where we express that. We get on all right. There's no doubting the professional abilities of Peter. I'm sure Peter would probably have got on the executive. But we are now changing the rules so that probably won't happen unless he is appointed from a Cabinet.'

This oblique suggestion from so senior a source prompted a

fresh wave of speculation about Mandy's future. Political correspondents began writing that Mandelson would eventually enter the Cabinet in succession to David Clark, as chancellor of the Duchy of Lancaster. The job, they suggested, would be broadened and strengthened. He would be in charge of a revamped Cabinet Office machine that would, in effect, become the prime minister's office. Or, to use an American analogy that would no doubt have pleased him, the executive arm of the Blair presidency.

It was a role for which he was uniquely well fitted. No one, with the possible exception of Alastair Campbell, was closer to the prime minister, or could read his mind more clearly. Mandelson was also immensely hard-working, a passionate, driven member of the government determined to see the Blair revolution succeed. He relished the prospect of being able to cut across departmental boundaries with a Cabinet brief to carry through the will of the centre.

Yet it was far too early for a ministerial reshuffle. The government had been in office for less than six months. Mandelson had to bide his time, though he naturally used it to best advantage by widening the scope of his network and delving deeper into the reaches of business and the establishment.

His political delivery improved, and his parliamentary appearances increased, but not by much. Mandelson attracted far more attention for his Svengali role at the heart of government than he did for his ministerial performance. He was particularly active in an almighty row over European monetary union and the single European currency. Citing 'ministerial' sources, the *Financial Times* predicted on 26 September that Britain was likely to join the single currency sooner rather than later. The impact of a splash story on page 1 of the *FT*, the City bible, was instantaneous. The pound fell in value, thereby helping the hard-hit manufacturing sector, while shares rose in value dramatically. Unfortunately, this virtuous cycle of events was confounded by the facts. Chancellor Brown, and a raft of other ministers, disowned the story. But the City refused to believe the denials, compelling Brown and Blair to agree a formula to lay the issue to rest. The government was horrified at the prospect of Europe haunting Labour as it had the Tories. So on 17 October, *The Times* was given an interview with the chancellor, in which he strongly hinted that the UK would not join the single currency for the lifetime of Labour's first Parliament. The story was also spun to several other titles, by Brown's PR man, Charlie Whelan, and by Number 10's Alastair Campbell. Whelan famously conducted his briefings by mobile phone on the pavement outside the Red Lion pub, across the road from the Treasury in Whitehall.

The story led *The Times* the day under a headline that ruled out UK entry during the current Parliament. Mandelson was incandescent. For once, he was out of the loop, and on an issue very close to his heart. So was his friend Roger Liddle, who is supposed to be Europe adviser to the Number 10 Policy Unit, and who reportedly threatened to resign over the matter. Yet here was the government embarking on a more Eurosceptical strategy, with neither of them being involved in the decision-making.

Amid Tory demands for a recall of Parliament, Brown and Blair decided on an early statement to the Commons to close down the issue. There was much speculation about what the chancellor would say. Then, an 'inside account' of the in-fighting appeared in the Europhile *New Statesman*, with Mandelson's fingerprints all over it. The article predicted that Brown would be more positive on EMU than expected, proposing an annual review of Britain's convergence with continental economies, which would permit a periodic reconsideration of the government's position. This was an option circulated in the City by Mandelson's people. The idea had no attraction for Brown, because it would feed speculation, rather than end it.

His first ministerial appearance at the Despatch Box was less than a success. On 10 November, he answered questions on the Millennium Experience for five minutes. The sketch-writers had a field day describing the smirks on the faces of Labour MPs behind him, and his nervousness before getting to his feet. Mandelson took repeated sips of water before being called by the Speaker, Betty Boothroyd. He took a deep breath and ran his finger round his collar.

Facing up to a full (and not particularly friendly) House of Commons is a truly daunting experience, and Mandelson appeared truly daunted, even though he was asked only one question, by Phyllis Starkey, the Labour MP for Milton Keynes South West. What, she wanted to know, would the minister be doing about the traffic jams around the Millennium Dome site in Greenwich? He was full of reassurances about queuing strategies for the 12 million people he thought would visit the Dome. He enthused about the 'once in a lifetime experience' awaiting Britons, but by common consent his delivery was nervous and wooden. Shadow heritage secretary Francis Maude noted that it was usual to welcome a minister on his first time at the Despatch Box, but it was not normal to have to wait six months to do so. 'If he continues to answer one question every six months we can be sure he will not outstay his welcome,' quipped Maude.

November was not his best month in government. Mandelson also had to put up with an emotional tirade from the comedian Harry Enfield, at a glitzy drinks party at Number 10. Enfield, fuelled by champagne, confronted the minister without portfolio, and told him, 'Nobody likes you. You're ghastly. You should resign . . . We're off to see the leader now to get you sacked.' The comedian urged Blair to get rid of his 'ghastly' spin-doctor: 'He got you into Downing Street – now stab him in the back. I speak for the nation.' Enfield's wife, Lucy, and fellow-comedian Ben Elton got him out of the prime minister's company, and Enfield later apologised for the affair, saying he was 'squiffy'. Mandelson accepted his apology, dismissing the incident as Enfield acting out his Tory Boy character. There was much chuckling at Westminster about *in vino veritas*.

Early in the new year of 1998, Mandelson was heavily involved in the handling of my biography of Gordon Brown, which caused a furore in the highest reaches of government for its candid portrayal of relations between Brown and Blair. The book was leaked to the *Guardian*, which naturally made the most of the revelation that Brown felt let down by Blair's breach of a promise that he would not steal the leadership nomination from him.

The book also disclosed the existence of Mandelson's secret letter to Brown, seeking to take him out of the leadership contest in 1994. The prime minister and his key advisers were all out of the country, on a politics-and-trade visit to Tokyo, but Mandelson was still minding the shop. The *Guardian*'s 'scoop' was written by Seumas Milne, the paper's labour editor, and a known contact of Mandelson. He quoted a 'well-placed government source' criticising Brown for co-operating with the biography. There were further, more hostile noises about the chancellor. Later, the story emerged that some of these quotations came from Mandelson. It is certainly most unlikely that Milne wrote his various stories without consulting Mandelson, of whom he once contributed a flattering profile to his paper. The most damaging comment of all, accusing Brown of having a 'psychological flaw', was wrongly attributed to Mandelson in a headline over Stephen Glover's weekly column on the media in the *Spectator*. Glover subsequently withdrew the charge (though the headline-writer, rather than he, originally made it) but insisted that Mandelson did have a hand in the story, which was based on a Downing Street briefing to Andrew Rawnsley of the *Observer*. Glover pointed out that a 'second, ministerial source' was quoted by the *Observer*, and wrote, 'This person says that Mr Blair believed that Mr Brown's decision to sanction the book was "a silly and serious move that weakens the government". Was this source our old friend Mr Mandelson? If so, I am sure he will not deny it.'[1] He has not done so. This was not a productive phase for Mandelson, and it got worse when he told an audience of Asian businessmen that Labour had reclaimed the Union Jack as an emblem of 'national pride and diversity'. The wrath of the tabloids was not slow in arriving. The *Daily Mail* found his 'egregiously impudent claim' another sign of the arrogance emerging in the behaviour of the Blair administration from a man 'for whom delusions of grandeur are never far away'.

Yet he still managed to retain the aura of a minister on the up-and-up. Speculation about his entry into Cabinet intensified in early February 1998. Leaks suggested that Blair was thinking of setting up a super-department in Whitehall charged with driving through his revolution. It would be headed by a new secretary of state for public services, who would replace the 'archaic' chancellor of the Duchy of Lancaster. Alternatively, it was suggested that the prime minister would create a powerful new Cabinet post of spokesman for the whole government, with a ministerial link to the Labour Party somewhat akin to the role of the Conservative Party chairman. The ideas came from a review of strategy carried out by leading figures in the Cabinet, but also including Mandelson. No prizes were needed to guess whose name immediately appeared in the frame to take up this role, in whatever manner it materialised. *The Times* tipped Mandelson, while admitting that he might have too many enemies in the Labour hierarchy to be accepted in such a high-profile role. The paper might have added that he was also too controversial, and too insistent on pushing party policy on Europe beyond the limits set by the Blair–Brown concord. As the perceived lieutenant of Blair, he embarrassed the prime minister with his call that month for Britain to surrender more power to the European Union, arguing that 'shared sovereignty' was the only way the EU could address issues of real concern in ordinary people's lives. He was further rebuffed when he speculated that Rupert Murdoch, the media mogul most hostile to the single currency, might be persuaded to say, 'OK, we've got to go in.'

It then emerged that Mandelson had his sights set on ousting Chris Smith as culture secretary. His ubiquitous 'friends' were wheeled out to insist that Mandy was getting fed up with being Blair's top troubleshooter. He was an ambitious politician, who wanted to emerge from behind the scenes to demonstrate that he could run a big department. The friends, acting on Mandelson's behalf, played down his ambitions to succeed David Clark. They emphasised his links with the arts world – contrasting his close relationship with the luvvies with Smith's 'increasingly acrimonious relationship with the arts lobby'. His love of ballet and the theatre was advertised, along with his closeness to John Birt, director-general of the BBC, which would help with the media dimension of the job. Smith, it was suggested, could be shunted off to Transport or Agriculture. In fact, Mandelson had made a public application for the job more than a year before, saying, 'If I ended up as Secretary for National Heritage one day, I would be absolutely thrilled. I do have a great interest in the arts, in Britain's creative economy and in producing a stable, long-term framework in which different broadcasters and organisations flourish. It represents a tremendous challenge.'[2]

Mandelson kept up his war of words with the media in a speech to journalists gathered for the annual *What the Papers Say* awards lunch at the Savoy Hotel in London on 27 February. He began with a reasonable joke. He told his sceptical – cynical, even – audience that he wanted to speak about a phenomenon whose future was very uncertain, possibly even doomed. Not the Dome, but himself. He talked about his prickly relationship with the media before embarking on a calculated putdown of the cream of British journalism. He claimed that Britain no longer had a prime minister obsessed by the newspapers. 'This may come as a blow to you, but I have to tell you it's true. Unlike John Major, Tony Blair does not go to bed fretting and worrying about what is in every jot and comma of the next morning's press.' He was more likely to turn to the sports page of the *Mirror* than its leader page, or the Bizarre pop gossip page of the *Sun* than its opinion column.

Nobody present believed this patent nonsense, any more than they swallowed his claim that the voters did not care about ministers' marriages or the cost of the lord chancellor's £400-a-roll wallpaper – 'the froth of jangling journalism', as he put it. The government, he insisted, would continue to keep its eyes set firmly on 'the big picture' of health, education, crime, jobs, business, living-standards, transport and public services: the issues on which New Labour had fought the last election. 'And they're what we'll win or lose on again.' It was an entertaining performance, more assured than his feats at the Despatch Box, but unduly patronising. It did not win him any friends.

Conjecture about Mandelson's future revived again in his favourite broadsheet outlet, the *Sunday Times*, on Easter Sunday, 12 April. Andrew Grice, the paper's political editor and close contact predicted that Mandelson would join the Cabinet within a matter of weeks as head of an expanded Cabinet Office with wide-ranging powers. Or, as the headline put it, as 'No 10 enforcer'. His role would be to ensure that Downing Street's writ ran throughout Whitehall. It seemed that Blair was frustrated that some of his policies had been delayed by in-fighting between departments. Mandelson's appointment was confidently forecast for the spring bank holiday, though 'close associates' of Blair – presumably Mandelson – believed it could come sooner. His elevation did not arrive on time. Instead, Mandelson had to put up with headlines that his Downing Street Champagne tormentor, Harry Enfield, was about to poke fun at him again in a new BBC TV satire featuring the megalomaniac MP, Norman Ormal.

Mandelson ploughed on with his own agenda, intervening behind the scenes to water down the white paper on employee and trade-union rights, *Fairness at Work*. The document was a draft of legislation implementing Labour's promise to grant statutory recognition to a trade union where a majority of the workforce wish it. Labour's new friends the employers were anxious that this formula be interpreted in the strictest possible manner so that recognition would be difficult to achieve. Trade-union leaders detected Mandelson's hand in the hard line taken by the Confederation of British Industry, a suspicion confirmed by leaks from the private office of Margaret Beckett, president of the Board of Trade, alleging that he was constantly on the phone right up to the date of publication, arguing for limitation of union rights. TUC officials believed his attitude was, in part at least, conditioned by his unhappy experience at Congress House two decades earlier – and possibly by a desire to emulate his grandfather, not usually regarded as a friend of the unions.

Yet Mandelson insisted at a May Day gala dinner in Newcastle that Labour had had a good first year in office, completing 50 of its 177 manifesto commitments and making progress on 109, leaving only 18 to be timetabled. If the party was to carry out its planned transformation of Britain, he declared, 'we'll need to plan for years not days – years of Labour government, not the truncated terms in office which cut us off in midstream at the end of the '40s, and the end of the '60s and at the end of the '70s.' It is at least arguable that all three governments had run out of steam by those dates, rather than being in mid-stream, but Mandelson was unapologetic. 'If that means being thoughtful and careful in government now, yes, even cautious, I would rather that than being bold and reckless at the beginning – and in Opposition again – before long.'

His self-congratulation was not shared by the voters. A *Guardian* poll in late May placed him at the bottom of the popularity ratings. Of those questioned, only 22 per cent said they were satisfied with his ministerial performance, while 32 per cent were dissatisfied, giving him a minus-10 satisfaction rating – making him twice as unpopular as Foreign Secretary Robin Cook, embroiled in controversy over arms-to-Africa and scandal in his private life. The question on MPs' lips was: why should Tony Blair promote his government's least-admired minister into the Cabinet? But the speculation about his future merely increased. The whole reshuffle was predicated on 'the Mandelson anomaly', which required the most ambitious member of the government to be placated. Rarely in modern times can a politician of such limited experience, with a track record of deep unpopularity, have had such a leverage on the prime minister's powers of patronage.

By early June, the press was reporting Mandelson's impending appointment to a beefed-up Cabinet Office as fact, but then the mood music emanating from the usual sources suddenly changed. John Prescott had been chafing behind the scenes, and he is a serious chafer. The on-off rancour between the two men is well documented, most obviously in the mitten-crab episode during the summer of 1997. Prescott had backed Mandelson for the Labour Party communications job, but was dismayed to find that he was a victim of Mandy's machinations. In a BBC 2 series, *The Wilderness Years* screened in December 1995, he accused advisers of trying to 'rubbish' him, and singled out Mandelson for particular criticism, saying he had 'extraordinary influence beyond what he should have exercised'. He was not the only target, and Kinnock used to deny what was going on, said Prescott. 'Well, we just all knew that frankly wasn't true.' In true style, Mandelson insisted he had only been trying to save politicians from themselves, and his office said flatly, 'There has never been a personal problem between Peter and John,' a statement plainly incompatible with the facts.

Now, Prescott was chafing at the prospect of Mandelson being promoted to be 'the Enforcer', a post which commentators suggested was the real deputy premiership. The incumbent was enraged, and his suspicions about extending the influence of the minister without portfolio were shared by Gordon Brown. Together, they made a formidable opposition. On 5 July, it emerged that Tony Blair had decided not to give his favourite courtier a strategic planning role across government. He would enter the Cabinet, but in charge of a ministry. He would not be a second deputy PM, or a rival to the chancellor ensconced next door. Of course, Mandelson would be able to say that this was what he had wanted all along, though he had by this time made semi-public applications for most jobs in the Cabinet, with the exception of Northern Ireland and Wales.

But on the very day that this intelligence surfaced (and in the same paper, the *Observer*) a fresh scandal broke over the government's head, dragging in Mandelson's name and that of his close friend Roger Liddle, the Number 10 adviser. The so-called 'cash for secrets' row overshadowed preparations for the Cabinet reshuffle, and at one time threatened Mandelson's position. The allegations were many, but the central charges involved Liddle and, separately, Derek Draper, Mandelson's former chief aide, who still enjoyed close links with him. Speaking to an undercover *Observer* reporter, Draper, now a lobbyist with the firm of GPC Market Access, boasted that he could get hold of market-sensitive information, could get access to government ministers and advisers and was intimate with every one of the seventeen most influential people in the Blair administration. He further claimed that Mandelson had control over his weekly column in the *Express*, Inside New Labour, telling the reporter, who (though Draper did not know it) was fitted with a tape-recorder: 'I don't write that column without vetting it with Peter Mandelson.' Bringing Mandelson's name into the frame was a major political faux pas, particularly when he bragged at the same meetings, 'I just want to stuff my bank account at £250 an hour.'

The allegation against Liddle, Mandelson's political ally, was even more serious. At GPC's annual summer bash for clients, politicians and the media, Draper introduced the undercover reporters to Liddle as potential GPC clients. The *Observer* pair were posing as Americans representing the electricity-generating business, which has a big stake in the UK, and is seeking more. They asked if Draper was as influential as he claimed. Liddle was quoted as saying, 'There is a Circle, and Derek is part of The Circle. And anyone who says he isn't is An Enemy. Derek knows the right people.' The reporters asked if Mandelson's former right-hand man could introduce them to policy-makers. In response, Liddle gave them his business card with Downing Street and home numbers. According to the *Oberver*, he then made an extraordinary offer: 'Whenever you are ready, just tell me what you want, who you want to meet and Derek and I will make the call for you.'[3]

The story was dynamite, coming as it did in the wake of revelations that Labour had given tacit approval to favoured lobbying companies, enlisting their services to boost party funds through business sponsorship. After the Bernie Ecclestone affair, for which Blair and Mandelson had had to apologise, here was another – potentially more serious – allegation of Labour 'sleaze'. Some also found the Draper face of New Labour – stuffing his bank account with £250 an hour – sickening. There was further unease about the financial affairs of the principals in the affair. Liddle was a co-founder and managing director of the lobbying group Prima Europe, and on joining the government he had been obliged to place his shareholding in a blind trust, in line with Cabinet Office rules. Prima was subsequently sold to GPC, a Canadian company, in February 1997, for £1.8 million, further diminishing Liddle's 'arm's-length' financial interest. Draper was in turn a valued executive of GPC – 'their only heavy hitter' in the UK, according to a rival – earning a reputed £100,000 a year working for a firm that counted among its blue-chip clients British Gas, US investment bank Salomon Smith Barney, and PowerGen. He had also benefited from the sale of Prima to GPC, to the tune of an estimated £400,000.

The Opposition was quick to seize on what rapidly became known as 'Dollygate'. Tory deputy chairman Michael Ancram wrote to Blair asking him to suspend Liddle pending an investigation into his affairs. The Conservatives also demanded a Commons statement and a top-level inquiry into the relationship between Labour and the lobbyists. The Opposition's move may have been opportunist, but that is what oppositions are for, and the government was caught in the embarrassing situation of having to defend itself against allegations of 'sleaze' of the very kind that had helped bring down John Major's government. There was no evidence that money had ever changed hands, as it certainly did with some Tory MPs, but the overall impression left by the disclosures was one of contempt for the political process and a readiness on the part of New Labour to exploit old contacts and friends. Liberal Democrat MP Paul Tyler, a member of the Commons Committee of Parliamentary Privilege, summed up the mood: 'The whole thing leaves an unpleasant stench.'

Naturally, Mandelson was volcanic that he, and his friend Liddle, had been drawn into the web of scandal. The media were quick to point up the network of links. Not only were Liddle and Draper close to each other, but they were both close to Mandelson. Liddle and Mandy had been friends for twenty years. They had written *The Blair Revolution* together. Draper had worked part- or full-time for Mandelson from 1992 until 1996, and in 1997 he was his campaign manager in his unsuccessful bid to win election to Labour's NEC. Later he worked on the Mandelson–Liddle book. Indeed, the pair said in the preface, 'Both of us owe a special debt to Derek Draper.' He had been closely involved with this project from the start and made a major contribution to the outcome at every stage. How fortunate was New Labour, the writers argued,

that it could boast a whole new generation with his quality of
organisational energy, political commitment and realistic vision.

Quite so. But not any more. A source close to the minister
without portfolio said he was 'furious' about Draper's remarks.
'Peter regards these boastful claims as typical Derek Draper hype,'
added the source, presumably Benjamin Wegg-Prosser, his closest
aide. Downing Street issued a statement on behalf of Liddle,
admitting that the meeting with the 'American businessmen' had
indeed taken place. 'I offered them my card and said I would be
happy to talk to them further about it.' Meeting business people
was an important part of his responsibilities, he insisted, and at no
time did he offer to make any introduction on behalf of GPC or
Mr Draper. *The Times* described his denials as 'weak and
unconvincing', while finding his behaviour foolish, naive and ill-
judged rather than evil, naive and corrupt. Even so, it is hard to
see why Tony Blair and Peter Mandelson rated his talents so
highly. Some Labour MPs argued that he should go, and backbencher Alice Mahon, a former PPS in the Blair administration,
wrote to the prime minister saying, 'I believe that the integrity of
your office and the Labour Party would be best served if he was
sacked at once.'

Behind the scenes, Mandelson became hyper-active. Unusually
for a spin-doctor who eats and sleeps newspapers, he did not know
about the allegations until he saw the issue aired on TV on *Frost
on Sunday*. According to a close contact, Mandelson first contacted
Wegg-Prosser to ask what was going on. He then got hold of
Draper in Italy, where he had just started his summer holiday, and
shouted down the phone: 'I told you your big mouth would get
you into trouble.' Mandelson's advice was to come back, do a
couple of '*mea culpa*' interviews with the broadsheet press and then
go back to Italy. Instead, Draper, once his nearest confidant,
emulated a whole flock of canaries. He sang so loud that
Mandelson thought he might be having a nervous breakdown.

On his return, Draper was suspended by a 'very concerned'
GPC, and Rosie Boycott, editor of the *Express* sacked him from his
£70,000-a-year column for the paper over his boast that it had

been 'vetted' by Mandelson. Columnists, she said, should be
independent, and should certainly not be discussing their column
in detail with a government minister. A spokesman for Mandelson
said that claims of vetting were 'an exaggeration and untrue'.
They could not have been both. The minister's office admitted
that Draper had visited Mandelson's office on at least two
occasions, having written his column, to check facts on 'difficult
subjects'. This partial confirmation merely fuelled speculation
that Draper was flying kites on Mandy's behalf – for instance, his
demand the previous weekend for Nick Brown, confidant of the
chancellor, be got rid of from his post as chief whip.

Draper sought to exculpate Liddle and Mandelson, apologising
to both that his big mouth had got them into trouble. He insisted,
'I've never even asked Peter Mandelson for inside information. I
never ask favours or get favours.' He had also talked to the
minister about his column, but 'there is no vetting'. It was all
rather too late. GPC finally sacked its talkative executive three
days after the storm broke.

The spotlight shone more sharply on Mandelson as the week
progressed. On 8 July, the *Independent*'s splash headline read, 'Now
the heat is on Mandelson'. He dismissed his former employee as 'a
bit of a showman', adding: 'He is a bit of a show-off and rather
good at selling himself and, in the course of that, making claims
and boasts that really don't stack up. But that is not the same as
saying that he breaks the rules or breaks the law or that he is a
congenitally dishonest person.' A far cry from the encomium of
his book preface, some noticed, but still not an absolute denial of
his former protégé. The columnist Suzanne Moore noted astutely,
'There are those who say that whatever Mandelson's public
reaction to this, he will always remain loyal to "his boy", as his boy
knows where the bodies are buried.'[4]

Mandelson urged his chiefs in Downing Street not to get
rattled. 'It will all blow over,' he told them. But each day brought
fresh, embarrassing revelations. Liddle's 'blind trust' set up on
Cabinet Office advice to look after his shares in GPC Market
Access, it emerged, was handled by his next-door neighbour,

Matthew Oakeshott, an investment manager and former political associate in the SDP. Shadow chancellor Francis Maude demanded a further investigation. Alastair Campbell promised a review. Amid what the tabloids called 'Blair's Worst Week' since taking office, the prime minister had a rough ride at Question Time. He insisted that 'not a single allegation in the *Observer* article is true', an astonishing assertion, which is open to question, since the bulk of the disclosures were not contested. Mandelson was not in the chamber to hear his boss grilled about Labour 'cronyism'. He was escorting Princess Margaret to a lunch party given by Drue Heinz, widow of the baked-bean magnate, in Mayfair.

On 10 July, Mandelson was due to appear before a select committee of MPs to answer questions on the Millennium Dome. He turned up to face his inquisitors with a jaunty air, rubbing his hands and quipping, 'It's nice to be back. There's nothing like a select committee to focus the mind magnificently.' He parried some soft questioning with New Labour-speak remarks about zones and access co-ordination, while growling at the Tory MP Michael Fabricant, who had the temerity to ask where all the private-sector sponsorship money was going to come from. With his parliamentary friend Gerald Kaufman in the chair, Mandelson did not have a rough ride. However, his smirking self-confidence did not go down well with *The Times*, which in a magisterial leader called on the prime minister to give him a proper job. Exclusivity, secrecy, conspiracy and implied intimidation were his stock-in-trade. He relished dissension at the heart of a government already riddle with feuds. 'None of this would matter very much if Tony Blair were not so close to him,' the paper argued. It would be a sign of the prime minister's political maturity if he could show that he could govern without Mandelson by his side.

The *Times* leader was only one of a number of signs that Mandelson's way of doing business, and the people he did it with, was becoming a political liability for Blair. The same day, it was disclosed that Draper had charged businessmen £150 a time to meet Mandelson and Liddle to discuss their book *The Blair Revolution*. Furthermore, the ticket proceeds were paid over to a company called 3C, set up by Draper to handle mail-order sales of the book. Three seminars were held, at Millbank, Labour's HQ, in the City and in Newcastle. The company had not lodged accounts in Companies House, as required by law, but Draper dismissed his inaction as 'no big deal'. Then, it was revealed that Draper and Mandelson's office were in fax contact on an 'almost daily basis', and that there were more links – though not very substantial ones – between GPC Market Access and the minister without portfolio.

Mandelson sought to clear the air in an interview with the very paper that was his chief tormentor – the *Observer*. The paper's political editor, Patrick Wintour, found him tired and sepulchral-white, sipping Lemsip and hot water for a cold and looking forward to five days in the sun in Brazil the following week. The minister was clearly bloodied, but unbowed. He offered the standard, shamelessly self-praising defence: it's not me they're after – it's the boss. 'I am a symbol of the modernisation and professionalism of Labour and a symbol of its success. The right-wing press attack me because we are Labour, and the left-wing attack me because I am New Labour. I think it's also cowardice. They dare not attack Tony Blair directly, so they go for the next best thing, which they think is me. I don't mind being a shield or a lightning conductor in this sense. But it has been very hurtful sometimes when people I know well, and who have been friendly to me in other circumstances, have chosen to attack me because they are playing to a particular gallery. It's very snide and it's very cowardly. It's designed to hurt and to injure and, in some cases, it does.'[5] Perhaps he had in mind the ex-SDP and now Blairite columnist Polly Toynbee of the *Guardian*, who had described him as 'a canker at the heart of the Labour government'.

What his remarks reveal is that far from having 'balls of steel' in a crisis (in Tony Blair's words), Mandelson is just as easily wounded as the next politician. Furthermore, his invariable formula of 'It's Tony they want – I am a proxy target' simply did not fit on this occasion. No-one was accusing Blair of anything. It was Mandelson who was being criticised by media and politicians alike. He was perceived as the *fons et origo* of Labour's 'crony culture', which was fast becoming a political catch-word in the same class as Tory sleaze. Mandelson admitted, 'The hysteria in the press is damaging for the government because it has led to the impression not merely that loud-mouthed lobbyists are getting something. Except at the margin, I know of no policy, no decision, no ministerial action, which has flown from the intervention of a lobbyist, not one.' He was not asked how wide the margin was, but he defended his own readiness to attend a private seminar for GPC Market Access to talk to its clients. This was no different from talking to the TUC or the CBI, or a voluntary organisation, he claimed. 'It is the job of a Minister to be open and take questions.'[6] Others took a less charitable view of the relative merits of these organisations.

Mandelson admitted he was unhappy about Dollygate, but he defended Liddle – 'on no occasion could he be seen to have acted improperly' – and refused to join in the general attack on Draper: 'I was saddened, but my natural instinct is to stand by someone in trouble, and not kick them when they are down.' But he was still angry with his one-time protégé, calling him a fool who should have seen he was being taken in. 'Derek should never have trusted an American who wears a trilby hat indoors' was his put-down. And, embarrassed at Draper's self-description as the minister's former chief political adviser, Mandelson forbade Dolly to link their names again in that way.

Finally, he conceded that Draper's disclosure of the so-called Magic 17 inner circle effectively running the government was damaging. 'We have to be very conscious, more than we have been, that in a government of 100 ministers there are bound to be MPs who feel there are things done without [them] being consulted. We must do more to overcome that.' He rejected charges that Labour was ignoring Parliament. 'It's just not true that we are drunk on power,' he said.[7]

However, a Gallup poll for the *Daily Telegraph* in mid-July signalled a shift in voter perception of the government. The proportion of voters believing that Labour was honest and trustworthy fell from 56 per cent to 50 per cent, while the doubter's share rose from 41 to 45 per cent – a fall in the 'trust factor' from 15 points to 5 in only two weeks. The loss of confidence was greatest among women and young voters, precisely the area originally targetted by New Labour in the run-up to the election.

Mandelson pursued his familiar theme in the *Mirror* and other newspapers the following day: he had enemies in the press because they thought they could strike at Tony Blair through him, but he could stand up to the pressure. The only fresh line was that he was the innocent victim of a 'war of the lobbyists', between the long-established companies like Sir Tim Bell's Pottinger Good Relations, and the new consultancies that had sprung up in the wake of New Labour's election victory. The idea of Mandelson as victim was certainly new, if difficult to swallow. But his political credibility had been diminished by a week of bad publicity, and doubts began to emerge over the correctness of appointing him to the post of Blair's Cabinet 'Enforcer'. The usual government sources said that his promotion to chancellor of the Duchy of Lancaster in charge of a strengthened Cabinet office was being reconsidered.

Naturally, Mandelson sought to turn this setback to his advantage by feeding speculation that he would be offered what he really wanted: a Cabinet post in charge of a high-spending department, where he could prove his transition from spin-doctor to big-time politician. The Tory press turned up the heat, with the *Daily Mail* headlining that Blair's troubleshooter 'sees power slipping from his grasp' amid revelations that Mandelson's office had tipped off Draper about the *Observer* scoop, and helped orchestrate his media fightback.

The first suggestion that Mandelson might go to the Department of Trade and Industry emerged on 13 July, but commentators regarded it as an unlikely move, given the commercial sensitivity of trade matters to lobbyists, and Mandy's connections with Dollygate. With few new disclosures of substance, the scandal-that-never-quite-was began to disappear from the front page. Mandelson was not around to feed it. He was on a four-day 'mission' to Brazil, including talks with President Fernando Henrique Cardoso. Quite why he was in South America was never really established, apart from his understandable love of foreign travel. His ministry had no obvious links with Latin America, yet here he was travelling unaccompanied at the invitation of the president, officially to promote a Portuguese version of Blair's own book, *New Britain: My Vision for a Young Country*. The edition had an introduction by Cardoso himself, offering the not very surprising view that he was a world leader creating a model to be followed by other countries. Mandelson had a packed itinerary taking in São Paulo, Bras'lia and Rio de Janeiro.

Nevertheless, he managed to hit the headlines, for the wrong reasons. At the end of his four-day trip, he gave a newspaper interview in which he sniffed at the Opposition Workers' party candidate, Lu's Ignácio da Silva – known as 'Lula' – as 'backward-looking' and out of tune with New Labour thinking. Uproar followed a university lecture that Mandelson gave in Brasilia, in which he supported re-election of President Cardoso, a disciple of Tony Blair's so-called 'third way' between the free market and traditional socialism. He followed up praise for the president with condescension towards Lula, calling him a 'retrograde who would leave me surprised if elected' and saying his party was 'retarded and with conservative ideas that are not compatible with the ideas of the new Left'.

The Workers' Party were understandably furious at being depicted as out-of-date no-hopers, and made a formal complaint to the British embassy about Mandelson's 'vulgar propaganda' on behalf of the ruling Centrist Party. In a statement, the party described him as 'an unquestioned marketeer for the current Brazilian president, gauging from the size of his bootlicking posture'. The press back home loved that, and 'bootlicker Mandelson' headlines sprouted before he could even get home. Downing Street poured oil on troubled waters, because Brazil is an important trading partner of the UK, and it is undiplomatic for ministers to appear to intervene in the domestic politics of foreign countries. Mandelson, said Alastair Campbell, had made no official comment while in Brazil. He had merely responded to a question about international reaction to an opposition victory by predicting that it would create surprise, 'but stranger things had happened'. Mandelson issued a statement dismissing the criticism from 'the old wing' of the Worker's Party.

The incident did nothing for his long-standing ambition to become foreign secretary, and while he was away the die was cast. Mandelson would not become the Enforcer. The job would be given to veteran minister Jack Cunningham, currently at Agriculture, who would take over a revamped Cabinet Office with a writ running across Whitehall, becoming effectively the government's chief spokesman. Downing Street 'let it be known' that Blair had heeded warnings from senior Cabinet colleagues that Mandelson should not be given such wide-ranging powers. Instead, he would go to the DTI, where he would continue to oversee the Millennium Dome.

At 44, he had finally made it. Extraordinarily, he heard of his promotion from the chancellor. Gordon Brown invited Mandelson round to his Westminster flat for a drink on the evening of Sunday 26 July, and gave him the good news. 'Congratulations,' beamed his former mentor. 'You will be a great success as secretary of state for trade and industry.' When he got the call, Mandelson had guessed it might mean a promotion to the Treasury, perhaps as chief secretary. He had been feeding speculation on these lines in private dinners and chats, but he was wide of the mark.

A source close to Brown said, 'He was amazed when Gordon broke the news and started talking in detail about the job. He kind of thought that he'd hear it first from Tony Blair. But Tony clearly thought this would be a smart way of getting the two of them off to a good start. Peter walked into Gordon's flat and Gordon got the wine out and said, "This is a big job, but you deserve it. It will be demanding and taxing, but I will help you as much as I can. The most important thing is that we do not say different things about the economy. If we do, we will damage the whole government." Peter listened very carefully and replied, "Look, that will simply never be allowed to happen. I agree with you on economic policy. Why should I take a different line?" They both agreed that this was a perfect opportunity to bury the hatchet and start again with a clean sheet. Peter knows that Gordon's the boss and he will defer to him, obviously. He wants to learn from him.' According to the chancellor's aide, the two men then shook hands, delighting Blair, who had been frustrated at these two 'great, talented friends' at each other's throats. 'He set up the meeting between them in the hope that they could iron out any differences between them. He is delighted with the way it went.'

Mandelson played his part perfectly, insisting, 'Gordon is a great Chancellor. We may have had our differences in recent times, but my friendship with him goes back a long way. I know that we will be working hard together for a common goal of a prosperous economy in which business can flourish.'

It was a wonderful piece of choreography, but it fooled no one in the Westminster village. It very soon emerged that Brown had got his way in preventing Mandelson's promotion to Enforcer, but had had to give way to Blair's insistence that he got the DTI portfolio. Within minutes of the 'luvvies' script being given, other government sources were cheerfully admitting that Brown and Mandelson did not have to like each other. 'They just have to realise that they have to get on.' That would not be easy, especially when it became clear that Mandelson had been spinning his appointment through the Sunday night. The *Sun*, virtually a house magazine for Mandelsonian New Labour, said in its first edition of 27 July that Brown was fighting the prime minister to prevent Mandy becoming trade secretary. After the 'summit' with Brown, Mandelson's assistant, Wegg-Prosser, tipped off the paper about his boss's promotion. Mandelson spoke to the *Sun*, which was able to lead its second edition with a front-page exclusive on 'President Mandelson' (it then being thought that he would keep the title vacated by Mrs Beckett). His old habits died hard. Indeed, they did not die at all.

Mandelson was now entitled to £61,650 a year on top of his

MP's salary of £45,066, improving his financial position very considerably. His arrival at the DTI's sumptuous offices in Victoria Street was greeted with mixed feelings. Some commentators thought him an odd choice, pointing out that his meddling in the department's policies on union recognition and the national minimum wage had not earned him any friends on the Labour backbenches. But *The Times* was kinder than usual, arguing that, while the DTI had become a shrivelled empire with a shrunken budget, it deserved to have a minister in charge who was unambiguously pro-business. 'Mr Mandelson at last has the chance to prove properly enterprising,' opined its first leader. Downing Street agreed that Mandelson would be 'the guardian of business interests' at the DTI.

In this, Blair's first ministerial reshuffle, four members of the Cabinet were sacked, including Mandelson's old boss David Clark, the mild-mannered chancellor of the Duchy of Lancaster. It was not a bloodbath, however, and the reconstruction drew praise from every quarter but the Opposition. Mandelson swiftly drew a line under the old regime with an announcement he would be known not as president of the Board of Trade, but simply as secretary of state for trade and industry. 'It's hard work to create prosperity for Britain's hard-working families that I am interested in, not pompous titles.' It was also noted that his promotion strengthened the pro-European single currency lobby within the Cabinet. On his plate now were thorny issues such as the future of the Royal Mail, and the government's white paper on competitiveness, due out in the autumn. It was assumed that he would look more kindly on at least partial privatisation of the Royal Mail than Mrs Beckett. But virtually his first decision was to bat away business pressure for a delay in the introduction of the European Working Time directive. He confirmed that the EU measure, which for the first time made statutory provision for holidays, rest breaks and maximum working-hours, would be implemented on schedule on 1 October, delighting the TUC.

15

THE FULL MANDY

Problems crowded on to Mandelson's plate as soon as he took office, testing not merely his administrative skills but the whole foundation of his political way of life. Whereas before there had been only faint murmuring about 'cronyism' and the Dome, there was now sharp-edged analysis of his links with the rich, famous and powerful. Commentators began to talk about conflicts of interest between his position as the minister in charge of regulation and competition in business, and his role in attracting private-sector sponsorship for the Millennium Experience.

And what of his circle of friends? It is all very well to dance the night away with Rupert Murdoch's daughter Elisabeth, but he was now also in charge of implementing Labour's *Fairness at Work* white paper to which the media mogul was totally opposed because it restored trade-union recognition rights. Murdoch's obsessive business expansionism also posed a potential threat, which was not long in coming.

Before he even had time to announce his new ministerial team, the skies over north-east England darkened with the news that computer chip-maker Siemens was pulling out of Tyneside. On 31

July, the German industrial giant announced that it was closing its state-of-the-art microchip company – just fifteen months after it had been opened by the Queen in a fanfare of publicity – with the loss of a thousand jobs. Mandelson, who was told of the impending catastrophe the day before it was made public, insisted, 'It's a setback, but it's not a disaster if we can find a new owner.'

It was a big 'if'. Siemens blamed the closure on the financial crisis in Asia, which had unloaded dirt-cheap microchips on the world market. Opposition trade spokesman John Redwood blamed Labour's economic policies, particularly high interest rates and the high value of the pound, and sought to portray Mandelson as the chief culprit. Tony Blair rode to his rescue: 'As Peter Mandelson has made clear, the decision to close the plant is absolutely nothing to do with the value of sterling or the state of British economy.' Mandelson loftily sought to put himself above the fray, saying, 'I am sorry that whether through ignorance or cynicism, John Redwood should choose to politick over this.' He set up a joint force between Siemens and the DTI, and also brought in key regional figures, to explore options for future ownership of the plant. There were no immediate offers.

An early crisis presented itself in the airline industry. British Airways had just concluded a highly lucrative alliance with American Airlines. The European Commission approved the deal, but only on condition that the two airlines gave up 267 'slots' at Heathrow airport to meet competition concerns. Having no option but to obey, the airlines then decided to sell the slots, worth an estimated £500 million, to other carriers. The Office of Fair Trading approved the sale, but on 10 August EU competition commissioner Karel van Miert ruled that such a move would contravene European regulations. Mandelson's ambiguous position aroused considerable concern. BA was an ally of New Labour. It had promised £6 million in business sponsorship to the Dome, and the company's chairman, Bob Ayling, was a friend of Mandelson. Mandelson was obliged to take advice from a senior civil servant at the DTI on whether it was appropriate for him to get involved in the issue, and was told that he could go ahead with a ruling. Airline unions predicted that consumer choice would suffer and air fares would rise by 10 per cent if Mandelson backed BA's sell-off strategy.

But the most awkward challenge came from his friends the Murdochs. *The Times*, Murdoch's flagship, disclosed on 7 September that Murdoch-owned satellite television station BSkyB was about to make a £575 million takeover bid for Manchester United. The acquisition raised serious questions about conflict of interest. BSkyB held the exclusive rights to show FA Carling Premiership matches. The company would be on both sides of the bargaining table at once – buying from itself the rights to show the most popular football club's matches.

The bid provoked anger from various quarters. Some analysts said the deal would be anti-competitive, requiring a referral to the Office of Fair Trading – if not the Monopolies and Mergers Commission. Joe Ashton MP, Labour chairman of the all-party parliamentary football group of MPs, said, 'If Parliament had been sitting, there would have been more than 100 MPs complaining very strongly about unfair competition.' United's fans rose in revolt. Shadow trade secretary John Redwood rushed out a statement, dismissing Mandelson's swift reference of the issue to the OFT as 'far too little too late', and calling on the minister to raise his game.

The DTI began floating the idea that politics should be taken out of competition policy, as they had been from monetary policy by Chancellor Brown's surrender of control over interest rates to the Bank of England. The job could be contracted out to an agency, freeing the politicians from awkward decisions. It was an appealing prospect. City competition lawyers, the *Financial Times* reported, said there was a prima facie case for Mandelson to step aside from the Manchester United decision. Not only was he a friend of BSkyB boss Elisabeth Murdoch and of BSkyB's head of communication, Tim Allan, a former aide to the prime minister, but BSkyB had signed up as a multi-million-pound sponsor of the Dome. Then another former aide to Mandelson during the general-election campaign, Andrew Sholl, joined BSkyB as a media adviser, prompting Tory Party chairman Michael Ancram to observe memorably: 'This shows that the culture of cronyism is alive and kicking. It is not only Tony's cronies, but Peter's cronies – and even the cronies' cronies.'

Faced with such conflicting calls on his loyalty, what could be more agreeable than to hand such hot potatoes to a third party? Meanwhile, Mandelson was stuck with the final decision. He struck a firm note, rejecting criticism of his closeness to Elisabeth Murdoch as 'exaggerated' and declaring that he been cleared by civil servants of any conflict of interest. He would consider all the issues with 'complete scrupulousness, objectivity and impartiality'.

He then embarked on a flag-waving tour of South Africa, selling the virtues of privatisation, British-style. Before leaving he impressed commentators with his 'Tory-like passion' for the policy once excoriated by Labour. 'I don't hear calls in this country for re-nationalisation of gas, water or electricity or people telling me BT should come back into state ownership or that BA would be better run from the DTI.' His choice of BA and BT – both large donors to his beloved Dome – may not have been inspired, but his audience got the message. He would sell 'the benefits and advantages of privatisation', which could be worth up to £20 billion to British business.

Mandelson decided on a high-profile appearance at the annual Trades Union Congress in Blackpool. He was picking up on an invitation originally issued to Margaret Beckett. She had arranged to appear on a long-range video link-up from South Africa. Mandy must therefore appear in person. It was like a state visit. He refused interviews and photo-calls, stayed overnight on the penthouse floor of the resort's best hotel, and next morning swept grandly past waiting snappers to the Winter Gardens. In *The Times* he was cartooned as an Indian maharajah riding on an elephant, while a man in dungarees labelled 'Unions' followed behind with a brush and pan.

Even for Mandelson, it was a speech of remarkable self-assurance. He began by telling delegates that twenty years previously, he had attended Congress 'as one of the TUC's youngest staffers'. This was technically true, since he was paid until the end of September 1978 – but only as a courtesy. His employment at Congress House had been terminated in August of that year.

Mandelson drew an immediate distinction between 1978 and 1998. Then, Prime Minister James Callaghan had unwisely taunted the unions by singing 'There was I, waiting by the church', hinting that he might call an early general election, when he did not so intend. Tony Blair, said a straight-backed Mandelson, would not repeat the mistakes of the 1970s. 'We should be close, but not *too* close,' he told delegates. His Labour government had good relations with the unions – but there was a critical difference with the bad old days. 'Those relations are not too close for comfort.' New Labour and the unions enjoyed a good dialogue 'but not under any duress'.

That was a recurring theme. Blair's government would not be 'a soft touch'. Labour would do its duty. 'We will never again contract out the governance of Britain to anyone, not to the TUC or its member unions, anymore than we would to big corporate interests,' he insisted. This was a shameless rewriting of history for his own purposes. Only in the febrile imagination of people like Peter Mandelson had the Labour government of 1974–9 'contracted out' the government of Britain (though he used the more pompous word, 'governance') to the TUC or the unions.

The trade secretary, standing stiffly at the lectern and with few body gestures, lectured the unions on their role. He offered them legitimate influence – or opposition. 'I know my preference,' he told them. 'It is for trade unions that draw increased strength from being modern, democratic, representative and influential.' He had his own definition of modernity: matching 'realism with responsibility' in dealings with employers and government. He looked ahead to 'the new unionism demanded by economic change'. It was a chilling prospect. The unions, still Britain's largest voluntary sector with 6.7 million members, were being relegated to a position of political sufferance.

For some union nabobs, like Ken Jackson of the engineering union AEEU, his message was perfectly acceptable. For many more, this was a *de haut en bas* performance by a secretary of state who had laid down fresh principles, requiring unions to conform to his view of the world if they wished to bring any influence to bear. Mandelson got a respectful, seated ovation for his long statement of political intent.

Shortly afterwards, Northern Ireland Secretary Mo Mowlam got not one but two standing ovations for her much more informal address on her hopes and fears for peace in the province. Talking of the time she spent with hospital staff and other public-service workers, she showed she knew how to find the labour movement's G-spots. Mandelson did not. If there had been a vote that morning, she would have been elected Labour leader. TUC staff tried desperately to put the best spin on Mandy's appearance. They briefed journalists after the morning session that Jim Hanna (Mandelson's former boss at Congress House) had marked him down as 'the next Prime Minister but three'. The story of his departure from Congress House was muddied with talk about them parting company by mutual agreement, though Mandelson had actually been fired.

The newspapers loved his performance at the TUC, showering praise on his firm line. However, the good publicity did not last long. On the day he spoke, it emerged that Mandelson had allowed his vanity to get the better of him on a Channel Four documentary presented by former Tory grandee, Michael Portillo. In the programme broadcast on 20 September, he attacked his Cabinet colleagues as political time-servers and creeps. 'They're always sitting on the fence. At the first sight of controversy, they run for cover,' he sneered. 'They're always there, sort of creeping about in the undergrowth in order to maintain their positions and keep their place in the Cabinet. Well, they are the majority. The minority are the people, the strong personalities, strong views, who are not cowards, who are risk-takers.' There was no question as to which camp Mandelson belonged. He told Portillo, 'You have paid the price for being a risk-taker – and so have I.'

Mandelson was in government, and might flourish. 'For you, the jury is still out,' he said with a smile.

It was an enlightening cameo. Two peacock politicians strutting their egos before the cameras, with Portillo flattering Mandelson as the man who 'stole from us the art of winning'. The programme went down rather less well with his Cabinet colleagues. It also upstaged his work as a minister, which was often relegated to the business pages of the broadsheets, whereas his *obiter dicta* on politics could virtually be guaranteed front-page treatment. This was true of his decision in late September to reject the proposed £375 million takeover by Ladbrokes of the Coral bookmaking chain. He made some mileage out of the ruling, posing as 'the punter's friend'. In an article for the *Sun* (owner: Rupert Murdoch) he said, 'I want the best prices and betting environment.' The paper linked his decision to reports that he was intent on diluting Labour's 'costly' pledges in *Fairness at Work*. Mandelson was said to be considering a £50,000 cap on unfair-dismissal awards by industrial tribunals, rather than unlimited compensation. A commentary called him 'a safer pair of hands' than Margaret Beckett, and the leader said, 'He's clearly the best Mandelson for the job.'[1] Some union leaders said the story confirmed their worst fears, but their knee-jerk reaction was misplaced. Mandelson had privately assured TUC bosses that the main planks in the white paper on union laws were 'a done deal'. At this point, he was in the business of making friends in the broad church of the Labour Party, not enemies.

He picked up the themes of his TUC speech in an address to the party conference in the same hall two weeks later, on 28 September, reminding delegates of New Labour's record: signing the EU social chapter, introducing the national minimum wage, and implementing – at his behest – the European Working Time directive that limits working hours and ensures paid holidays. He guaranteed to correct the 'basic imbalance' of power in the workplace, and revealed that he had become a revolutionary. Before the hollow laughter died down, he added, 'Don't worry, not a Marxist revolutionary, but a modern industrial revolutionary.'

He promised a new industrial revolution, based on the creation of a 'knowledge-driven economy', and cracked more jokes, including a risqué reference to Monica Lewinsky, President Clinton's former mistress. He insisted that the promotion of enterprise had to be at the heart of his ministry, dealing with tax, or pay and profits, or pensions, or housing, or planning, 'and so I could go on'. Indeed, he did. Enterprise would even be at the heart of education. He would 'put the future on Britain's side' (whatever that meant) but to be part of this brave new world 'we must demonstrate revolutionary discipline'. Alongside Blair's agenda of 'education, education, education', he offered 'enterprise, enterprise, enterprise' and received the same polite, seated ovation that the TUC brothers had given him. But when he took his place on the platform, Mandelson had to listen white-faced to the postal workers' leader, Derek Hodgson, attacking the 'faceless, unrepresentative spinner' who had leaked speculation about the future of the Royal Mail. The papers that morning had been full of stories that every Post Office worker would be given £2,000 of shares in a flotation of the Royal Mail. 'No more speculation, no more spin, no more delay. Tell us the Post Office is not going to be privatised or sold off,' bellowed Hodgson, for which he received a prolonged standing ovation. Mandelson forced a smile. His media sidekick later insisted it had all gone well, remarking, 'After all, you can hardly expect Labour conference to go wild when you say it is all about enterprise and entrepreneurs,' but Mandelson skipped the communication workers' party.

The lapdog *Sun* reported that the trade secretary had delegates rolling in the aisles, which no other paper noticed, and Mandelson privately congratulated the reporter for being 'a stout fellow' when he complained that pressmen were ridiculing him. In fact, despite promising the TUC conference 'no more spin, honest' Mandelson was as busy as ever behind the scenes. He was noticed hovering in the media area, and after Tony Blair's famous 'no backing down' speech earlier in the week, he confided to the *Daily Telegraph*'s Boris Johnson: 'Basically, it's Tony's equivalent of the "Lady's not for turning" speech of 1981.' In truth, Mandelson could not slough off his spin-doctoring self. It was still as much a part of him as his modernising instincts. He remained in regular contact with his 'captured castles' (as he derisively called his key contacts in the press). Staff in the Westminster office of the *Independent*, for instance, noticed that Mandelson spoke 'two or three times a day' to political editor Andrew Grice, newly arrived from the *Sunday Times*.

Nor could he leave Blackpool without a ritual tilt at Old Labour. Speaking at a fringe meeting with the catchy title 'Is Middle England getting too much?', Mandelson suggested that 'blue-collar, working-class, northern, horny-handed, dirty-over-alled people' should not be selected as parliamentary candidates. His heavy irony did not go down well with delegates, many of whom fitted the stereotype (as did his electors in Hartlepool). There are still almost 22 million people in socio-economic groups C2, D and E, which roughly correspond to the working class, and the engineering union AEEU had just announced it was setting aside £1 million to get more of them into a middle-class-dominated Parliament. The union's general secretary, Ken Jackson, observed acidly, 'I think Peter was trying to be constructive, but let's face it, he has never got his hands dirty working.'

There was an entertaining diversion when Mandelson was discovered that week trying to sell his car on the cheap. Instead of advertising in the local paper, he put a hand-written 'For Sale' sign in the window of his Hartlepool home, offering his five-year-old metallic green Rover saloon for £4,200, which car-trade experts said was about £1,000 below book price. His agent, Steve Wallace, talked up the bargain: 'Some well-known people have sat in the car, including Tony Blair.'

Mandelson had a reasonable conference, rather than a brilliant one. He then set about the task of making a splash while the Tories held their conference in Bournemouth the following week. He decided to play the role of Old King Coal. His department's long-awaited review of Britain's savagely diminished mining industry was published on 8 October. Mandelson threw coal a lifeline, by ordering an indefinite moratorium on new gas-fired electricity generating-stations to safeguard the 21 remaining deep pits employing 15,000 men. The 'dash for gas' had distorted the energy market, and Richard Budge, chief executive of RJB Mining, owners of most of the privatised coal industry, welcomed Mandelson's move, saying it would 'enable coal to be an equal partner'. The trade secretary also scrapped the electricity pool, a marketplace for electricity, and announced a new push for coal to find new markets in Europe through the export of electricity via the undersea cable interconnector with France. Ever since his brief visit to Kellingley colliery in Yorkshire, the newspapers had loved using macho pictures of Mandy the Miner. They all came out again to illustrate his plan for coal.

Not everyone agreed with his solution, however. The gas-station builders said the reprieve for coal would lose more jobs than it saved. Experts said Mandelson had missed an opportunity to restructure the energy market completely. And the story was chiefly tucked away on the business pages. There was almost as much interest in his new office furniture, and a conference table and chairs, ordered from the Conran Shop (*not* Habitat, which sounds more vulgar) at a cost of £16,000.

By now, Mandelson was learning to throw his weight around in Cabinet. He notched up a victory over Foreign Secretary Robin Cook with a decision that the Foreign Office could not publish an annual list of firms whose applications to sell arms it had vetoed on human-rights grounds. Mandelson argued, successfully, that such a 'list of shame' might embarrass both potential overseas customers and British arms-exporters.

He also brought a new panache to international politicking, making a speech in New York in October on reform of the bankruptcy laws that made headlines back home. He said he wanted to make it easier for business people who go bust to start up again. The idea caused some dismay, but Mandelson reassured his critics that he was not offering 'a licence to leave creditors in the lurch'. His remarks could have been better timed, appearing as they did the day after the DTI reported that its Insolvency

Service had disqualified more than a thousand company directors, and issued writs against many more. It was particularly proud of a campaign against 'phoenix directors' who move from one failed company to the next, leaving creditors out of pocket. As the City editor of *The Times* observed, 'Mandelson says villains are heroes.'

Being a Cabinet minister brought Mandelson immense satisfaction. The sheer pleasure of getting round the big table in Downing Street was the icing on the cake of years of intrigue and political machination. But it also had its down side. As manufacturing industry lurched into recession, he had to take responsibility. It was his misfortune that the German-owned car-makers Rover should announce massive redundancies in the week that MPs came back to Westminster after their thirteen-week summer break.

On 20 October, BMW, Rover's parent company, said it would have to sack 2,500 men at the giant Longbridge plant in Birmingham, whose survival was in jeopardy. Mandelson blamed the firm's problems on low productivity, and ruled out financial intervention by the DTI. He called on Rover's management and worker's to 'sharpen up their act', which infuriated people on the shopfloor. They blamed the high pound, and the government's failure to bring it down.

Mandelson was compelled into making an emergency Commons statement promising to bring the parties together for crisis talks on the company's future. He back-tracked on his criticism of management and workers, retreating into business platitudes. John Redwood, the shadow trade secretary, described his performance at the Despatch Box as patronising and complacent, comparing him to 'an undertaker denying all knowledge of the reasons for death when it was the government's policy that was throttling industry'. It also emerged that he had persuaded the Motor Show in Birmingham to open up an hour early on the day of his statement – 21 October, his forty-fifth birthday – so he could pay a flying visit and get back in London for a private lunch. Alas, the lunch had to be cancelled.

Mandelson's relations with Rupert Murdoch nosedived days

later, when he was obliged to refer the media magnate's bid to purchase Manchester United to the Monopolies and Mergers Commission, delaying the bid for at least four months. Mandelson was only following the advice of the Office of Fair Trading – he had no real alternative, particularly given his links with the Dirty Digger's daughter. Murdoch was furious, lambasting the decision as 'politically motivated', though he tried to exculpate his friend the trade secretary: 'I am not blaming Mandelson in the least . . . Obviously, it's an excess of caution. I mean, to be influenced by a few paranoid hacks on Fleet Street is ridiculous.' Most United fans were overjoyed, but few City analysts expected the MMC to rule out the takeover. The final decision would be Mandelson's.

Scenting a minister under pressure, the Tories stepped up their attack on Mandelson, particularly in relation to the Dome. Shadow trade spokesman Christopher Chope called on him to stand aside from any regulatory role which might affect Dome sponsors. Of the £100 million so far raised £48 million had come from companies facing competition inquiries of one kind or another. How could Mandelson be an objective regulator? 'There is a danger that he will have to find against the company to avoid accusations of cash for favours . . . Mr Mandelson must stand aside. If he wishes to carry on with the Greenwich project he cannot be the country's chief business regulator as well.'[2] Chope had a fair point, but Mandelson brushed it aside.

16

THE PROJECT

In the autumn of 1998, a sequence of events began to unfold that signalled a shift of gear in Mandelson's long-term game plan. In themselves, they amounted to very little: an article here, a friendly notice there, a book that flatteringly rewrote his role in recent political history. But cumulatively, they indicated that Mandelson believed he could go further than his mid-term ambition to oust Robin Cook and become foreign secretary.

There had always been a Blair Project: modernisation of the Labour Party, followed by a realignment of British politics with the Liberal Democrats that would give a centrist coalition perpetual supremacy over the Conservatives. Not that it was put like that, of course. It was merely 'inclusiveness', which could even find a place for ex-chancellor Kenneth Clarke and former deputy prime minister Michael Heseltine. Now, however, there emerged from the shadows the Mandelson Project. In outline, it ran as follows. Mandelson could supplant Gordon Brown as chancellor, and succeed Tony Blair, his patron-cum-protégé (he is different things on different days) as leader of the Labour Party and prime minister of his country.

Initially, it seemed a preposterous idea. Mandelson arouses visceral hatred among a large section – probably still a majority – of the parliamentary Labour Party. He is viewed with deep suspicion in the trade-union movement. And he has still not won the support of the constituency parties which he so spectacularly failed to mobilise in his bid to secure election to the NEC. In short, the Labour Party in late 1998 was a long way from 'loving' Peter Mandelson – the test set by Blair for its final maturity. Wisely, the prime minister did not nominate him as one of his ministerial place-men on the NEC at the party conference in Blackpool, preferring his understudy Ian McCartney, minister of state in Mandy's DTI.

And yet, and yet . . . Mandelson began to prepare for greater things. Gordon Brown was beginning to suffer the political backwash of the global economic downturn. Tens of thousands of jobs disappeared in manufacturing industry. The chancellor was obliged to revise sharply downwards his predictions of economic growth. The Tories intensified their attacks, and Brown's position weakened visibly. If he could be blamed for the economic slowdown – if it could become identified as 'the Brown recession' – he might be vulnerable.

The first signs of the strategy appeared in the *New Statesman*, ironically owned by Brown's friend and ministerial colleague at the Treasury, Paymaster-General Geoffrey Robinson. John Edmonds, leader of the GMB and a self-appointed mover and shaker in the Labour world, gave an interview to the magazine's political editor, Steve Richards. Edmonds, who had gifted Hartlepool to Mandelson, said he 'had a problem with Gordon', despite the chancellor's known warmth towards the unions. He claimed to suffer from 'extended spinning' in advance of meetings with Brown, in which the union leader's views were rubbished (presumably by Brown's press secretary, Charlie Whelan). 'It would be nice to be at least listened to without reading that it's nonsense before we have opened our mouths,' he said.[1]

By contrast, Mandelson, who had lobbied intensively to dilute both the minimum wage and the rights at work policy, came out as the good guy. 'Peter went out of his way to ask the TUC to see him immediately after he was appointed, literally within minutes,' Edmonds disclosed. 'The day we had arranged to see him, he had every excuse to cancel because he was dealing with the announcement of job losses at Siemens, but the meeting went ahead. He went out of his way to reassure us that the *Fairness at Work* white paper was government policy and that people who thought he would automatically side with the employers on any issue in the consultative paper were wrong. And, of course, in one of the most important areas of policy, the single currency, there is common ground.'[2]

Mandelson seemed to be 'going out of his way' quite a lot. In fact, his artifice was transparent. He needed allies in the party at large, and Edmonds was as good a place to start as any. Just in case the emphasis was not noticed, the GMB leader drew it to Richards' attention, and told him that was the message he wanted to get across. It was duly conveyed: 'Blair and Mandelson the good guys, Brown the villain.' No matter that the chancellor had delivered the New Deal for jobless young people, and mulcted the privatised utilities – the object of a sustained GMB campaign against 'fat cats' – of £3.5 billion to pay for it. Brown was out of favour. Mandelson was installed in his place as the unions' favourite minister.

A month later, in the rival *Spectator*, Brown received another drubbing, this time at the hands of Rupert Murdoch's favourite economics guru, Irwin Stelzer. Headlined 'Gordon's Decline is Peter's Rise', the article said that the chancellor had gone from 'champ to chump' in a matter of weeks and now risked being marginalised. Unless he had a radical rethink on tax, Brown would have passed the role of principal economic policy-maker to his old enemy Peter Mandelson. 'It is Mr Mandelson's Department of Trade and Industry that presides over the areas that matter to Britain's future . . . With Brown sidelined with self-inflicted wounds, Mr Mandelson is Britain's latest and best hope for economic growth,' wrote Stelzer.[3]

The picture could not be clearer. Brown is responsible for the recession. If there is an upturn, it will be Mandelson's handiwork. So, the scenario at Westminster ran, Blair will 'regretfully' move his chancellor to the Foreign Office some time before the general election, which will come earlier than expected, in 2001. He will then install Mandelson in the Treasury, where he will be seen as the heir apparent to the leadership – which Blair has occasionally confided he does not want to shoulder for ever. He could lead Labour to victory, and then hand over to Peter Mandelson, who might have difficulty in winning an election.

The rewriting of the Mandelson myth was taken a stage further in October 1998 with the publication of *The Unfinished Revolution*, the memoirs of his close political friend Philip Gould. The book was serialised in *The Times*, whose political editor assured his readers that this account was regarded by Tony Blair as 'the most accurate account yet' of the dramatic days after Smith's death. It was nothing of the sort. It was, however, as *The Times* went on to say, 'the most concerted effort so far to absolve Mr Mandelson of the charges of treachery and duplicity levelled at him by friends of Mr Brown'.

Gould claimed that until Smith's death Mandelson had seen Brown as the natural heir to the party leadership. He quoted Mandelson as saying how committed he was to Brown; how he worked for him, day in day out; how, in his years at Walworth Road and afterwards, he had made sure 'the machine' (as he described the Labour Party) worked for Brown, as well as Blair. To an extent this is certainly true. He pushed both modernisers to the forefront of media exposure, at the expense of more traditional figures such as John Prescott or Michael Meacher. But in private he called Brown and Blair 'my boys'. He saw them as *his* protégés, not the other way round. Had they not espoused his political outlook, they would have been left firmly out of the limelight.

So far from it being 'always Brown one, Blair two', the order of preference switched after the 1992 election that brought Mandelson into Parliament. Brown's people knew that Mandy was busily promoting Blair on the metropolitan dinner-party circuit, while the shadow chancellor was rewriting Labour's tax-and-spend strategy to make the party electable – and catching media flak and backbench unpopularity for so doing. In late 1998, Brown's circle were incensed at what they saw as a Stalinist rewriting of history, aimed at rehabilitating Mandelson at the expense of the chancellor, who was too heavily involved in coping with the economic slowdown and too conscious of the need not to precipitate yet another bout of internal party warfare just to correct the Mandyfication of the facts. Nevertheless, Brown fumed.

As well he might, for the Gould hagiography of Mandelson's role exposed an interesting dimension to the Blair plot. Gould disclosed that on 18 May 1994 he had written a memorandum to Mandelson, arguing the case for Blair to succeed John Smith and stressing the dangers of a Gordon Brown candidacy: the huge political cost, the damage to the shadow chancellor's relationship with Blair, the damage to the cause of the modernisers and the potential backlash against Brown. The memo bears an uncanny resemblance to a one-page subversive message from Mandelson, which had *already* been sent to Brown two days previously. No doubt these two great minds think on the same lines. But it is interesting that they even use the same words. So far from exonerating Mandelson of the charge of duplicity and treachery, the Gould book merely reinforces the clear impression that he undermined Brown's position – and shows that he had powerful friends driving in the same direction.

Ironically, the Mandyfication of history by Gould came out only three days after *The Times* predicted the demise of Mandelson's dream of a 'centre-Left' political hegemony in Britain – sometimes nastily compared to Hitler's fantasy of a thousand-year Reich. The paper claimed that Paddy Ashdown, the Liberal Democrat leader, had privately accepted that New Labour had decided to delay electoral reform at Westminster for the foreseeable future. There would be no referendum on proportional representation in the current Parliament. The Jenkins report on electoral reform, the fruit of more than a year's work, would effectively be shelved.

This was very bad news for Mandelson. His vision of a 'longer-term stable left of centre government', outlined in the confidential proposal for his book in 1995, was founded on an 'understanding' – an electoral pact, even – between New Labour and the Liberal Democrats. Mandelson had warned that to see his whole programme of 'renewal' to completion would take more than one five-year Parliament 'and the government will be facing re-election by a possibly sceptical or hostile public before the results have been achieved'. Accordingly, he favoured a deal with the Liberal Democrats, who had support 'that even Blair cannot touch'. However, there was never any prospect of a pact between the two parties unless Blair delivered substantial progress on electoral reform. Ashdown committed himself heavily to achieving a referendum on proportional representation during Labour's first Parliament, courting unpopularity in his own party for cosying up the Blair to achieve this goal.

But Downing Street was aware that proportional representation for Westminster elections was anathema to a large and growing body of opinion of Labour backbenchers, up to a hundred of whom might lose their seats in the doubtful name of 'fair votes'. They did not see it, as Mandelson and his co-author Roger Liddle did, and as the Tories feared, as a magnificent political opportunity to end the historic dominance of the Conservative Party. They saw the prospect of the dole, a poor reward for the blind loyalty they were expected to give to party leadership. In their twos and threes, and then their dozens, they gathered discreetly in the Commons to torpedo the proposal, and left the whips in no doubt about their feelings. They would rebel, and in the teeth of Tory hostility the government could not be sure of getting the necessary legislative changes through the House, even with the support of 50-plus Liberal Democrat MPs.

It was the end of the Project, or at least that vital dimension of it which sought to extend indefinitely the life of a Mandelson-model government by means of changing the voting system. This was no bad thing. The idea of Britons having a government of a Mandelson stripe for the foreseeable future, and certainly well into the next millennium, was not only depressing but profoundly undemocratic. It was a negation of democracy so to arrange the electoral system that one major party and its dependent coalition ally should enjoy uninterrupted government. Fortunately, it would never have worked, because voters are not the focus-group automatons that figure so largely in Mandelson's view of the world. They are awkward, perverse, unpredictable men and women who are just as likely to vote for 'the other lot' if they feel that New Labour is being thrust down their throats by a gang of smart-Alecs who believe they have a virtually divine mission to govern the country according to their own theories.

Mandelson's own personality is an important factor in this assessment. Though he has been a Cabinet minister for more than six months, he is still seen as a manipulative spin-doctor who insists that the world takes him on his own estimate. His intervention in the Pinochet affair in the autumn of 1998 was regarded at Westminster as a further manifestation of his campaign to win wider support in the parliamentary Labour Party. The former dictator of Chile, General Augusto Pinochet, languished under armed guard in a London hospital, claiming diplomatic immunity against an extradition warrant from a Spanish judge to stand trial for atrocities during the rule of his junta. On the BBC 1 Programme *Breakfast With Frost* on 18 October, Mandelson declared, 'I think the idea that such a brutal dictator as Pinochet should be claiming diplomatic immunity is for most people pretty gut-wrenching stuff.' He was in unusual company that day. Left-wingers Ann Clwyd MP, chair of the all-party human rights group at Westminster, and Jeremy Corbyn MP both demanded that Pinochet stand trial for human rights abuses. From them, it was expected. From Mandelson, it was not. MPs noted his remarks, which they assumed had been cleared with Downing Street, and interpreted his intervention as a move to bolster his political credibility with the Left. *The Times* was taken in. Its City editor observed that Mandelson sounded 'like an old-fashioned Leftie'.

A further piece of the Mandy mosaic slotted into place on 2

November 1998, when Mandelson upstaged Chancellor Brown at a CBI conference in Birmingham with a speech on the European single currency. Brown, cautious as ever, announced his intention to publish a national changeover plan that would promote 'practical steps' for joining the euro. Speaking after the Chancellor, Mandelson raised the government's game: 'We have made clear that we will join the single currency when it is in Britain's interest to do so.' He denied announcing any strategic shift, but commentators noticed the unsubtle move from 'if' to 'when' and concluded that they had seen a significant change of emphasis in policy. The *Sun*'s front page yelled, 'Outed!' On this occasion it was referring to the minister's attitude towards the single currency, not Mandelson's homosexuality.

The satirists have identified Mandelson as both cruel and a figure of fun. Rory Bremner created a memorable Virtual Mandelson in his TV show in winter 1997. The comedian fed into a computer information from six cameras mounted round his face, and the computer turned the images into a cartoon Mandy. Bremner's virtual reality puppet – a comic inversion of reality – whispered constantly in Blair's ear. His eyes bulged and his head spun round 360 degrees at the sound of the world 'Prescott'. The comedy programme *Have I Got News For You*, made for the BBC by an independent company, mercilessly lampooned him in the first showing that followed the BBC 'omertà' edict on Mandelson's sexuality, sailing as close to the wind as the corporation's lawyers would allow. Even Granada's sober-sided *What the Papers Say*, also made for the BBC, made pointed satirical references to the ban on mentions of his private life.

For satirists it is always open season on Mandelson, but behind the comedy lies his covert ambition to rise to the top, and to implement his own agenda on the way. A vital part of the Mandelson Project is Europe. Apart from his enthusiasm for the euro, he has a broader perspective on the EU. He outlined it in a speech to the European Institute in Florence in January 1998, before he had joined the Cabinet. Mandelson wants more 'shared sovereignty' in Europe, which would mean Britain giving more powers to Brussels. 'Loss of sovereignty only concerns people if they think they are giving it up to no good purpose,' he lectured his audience. His message was faintly reminiscent of the Tories in the dying days of the Major administration: that the policy was fine, and only the presentation was at fault. This was the opposite of his normal message that style was no good without substance. He went on, 'We have not demonstrated clearly enough that the purpose of pooling sovereignty is to address issues that are of real concern to people's lives.' In Mandelson's view, this would bring about a European superpower, rather than a European state.

Like Blair, Mandelson harbours a not-very-discreet admiration for Margaret Thatcher. He has met her only once, at an international conference on the relationship between Europe and the USA. 'You couldn't fail to be struck by her intensity, her single-mindedness of view,' he said later, in a manner that invited comparisons with his own intensity of purpose. He also identifies himself with her pioneering strategic view. 'She saw things and reached conclusions before the rest of us. I think the confronting of some trade union practices was necessary.' Her industrial relations law was perhaps 'a mite too far, but in principle, right'.

The broadcaster Trevor Phillips, a long-standing friend, and front-runner for Labour's nomination as mayor of London, argues that if Mandelson has any historical parallel, it is Robespierre, the architect of the Terror. 'Without his zeal and cool passion for the rights of the French people, the *ancien regime* would almost certainly have reasserted itself. His defence of the ideals of the revolution was absolute and unmoving. It won him no friends, and eventually swallowed him.' It would be a tragedy if Labour did the same to the architect of its own revolution, he thinks.

The boosting of Mandy reached a climax in November, when *The Times* ran a leader-page article with the headline 'Blair's heir apparent?' Written by the paper's political correspondent, Roland Watson, a recent arrival from the *Express* and not the most senior man in the paper's Westminster team, the article constructed a plausible scenario in which Mandelson became foreign secretary and then, after a third Blair election victory, slid effortlessly into

Number 10. 'Over-imaginative, perhaps,' mused Watson. 'But *impossible*? Six years ago he was not even an MP.' He reflected that Blair had recently said, in a little publicised speech, that when he retired he would be replaced by a moderniser who would make him look 'positively old-fashioned'. And who could that be? Watson wrote that the outing of Mandelson on *Newsnight* had been described by one Downing Street source as 'the most significant thing that has happened for a long time, both politically and sociologically', and further conjectured, 'It may no longer be unthinkable that modernising Britain may culminate in electing a gay Prime Minister.'

The article raised eyebrows at Westminster, but not many. Most political correspondents interpreted it as an interesting exercise in futurology, and nothing more. Only the placing of it in the most prominent slot in the paper gave it any real weight, and much of that was lost by the giveaway question mark in the headline. In fact, the piece was a cobbling together of unused information from *The Times*'s serialisation of Gould's hymn of praise to the great moderniser, plus a background piece written by Watson that had not found a home. Yet the article delighted Mandelson's supporters, who pointed it out as proof that their man was being seriously considered as a potential premier.

What would a Mandy premiership look like? If his analysis of the future is anything to go by, it is a chilling prospect: rule through a mixture of focus groups, referendums and the Internet. Parliament's days as the supreme forum of the people might be over. During a brainstorming session in a *Schloss* overlooking the Rhine in February 1998, Mandelson said, 'It may be that the era of pure representative democracy is slowly coming to an end.' His interlocutor, Wolfgang Schäuble, a prominent German Christian Democrat disagreed sharply. He argued that politicians were elected to take decisions, not to keep going back to the ballot box for a fresh mandate for every new policy.

Mandelson examined the development of representative democracy, and found it wanting. 'We entered the twentieth century with a society of elites, with a very different class structure. In those days, it seemed natural to delegate important decisions to members of the land-owning elite, or the industrial elite or the educated elite. When, in Britain, Labour emerged as the party of the working class, it quickly developed its own elite of trade union bureaucrats, city bosses and socialist intellectuals. But that age has passed away. Today people want to be more directly involved.'

His radical agenda looked to different structures: plebiscites, focus groups, lobbies, 'citizens' movements', and the Internet. New Labour had at that time carried out two referendums, on Scottish and Welsh devolution, and three more were in prospect. 'Democracy and legitimacy need constant renewal. They need to be refined with each generation . . . Representative government is being complemented by more direct forms of government, from the Internet to referenda . . . That requires a different style of politics and we are trying to respond to these changes . . . People have no time for a style of government that talks down to them and takes them for granted.'

Mandelson suggested that there was a choice between dying democracy and direct democracy. Superficially, his analysis meets the spirit of the times. But is the cry of the despot down the ages, of the banana republic dictator who knows what's best and seeks approval for his reign through a series of contrived popular votes whose objective is to bolster his power rather than to implement the wishes of the people. New Labour has made extensive use of focus groups for a decade or more, to hone its policies for winning power. The referendums held since then, in Scotland, Wales and London (on the principle of electing a metropolitan mayor), were all Yes/No verdicts on government policy, not exercises in identifying popular sentiment. And, given New Labour's obsession with controlling the political programme, it is unlikely that the Mandelson agenda would be any more than an instrument for extending control, not ceding it to Internet subscribers. Far from being the abdication of leadership, a strategy for 'cowardly politicians' envisaged by Wolfgang Schäuble, rule by Mandy would be a sovereignty of the self-chosen New Labour elite. If, that is, it ever comes about – for there are cogent reasons for believing that the Mandelson Project will fail.

Mandelson has a fatal flaw: a limitless self-belief that may one day prove his downfall. His hubris prevents him from seeing that the Mandy network, assembled so ingeniously over the decades, is incapable of delivering the leadership. The New Establishment – even assuming it holds together for more than New Labour's salad days – is an audience, not an electorate. Andy McSmith points out that Mandelson is a compulsive politician, with no private life, no personal hinterland and no political base of his own to sustain him should he ever fall out with his party leader. Mandelson is certainly clever, he observes, 'but not perhaps as shrewd as others who are playing the same game'.

Mandy insists that there is no Mandelson Project. 'I have never had a career plan. I don't calculate where I will be in ten years' time.' Then, in the same breath he admits to being driven. 'Let's not use the word "plot" but say I like to be ahead of the game.' This characteristic self-praise does not universally impress. The former leadership contender Bryan Gould, who worked closely with Mandelson, observes, 'I would expect Tony Blair to be totally beholden to Peter. On the other hand I can think of very few politicians who are less suited to be Secretary of State for Industry than Mandelson. In terms of what is needed to turn round the British economy, he is completely at sea. I have never heard him say anything to show he really understands how the economy works.'

Nor does Gould have much time for Mandelson's agenda. 'He is instinctively brilliant on the manipulation of politics. He understands that. He can identify a short-term political objective and secure it very very well. But he is not in any sense an original political thinker. He was always disappointing as someone who is said to be a visionary for the Labour Party. He had a vision of how Labour could win an election, but not too much idea of how to change society. Mandelson has been very lucky. For the time being, New Labour straddles the whole of the political centre, and there is hardly any room on the Right for the Tories and no room on the Left for some left-wing presence appearing.' This is convenient for Mandelson, Gould says, because he is only interested in the machinery of politics, and getting into government. 'It doesn't matter what you do in government in Peter's mind.' Mandelson's main campaign since 1 May 1997 is to be re-elected. 'Certainly this is the strongest example of a government seeing its first, major aim is to be re-elected.'

Geoffrey Goodman, who was a referee for his Labour Party job application, shares the apprehension that Mandelson will overreach himself: 'I still feel he will be an albatross round Tony Blair's neck. Something will come up that will make it very, very rough.' Others are more brusque. Joy Johnson, former director of communications, has told friends, 'He hasn't a democratic impulse in his body.'

Mandelson constantly invites comparison with his famous grandfather – 'from a very early age I was my grandfather's grandson' – though this was not always the case. He deliberately distanced himself from Herbert Morrison during his twenties, only to revive the relationship later. It was years before he identified Morrison as his grandfather in *Who's Who*. In some respects, he is a chip off the old block, but the comparison is easily strained. Morrison was very much a party man, revelling in his role as scourge of the Bevanite Left on the NEC and in the shadow Cabinet during the lean years of the early fifties. He was a hard-line home secretary, an undistinguished foreign secretary, and was ultimately prevented by Clement Atlee from succeeding to the leadership.

Mandelson is busily re-engineering his grandfather, to rehabilitate his memory and to ensure that the grandson does well out of the comparison. 'My grandfather was an early moderniser. He always argued that Labour's ideas had to be refreshed,' he says. 'He was heavily involved with large-scale nationalisation after the war, but if he were alive today he would be the last person to argue for it.' This retrospective logic will not wash, though Mandelson is on firmer ground when he considers Morrison's inclusiveness. Towards the end of his political life, when he had become one of them, Morrison was loud in his defence of the middle class.

'I always this of him as decent, solid and loyal,' says Mandelson. 'It is an image which has firmly impressed itself on me. That is how I would like to be remembered as well.' It is too early to say what epitaph history will give Peter Benjamin Mandelson. But it is most unlikely to be that.

NOTES

1 Scandal!

1 *Daily Telegraph*, 2 March 1996.
2 Interview, 1 July 1998.
3 *Hartlepool Mail*, 11 February 1998.
4 Ibid, 20 February, 1998.
5 *Punch*, 28 February 1998.
6 Ibid.
7 Ibid, 13 February 1998.
8 *Daily Telegraph*, 2 November 1998.
9 Stephen Bayley, *Labour Camp* (Batsford, 1998) and interview, 3 November 1998
10 *Pink Paper*, 6 November 1998, and interview, 22 November 1998.

2 Red Spoon

1 *Punch*, 12 September 1998.
2 Obituary of Herbert Morrison, *The Times*, 8 March 1965.
3 Bernard Donoughue and G. W. Jones, *Herbert Morrison: Portrait of a Politician*. (London: Weidenfeld & Nicholson,

1973), p.71.

4   *Punch*, 12 September 1998.
5   Lady Morrison of Lambeth, *Memories of a Marriage* (London: Muller, 1977), p.42.
6   Donoughue and Jones, *Herbert Morrison*, p.51.
7   *Punch*, 12 September 1998.
8   Donoughue and Jones, *Herbert Morrison*, p.173.
9   *Jewish Chronicle*, 23 May 1997.
10   *Financial Times*, 7 June 1997.
11   Lady Morrison, *Memories of a Marriage*, p. 41.
12   Donoughue and Jones, *Herbert Morrison*, p. 255.
13   Lady Morrison, *Memories of a Marriage*, p. 41.
14   *Financial Times*, 7 June 1991.
15   Ibid.
16   Ibid.
17   *Daily Telegraph*, 17 December 1997.
18   *Daily Mail*, 18 December 1997.
19   *Punch*, 12 September 1998.
20   Heather Bell, interview, 19 October 1998.
21   Paul Marginson, interview, 9 March 1998.
22   Ibid.
23   Ibid.
24   *Challenge*, 24 November 1970.
25   Peter Mandelson, interview with Oliver James, *The Chair*, BBC 2, 2 June 1997.
26   Heather Bell, interview, 19 October 1998.
27   Bob Labi, interview, 1 July 1998.
28   *Independent on Sunday*, 4 February 1996.
29   Tom Bell, statement, 23 September 1998.
30   *Guardian*, 11 February 1994.
31   Paul Marginson, interview, 9 March 1998.
32   Heather Bell, interview, 19 October 1998.

3 Dreamer, Calculator

1   *Daily Telegraph*, 17 November 1997.
2   Paul Marginson, interview, 9 March 1998.

3   *Independent on Sunday*, 4 February 1996.
4   Lord Newby, interview, 2 June 1998.
5   Ibid.
6   Ibid.
7   Interview, March 1998.
8   Tony Benn, *Conflicts of Interest: Diaries, 1977-80* (London: Hutchinson, 1992), p.54.
9   *Youth Unemployment: Causes and Cures*, British Youth Council, (1977), p.viii.
10 Ibid, p.x.
11 Ibid, p. 103.
12 *Sunday Telegraph*, 15 March 1992.

4 Brothers Fall Out
1   David Lea, interview, 19 March 1998.
2   Peta van den Bergh, interview, 23 February 1998.
3   *Guardian*, 4 July 1977.
4   David Hencke, interview, 23 March 1998.
5   *Guardian*, 7 August 1978.
6   *Independent*, 20 August 1997.
7   David Lea, interview, 19 March 1998.
8   Paul Ormerod, interview, 19 June 1998.
9   Letter to the *Guardian*, 4 October 1989.
10 Interview, summer 1998.
11 Ted Knight, interview.

5 Fixer, Spinner
1   Albert Booth, interview, 30 June 1998.
2   Ibid.
3   Ibid.
4   Bryan Gould, interview, 13 August 1998.
5   David Aaronovitch, interview, 7 July 1998.
6   Ibid.
7   *Observer*, 31 May 1987.
8   *Guardian*, 2 October 1989.
9   Pearl Bevis, interview, 10 May 1998.

10   Charles Clarke, interview, 31 March 1998.
11   Geoffrey Goodman, conversation with the author, 14 August 1998.
12   *Guardian*, 23 September 1995.
16   *New Statesman*, 15 May 1998.

6 Roses All the Way

1   David Owen, *Time to Declare* (London: Penguin, 1992), p. 640.
2   Andy McSmith, interview, 24 March 1998.
3   John Booth, interview, 29 March 1998.
4   Ibid.
5   Andy McSmith, interview, 24 March 1998.
6   Colin Hughes and Patrick Wintour, *Labour Rebuilt* (London: Fourth Estate, 1990), p. 54.
7   Tony Benn, *The End of an Era: Diaries, 1980-1990* (London: Hutchinson, 1992), p. 442.
8   John Booth, interview, 29 March 1998.
9   Letter in the possession of the author.
10   John Booth, interview, 29 March 1998.
11   *PR Week*, 9 October 1986.
12   Andy McSmith. *Faces of Labour: The Inside Story* (London: Verso, 1996), p.248.
13   Carole Boardman, interview, 21 July 1998.
14   Bryan Gould, interview, 13 August 1998.
15   Tony Benn, *The End of an Era: Diaries, 1980–1990* (London: Hutchinson, 1992),
16   Ibid p.494.
17   Bryan Gould, *Goodbye to All That* (London: Macmillan, 1995), p. 179.
18   Bryan Gould, interview, 19 August 1998.
19   Bryan Gould, *Goodbye to All That*, p. 191.
20   Ibid.
21   *Blitz*, October 1989.
22   Ibid.
23   *Guardian*, 2 October 1989.

24 David Butler and Denis Kavanagh, *The British General Election of 1987* (London: Macmillan, 1988), p. 260.
25 Ibid p. 259.

7 Outed!

1 Andy McSmith, interview, 24 March 1998.
2 Steve Wakelam, interview, 24 August 1998.
3 Ibid.
4 Peter Tatchell, interview, 1 March 1998.
5 Peter Tatchell, interview, 1 March 1998.
6 Bryan Gould, *Goodbye to All That* (London: Macmillan, 1995), p. 185.
7 Ibid, p. 189.
8 *Sun*, 23 August 1995.
9 Bryan Gould, interview, 13 August 1998.
10 *Punch*, 31 January 1998.
11 Peter Tatchell, interview, 1 March 1998.
12 *Daily Telegraph*, 17 December 1997.
13 Steve Wakelam, interview, 24 August 1998.
14 Interview, 29 July 1998.

8 Hartlepool Coup

1 Bryan Gould, interview, 13 August 1998.
2 *Daily Mirror* colour magazine, September 1988.
3 *Daily Express*, 4 November 1989.
4 *Independent*, 11 December 1989.
5 Ibid.
6 *Hartlepool Mail*, 14 December 1989.
7 Undated briefing note, pp. 1–2.
8 Ibid.
9 Charles Clarke, interview, 31 March 1998.
10 *Sunday Times*, 19 August 1990.
11 *Hartlepool Mail*, 27 October 1990.
12 *Independent on Sunday*, 2 June 1991.
13 Bryan Gould, *Goodbye to All That*, (London: Macmillan, 1995), p. 226

14   Ibid, p. 226.
15   Quoted in Andy McSmith, *Faces of Labour: The Inside Story* (London: Verso, 1996), p. 267.
16   Conservative Party Central Office press release, 7 June 1991.
17   *Hartlepool Mail*, 6 June 1991.
18   Ibid, 26 September 1991.
19   *Sun*, 26 September 1991.
20   *Sunday Telegraph*, 15 March 1992.
21   *People*, 12 April 1992.

9 Backbench Novice

1   *Fabian Review*, vol. 104 (1992), no. 33.
2   *People*, 19 April 1992.
3   *Hansard*, 14 May 1992.
4   *Hansard*, 14 May 1992, cols. 802-6.
5   *People*, 21 June 1992.
6   Ibid, 27 September 1992.
7   *Sunday Times*, 22 November 1992.
8   *Evening Standard*, 24 November 1992.
9   *The Times*, 16 December 1992.
10   Ibid.
11   *Hansard*, 29 January 1993, cols. 1306, 1347, 1349.
12   *Sunday Telegraph*, 25 April 1993.
13   Ibid, 9 May 1993.
14   Andy McSmith, *Faces of Labour: The Inside Story* (London: Verso, 1996), p. 271.
15   *Independent*, 3 August 1993.
16   *Hartlepool Mail*, 14 February 1994.
17   *The Times*, 7 January 1994.

10 The Blair Plot

1   Alastair Campbell's column, *Today,* 6 October 1994.
2   John Rentoul, *Tony Blair* (London: Little, Brown, 1995), p. 369.
3   Derek Draper, *Blair's 100 Days* (London, Faber, 1997), p. 21.
4   Ibid.

5   *Hansard*, 19 July 1994.
6   *Today*, 6 October 1994.
7   *Daily Mail*, 7 October 1994.
8   Quoted in the *Hartlepool Mail*, 6 October 1995.
9   *On the Record*, BBC, 25 February 1996.
10 *Guardian*, 27 February 1996.
11 *Sunday Times*, 20 April 1997.
12 *Spectator*, 19 April 1997.
13 *Guardian*, 14 April 1997.

11 The Greatest Showman on Earth
1   Bernard Donoughue and G. W. Jones, *Herbert Morrison: Portrait of a Politician* (London: Weidenfeld & Nicholson, 1973)
2   *Daily Mail*, 25 August, 1997.
3   *Evening Standard*, 19 December 1997.
4   *Daily Mail*, 16 February 1998.
5   *Sun*, 23 February 1998.
6   *Independent on Sunday*, 26 April 1998.
7   *Hansard*, 29 June 1998.
8   Stephen Bayley, *Labour Camp* (London: Batsford, 1998), p. 60.

12 Interesting Friends, Funny Friends
1   Tom Shebbeare, interview, 30 July 1998.
2   *The Times*, 16 December 1992.
3   *People*, 26 April 1992.
4   Ibid, 17 May 1992.
5   Ibid, 20 August 1992.
6   *Daily Mail*, 27 August 1992.
7   Tom Shebbeare, interview, 30 July 1998.
8   *The Times*, 10 July 1998.
9   Ibid, 11 September 1997.
10 *Daily Mail*, 7 January 1994.
11 *Mail on Sunday*, 24 August 1997.
12 Ibid.

13   Stephen Dorril, statement to author, 1 October 1998.
14   *Guardian*, 22 September 1997.
15   Stephen Dorril, statement, 1 October 1998.
16   *Mail on Sunday*, 28 September 1997.
17   Ibid.
18   Ibid.
19   Ibid.
20   Stephen Dorril, statement, 1 October 1998.
21   Ibid.
22   Ibid.
23   Julian Lewis, statement to author, 12 January 1998.
24   Julian Lewis, interview, 21 July 1998.
25   Robin Ramsay, *Prawn Cocktail Party* (London: Vision Paperbacks, 1998), p. 113.
26   *Tribune*, 29 September 1989.
27   Ramsay, op. cit., p. 78.
28   New Labour, TUCETU, occasional paper (1996) p.4.

13 Carry On Being Peter

1   Derek Draper *Blair's 100 Days* (London: Faber, 1997), p. 20.
2   Ibid, p. 24.
3   *The Times*, 4 June 1997.
4   Ibid.
5   *Sunday Times*, 20 July 1997.
6   *Daily Mail*, 19 August 1997.
7   *Guardian*, 20 August 1997.
8   *Independent on Sunday*, 24 August 1997.
9   *Daily Telegraph*, 12 September 1997.
10   *Evening Standard*, 20 September 1997.
11   *Daily Mirror*, 20 September 1997.

14 Cabinet

1   *Spectator*, 31 January 1998.
2   *New Statesman*, 21 January 1997.
3   *Observer*, 5 July 1998.
4   *Independent*, 8 July, 1998.

5   *Observer*, 12 July 1998.
6   *Observer*, 12 July 1998.
7   Ibid.

15 The Full Mandy
1   *Sun*, 24 September 1998.
2   *Conservative Party News*, 29 October 1998.

16 The Project
1   *New Statesman,* 11 September 1998.
2   Ibid.
3   *Spectator*, 17 October 1998.

INDEX